Revisiting the Regulation of Human Fertilisation and Embryology

The Human Fertilisation and Embryology Act 2008 was a major update to the UK's laws on the use and regulation of reproductive technology and assisted reproduction. Since the enactment of the new law, the sector's regulatory body, the Human Fertilisation and Embryology Authority (HFEA), has also consulted on various related topics including barriers to egg and sperm donation in the UK, multiple births/single embryo transfer and using IVF technology to prevent mitochondrial disease.

This book critically considers recent developments in human fertilisation legislation, asking whether the 2008 Act has achieved its stated aim of being fit for purpose. Bringing together a range of international experts, the book evaluates the fresh risks and challenges emerging from both established and existing technologies and techniques in the field of human fertilisation and embryology, as well as offering valuable insights into the social and regulatory challenges that lie ahead. Key topics include problems with DIY assisted conception; the lack of reform in respect of the regulation of surrogacy arrangements; and mitochondrial DNA transfer.

As a review of the status of assisted reproduction legislation, this book will be of great use and interest to students, researchers and practitioners in medical law, bioethics, medicine and child welfare.

Kirsty Horsey is Senior Lecturer in Law at the University of Kent, UK.

Biomedical Law and Ethics Library
Series Editor: Sheila A. M. McLean

Scientific and clinical advances, social and political developments, and the impact of healthcare on our lives raise profound ethical and legal questions. Medical law and ethics have become central to our understanding of these problems, and are important tools for the analysis and resolution of problems – real or imagined.

In this series, scholars at the forefront of biomedical law and ethics contribute to the debates in this area, with accessible, thought-provoking and sometimes controversial ideas. Each book in the series develops an independent hypothesis and argues cogently for a particular position. One of the major contributions of this series is the extent to which both law and ethics are utilised in the content of the books, and the shape of the series itself.

The books in this series are analytical, with a key target audience of lawyers, doctors, nurses and the intelligent lay public.

Available titles:

Human Fertilisation and Embryology
Reproducing regulation
Kirsty Horsey & Hazel Biggs

Intention and Causation in Medical Non-killing
The impact of criminal law concepts on euthanasia and assisted suicide
Glenys Williams

Impairment and Disability
Law and ethics at the beginning and end of life
Sheila McLean & Laura Williamson

Bioethics and the Humanities
Attitudes and perceptions
Robin Downie & Jane Macnaughton

Defending the Genetic Supermarket
The law and ethics of selection the next generation
Colin Gavagham

The Harm Paradox
Tort law and the unwanted child in an era of choice
Nicolette Priaulx

Assisted Dying
Reflections on the need for law reform
Sheila McLean

Medicine, Malpractice and Misapprehensions
V.H. Harpwood

Euthanasia, Ethics and the Law
From the conflict to compromise
Richard Huxtable

The Best Interests of the Child in Healthcare
Sarah Elliston

Values in Medicine
What are we really doing to patients?
Donald Evans

Autonomy, Consent and the Law
Sheila A.M. McLean

Healthcare Research Ethics and Law
Regulation, review and responsibility
Hazel Biggs

The Body in Bioethics
Alastair V. Campbell

Genomic Negligence
An interest in autonomy as the basis for novel negligence claims generated by genetic technology
Victoria Chico

Health Professionals and Trust
The cure for healthcare law and policy
Mark Henaghan

Medical Ethics in China
A transcultural interpretation
Jing-Bao Nie

Law, Ethics and Compromise at the Limits of Life
To treat or not to treat?
Richard Huxtable

Regulating Pre-Implantation Genetic Diagnosis
A comparative and theoretical analysis
Sheila A.M. McLean & Sarah Elliston

Bioethics
Methods, theories, domains
Marcus Düwell

Human Population Genetic Research in Developing Countries
The Issue of Group Protection
Yue Wang

Coercive Care
Rights, law and policy
Bernadette McSherry & Ian Freckelton

Saviour Siblings
A relational approach to the welfare of the child in selective reproduction
Michelle Taylor-Sands

Human Population Genetic Research in Developing Countries
The issue of group protection
Yue Wang

Stem Cell Research and the Collaborative Regulation of Innovation
Sarah Devaney

End of Life Decision Making for Critically Impaired Infants
Resource allocation and difficult decisions
Neera Bhatia

Forthcoming titles include:

The Jurisprudence of Pregnancy
Concepts of conflict, persons and property
Mary Neal

Regulating Risk
Values in health research governance
Shawn Harmon

The Umbilical Cord Blood Controversies in Medical Law
Karen Devine

The Legitimacy of Medical Treatment
What role for the medical exception?
Sara Fovargue and Alexandra Mullock

Revisiting Landmark Cases in Medical Law
Shaun D. Pattinson

The Ethical and Legal Consequences of Posthumous Reproduction
Lewis Browne

Pioneering Healthcare Law
Essays in honour of Margaret Brazier
Catherine Stanton, Sarah Devaney, Anne-Marree Farrell and Alexandra Mullock

Birth, Harm and the Role of Distributive Justice
Burdens, blessings, need and desert
Alasdair Maclean

About the Series Editor
Professor Sheila McLean is International Bar Association Professor of Law and Ethics in Medicine and Director of the Institute of Law and Ethics in Medicine at the University of Glasgow.

Revisiting the Regulation of Human Fertilisation and Embryology

Edited by Kirsty Horsey

Routledge
Taylor & Francis Group
LONDON AND NEW YORK

First published 2015
by Routledge
2 Park Square, Milton Park, Abingdon, Oxon, OX14 4RN

and by Routledge
711 Third Avenue, New York, NY 10017

Routledge is an imprint of the Taylor & Francis Group, an informa business

British Library Cataloguing in Publication Data
A catalogue record for this book is available from the British Library

Library of Congress Cataloging-in-Publication Data
A catalog record for this book has been requested

ISBN: 978-1-138-02189-1 (hbk)
ISBN: 978-1-315-76789-5 (ebk)

Typeset in Baskerville MT Pro by
Servis Filmsetting Ltd, Stockport, Cheshire

MIX
Paper from responsible sources
FSC www.fsc.org FSC® C013056

Printed and bound in Great Britain by
TJ International Ltd, Padstow, Cornwall

Table of Contents

Preface

In 2007, many of the authors in this volume contributed to a collection of work critiquing the then state of play with regard to the Human Fertilisation and Embryology Act 1990 and how it was faring, in the light of the Government's announced intention to review it and the launch of the public consultation, 'with particular emphasis on those [issues] that were either not considered or were under-considered when the Human Fertilisation and Embryology Act was passed in 1990' (Horsey and Biggs, 2007: xii). Chapters in the collection were written by a mixture of established and emerging scholars, as well as others external to academia with an interest in the field. They covered the law's role in regulating reproduction, postmenopausal pregnancy, welfare of the child considerations, payment to gamete donors, access to IVF and related treatments, preimplantation genetic diagnosis (PGD), embryo donation, legal parenthood, surrogacy and abortion. Our aim then was to inform and contribute to the debates on re-regulation, although we anticipated even at that time that many issues would be unresolved, and would continue to generate discussion and debate once the new legislation was passed.

Draft legislation was published in 2007 and parliamentary debate commenced.[1] The Human Fertilisation and Embryology Act was passed in 2008. This was legislation which, according to the ministers responsible for introducing it, was intended to 'ensure that the law remains effective and fit for purpose in the early 21st century' (Department of Health, 2005: 5). However, many scholars and other commentators in the area were perplexed by the fact that a piece of amending legislation was passed, rather than making the final outcome far less complex by repealing the original 1990 Act and re-legislating (Elliston, 2009). Added to this the fact that the 2008 Act came into force in various stages between April 2009 and April 2010, and that the two statutes have to be read alongside each other in order to make any kind of sense, the question arises as to exactly how 'fit for purpose' the law can currently be, notwithstanding the number of provisions that expressly give power for future Regulations. As noted by Sarah Elliston (2009), 'attempts to test

1 The original draft legislation was known as the Human Tissue and Embryos Bill, as it was originally intended to merge the functions of the Human Fertilisation and Embryology Authority (HFEA) with the Human Tissue Authority in one piece of legislation.

the limits of the legislation and its application seem extremely likely' in the courts and elsewhere, and the 'implementation of the HFE Act 2008 may thus be seen as the start of its real examination, rather than its end'.

Furthermore, since the enactment and coming into force of the new law, the sector's regulatory body, the Human Fertilisation and Embryology Authority (HFEA), has continued to consult on various aspects of the provision of assisted reproductive technologies (e.g. barriers to egg and sperm donation in the UK, multiple births/single embryo transfer) and embryology (including using IVF technology to prevent the transmission of mitochondrial diseases (recommendations on this came in March 2013)), suggesting that future regulatory changes will need to be made. The HFEA also survived the Government's review of arm's length bodies (also dubbed 'the bonfire of the quangos'), with the announcement in January 2013 that it was to be retained as the independent regulator for assisted reproduction treatments, recognising the opinion of the majority of respondents to the government's consultation on this. In making the announcement, the Department of Health said that further changes to the governance of assisted reproduction and the use of human embryos and tissues in the UK would be required, but that it had chosen to focus on improving and streamlining the existing regulatory bodies, rather than curtailing their activities (Department of Health, 2013a). Thus, it announced further independent review of the HFEA's activities, alongside those of the Human Tissue Authority (HTA), with a view to potentially merging the activities of the two agencies. However, this review, when the results were published by the Department of Health in July 2013, found little practical overlap in the work carried out by the HFEA and HTA (Department of Health, 2013b). The review noted that there was a need to maintain public confidence in the sensitive areas that the HFEA regulates, which again suggests that further changes to the way the sector is governed will become necessary, and continue to be so.

This volume is a recognition that the law in this area cannot and should not remain static. It contains a new selection of essays, which seek to critically evaluate many of the changes that were made to the law by the passage of the Human Fertilisation and Embryology Act 2008. It does not claim to do this exhaustively; there are some aspects of the new law that are not covered here, such as abortion, human reproductive cloning or embryo stem cell research, including the creation of and research into human admixed embryos, which proved to be a highly controversial part of the parliamentary debates, as well as causing controversy outside of the debate context after the HFEA licensed such research.[2] As a collection, the book looks to examine whether the 2008 Act achieved the stated aim of making the law governing assisted reproductive technologies and the science of embryology 'fit for purpose' in the twenty-first century or, if not, what could or should be done to improve it. Various features of the law as it is currently formulated might still be critiqued, as might some aspects of (or areas related to) fertility treat-

2 See *Quintavalle & Another, R (on the application of) v Human Fertilisation & Embryology Authority (HFEA)* [2008] EWHC 3395 (Admin).

ments that remain outside the parameters of the law as it currently stands. The book, which brings together an inter-disciplinary group of international scholars, includes chapters on many of these, as well as chapters that look comparatively at the law in the UK as it compares with for example Canada or Australia, in order to get a broader flavour of the kinds of flaws that the current legislation might contain. It is hoped that the collection of essays in this volume make a valuable addition to the literature. We hope it will be of interest to scholars in medical and family law generally and of assisted reproductive technologies in particular.

References

Department of Health (2005) *Review of the Human Fertilisation and Embryology Act: A public consultation* (London: Department of Health).

Department of Health (2013a) *Fertility and tissue regulators to be reviewed following consultation* (Press release, 25 January 2013).

Department of Health (2013b) *Review of Human Fertilisation and Embryology Authority and Human Tissue Authority* (London: Department of Health).

Elliston, S. (2009) 'The HFE Act 2008 – An end or a beginning?' *BioNews* 530 (London: Progress Educational Trust).

Horsey, K. and Biggs, H. (eds) (2007) *Human fertilisation and embryology: Reproducing regulation* (Abingdon: Routledge-Cavendish).

Notes on contributors

Antony Blackburn-Starza is a PhD candidate at Kent Law School, Canterbury, UK, where he teaches the Law of Obligations. His thesis is concerned with the use of race in gamete donor matching. He is also legal editor at *BioNews*, a weekly web- and email-based service providing news and comment on developments in assisted reproduction and genetics, published by the charity Progress Educational Trust. He has also taught Medical Law at the London School of Economics. Antony's research interests lie in tort and medical law, and he has previously written on versions of reproductive autonomy in the fertility context.

Eric Blyth is Professor of Social Work at the University of Huddersfield, UK, a position he has held since 2000. He has held visiting professorships at the Hong Kong Polytechnic University and the National University of Singapore. For more than 20 years he has been involved in research and policy development in assisted human conception. He was a founder member of the British Infertility Counselling Association (BICA) and is currently a member of the Victorian Assisted Reproductive Treatment Authority (VARTA) Advisory Panel (Australia) and the British Association of Social Workers Project Group on Assisted Reproduction (PROGAR).

Helen Codd is Professor of Law & Social Justice at the Lancashire Law School, University of Central Lancashire, UK. She also holds an Associate Research Fellowship at the University of London's Institute of Advanced Legal Studies. Helen has written and published many journal articles on issues relating to women, families, prisons and criminal justice, and is the author of *In the Shadow of Prison: Families, Imprisonment and Criminal Justice* published by Willan Publishing in 2008, and *Controversial Issues in Prisons* (2010) (co-authored by Dr David Scott). Her research on reproductive rights was cited with approval by the Grand Chamber of the ECtHR in their judgement in the *Dickson* case. She is currently a Lay Adviser to the Lancashire MAPPA Strategic Management Board, and has extensive experience of working with NGOs in relation to issues concerning children, poverty, homelessness and access to justice.

Karen Devine is a Senior Lecturer at Kent Law School, Canterbury, UK. She teaches Law and Medical Ethics and the Law of Obligations; while her main research interests lie in medical negligence, in particular the relationship between legal obligations and bodily integrity, and the role of informed consent. Her latest interests have centred upon the notion of property within the body and the ability for participants to enter the 'exchange marketplace' for bodily material, such as arises in egg-share agreements and organ donation. She has published a number of articles in her specialist area of umbilical cord blood stem cell collection, which have focused largely on the dichotomy between public and private bio-banking and the legal protection of health-care professionals who perform the collection procedures, as well as broader socio-legal work. Karen is currently the course convenor of the undergraduate module, Law and Medical Ethics; the Director of the Certificate in Law programme; and Deputy Director of Learning and Teaching for Medway. She was the winner of the Oxford University Press Law Teacher of the Year National Award 2012.

Lucy Frith is a Senior Lecturer in Bioethics and Social Science at the University of Liverpool, UK. Her research focuses on the social and ethical aspects of health-care decision-making and policy with a particular interest in combining empirical methods with ethical analysis. She has carried out research in women's health, pregnancy and childbirth, and reproductive technologies (gamete and embryo donation). She is interested in the socio-ethical aspects of health-care organisations: how the organisational aspects of health-care delivery impact on the ethical and social aspects of the practitioner and patient experience, and how new forms of health-care delivery will manage the ethical aspects of practice. She is empirical ethics section editor of the journal *Clinical Ethics*.

Colin Gavaghan is Director of the New Zealand Law Foundation Centre for Law and Policy in Emerging Technologies, and Associate Professor at the Faculty of Law, at the University of Otago. He is the author of *Defending the Genetic Supermarket: The Law and Ethics of Selecting the Next Generation* (Routledge-Cavendish, 2007), and of numerous articles and chapters on a range of topics, including legal questions around reproductive and genetic technologies, the role of neuroscience in criminal law, and assorted medico-legal issues.

Kirsty Horsey is a Senior Lecturer at Kent Law School, Canterbury, UK. She teaches the Law of Obligations at undergraduate level, having previously also taught aspects of family law and medical law. Her research interests lie primarily in the area of the regulation of assisted human reproduction and genetic technologies, particularly where these overlap with issues in family law; and the law of obligations, in particular those obligations based on 'relationship' and/or imbalances of power. She has previously published a number of articles and chapters on the regulation of surrogacy, and is co-author of *Tort Law* (4th ed, Oxford University Press, 2015).

Emily Jackson is Professor of Law at the London School of Economics and the author of *Medical Law: Text, Cases and Materials* (3rd edition, Oxford University Press, 2013). She is a member of the BMA Medical Ethics Committee. From 2003 to 2012, she was a member of the Human Fertilisation and Embryology Authority and from 2008, she was its Deputy Chair. Since 2014, she has been a Judicial Appointments Commissioner.

Isabel Karpin is a Professor in the Faculty of Law at the University of Technology, Sydney, Australia. She teaches and researches in the areas of feminist legal theory, health law, disability and the law, genetics and the law, reproduction and the law, and law and culture. She (with K Savell) is the author of *Perfecting Pregnancy: Law Disability and the Future of Reproduction* (Cambridge University Press, 2012) and is currently involved in several major research projects in the areas of reproductive technology and disability, including two Australian Research Council Grants.

Aikaterini (Katia) Neofytou is a PhD candidate at Kent Law School, Canterbury UK, and a graduate teaching assistant in the undergraduate law module of Introduction to Obligations. Her research interests involve issues of medical law, particularly ethical and legal aspects of assisted human reproduction and reproductive rights. Katia's thesis is a socio-legal study of surrogacy in Greece and the UK. She has previously worked at the London School of Economics as a research assistant for a project on surrogacy (McCandless J., et al., 'A Comparative Study on the Regime of Surrogacy in EU Member States' (May 2013, published by the European Parliament)), and later worked at the Commissioning Support Unit at NHS South London. In 2013, she was called to the Bar in Thessaloniki, Greece, but decided to pursue her PhD studies in the UK. Katia has completed an LLM in Medical Law and Ethics at Kent Law School, in which her thesis was on childlessness and NHS funding for fertility treatments.

Laura Riley leads the Ethics workstream at Genomics England, a company formed in 2013 by the Department of Health to implement the 100,000 Genomes Project. Prior to this she conducted the Nuffield Council on Bioethics project 'Mitochondrial Donation: Ethical Issues', also writing the final report. Laura was formerly a Director of the charity Progress Educational Trust. She has also worked in health policy and communications at the King's Fund, and the British Pregnancy Advisory Service (BPAS). Laura holds an MA in Medical Ethics and Law from King's College London. She has contributed chapters to *Human Fertilisation and Embryology: Reproducing Regulation* (Routledge-Cavendish, 2007) and *Regulating Autonomy: Sex, Reproduction and Family* (Hart Publishing, 2009). Laura is a Trustee of the Progress Educational Trust and a member of the Research and Ethics Committee at BPAS.

Jeanne Snelling (PhD) is from the University of Otago, New Zealand. Jeanne's research interests fall within the general health law field, in particular legal responses to issues arising from human reproduction, both unassisted and assisted. More recent research interests include the implication of behavioural genetics and neuroscience on the law. She is currently completing a three-year Research Fellowship in Bioethics and Health Law at the University of Otago's Bioethics Centre. Jeanne is also an adjunct lecturer at the University of Otago's Faculty of Law and teaches medical law to undergraduate medical students. She is currently a Principal Investigator on the New Zealand Law Foundation-sponsored project: *The Future of Preimplantation Genetic Testing.*

Anita Stuhmcke is a Professor in the Faculty of Law at the University of Technology, Sydney, Australia. She has had a longstanding interest in the legal regulation of surrogacy in Australia. Her scholarship in this area explores social exclusion and public access to services, such as the ongoing issue of accessing reproductive services – especially with respect to surrogacy. Anita has contributed to law reform inquiries across many Australian jurisdictions on this issue. The central premise of her research is to conceptualise the ways in which law operates as a continuum of effectiveness, the basic argument being that black letter law is just one regulatory option available to policy makers.

Pamela White is a PhD candidate and specialist associate lecturer at Kent Law School Canterbury, UK. She holds a PhD in Human Geography, McGill University and an LLM from the University of Kent. She works at the interface of medical law, ethics and clinical population health applications with a special interest in reproduction and the beginning of life, electronic health records, privacy and data protection. Her current research activities draw on her extensive experience in the Canadian federal government where she was a senior Director managing health, social and demographic research, and data access for Statistics Canada. She has held assignments with federal Privacy Commissioner and as Director, Assisted Human Reproduction Canada and has taught as a sessional lecturer at Carleton University. Since leaving the federal government she has worked as Research Associate, Population Health and Genomics Foundation, Cambridge and as a Researcher, Eggs and Embryos for Research Project, NovelTechEthics, Dalhousie University.

1 Revisiting the regulation of human fertilisation and embryology

Kirsty Horsey

Introduction

Since the technological breakthrough in reproductive technology that enabled the birth of the world's first 'test-tube baby', Louise Brown, in 1978, the development of assisted reproductive technologies (ART) has been increasingly rapid. Advancements in ART since then have opened up a world of possibilities for infertile heterosexual couples, same-sex couples and even single women (and, less often, men) to have the children they desire. Scientific offshoots of these technologies continue to be researched and often, in turn, lead to new or more effective forms of treatments, or new aspects or species of a particular type of treatment. However, because what researchers and fertility specialists work with is the material of human life and the formation of families is a time-honoured battleground for conflicting versions of social expectations and identities, inevitably social, moral and ethical considerations are raised.

The law in this area has a difficult task – it must manage ethical expectations against the progress of science and the goal of creating families for those who need assistance. The law of course is also formed by parliamentarians who may themselves reflect, or may seek to shape the social meaning attributed to the technologies at hand, or to prescribe the circumstances in which they believe these should be used. It must, therefore, be kept under review at all times, to ensure it continues to facilitate family formation while offering the right protections for the parties concerned, as well as not hindering scientific progress. This book considers whether the latest changes to the law in this area, namely the Human Fertilisation and Embryology Act 2008 (hereafter 'the 2008 Act') achieve this. It starts by outlining in this chapter how we reached the position we are in today, first by considering how the areas of ART and embryology, the science behind IVF, were first regulated. The chapter then goes on to consider some of the perceived flaws with that original legislation, despite its initial success and rightful description as a legal landmark and a triumph for progress over conservatism. It then considers the changes made to the law in 2008, and whether these adequately – or at all – address the issues arising from ART and embryology in the twenty-first century. Initially, this critique is on general terms, before introducing the specific focus taken in each of the subsequent chapters. The coverage of areas regulated by the

2008 Act is not exhaustive; there are no chapters addressing, for example, abortion, human cloning or research using human admixed embryos. However, what is included allows for a good overview of the Act and its effectiveness as a regulatory tool looking into the future.

Regulating human fertilisation and embryology

UK law rigorously regulates the use of gametes and embryos for both treatment and research purposes. The Human Fertilisation and Embryology Act 1990 (hereafter 'the 1990 Act') provided a framework of legislation on which other nations have since mirrored their own law.[1] The 1990 Act was based largely on the recommendations of the Warnock Report – a report commissioned by the Government in 1982 to enquire into the technologies of IVF and embryology amidst mounting concern at the speed in which these developments in a largely unregulated – and ethically sensitive – area were advancing. The committee of inquiry, led by philosopher Mary Warnock (later to become Baroness Warnock), was tasked with investigating 'recent and potential developments in medicine and science relating to human fertilisation and embryology' and considering the 'policies and safeguards [that] should be applied, including consideration of the social, ethical and legal implications' (Warnock Report, 1984: 4). The Warnock Committee reported its findings in 1984, immediately prompting academic, social and ethical discussion, and eventually parliamentary debate. Its report advocated a stricter form of regulation than was at that time offered by professional codes, recommending a regulatory authority to oversee and licence all activities relating to research and treatment services involving the creation, storage and use of human embryos outside the body, the use of donated gametes and embryos, and related research.

Despite some flaws, the Warnock Report advocated a permissive arena in which research and treatments could continue to develop and thrive, and which would help maintain the UK as a world leader in the twin spheres of ART and embryology. Having such a permissive – yet controlled – framework recommended was potentially a factor leading to the defeat of various Private Members' Bills laid before Parliament in the latter half of the 1980s, most notably Enoch Powell MP's Unborn Children (Protection) Bill 1985. Had this Bill been passed, all research into ART would have been halted, as any 'manipulations' of an embryo would only be allowed if that embryo was then to be used in an actual fertility treatment. So, while IVF would have been permitted, research into making IVF more effective would not. While it is not difficult to argue that such a law would hardly be beneficial to women and families in the UK in the long run, given the ethical and moral considerations that attach to the use of human embryos and the creation of life, it is hardly surprising that Powell's Bill had strong support – it progressed easily to its third reading. It took vigorous and dedicated campaigning to defeat it, alongside the voluntary creation of a licensing authority by professional organisations

1 For example the Australian state of Victoria's Infertility Treatment Act 1995, and even Canada's much later (though maligned) Assisted Human Reproduction Act 2004 (see White, this volume).

(the Medical Research Council and the Royal College of Obstetricians and Gynaecologists) along the lines of Warnock's recommendations. This Voluntary Licensing Authority (later the Interim Licensing Authority (ILA)) issued guidelines setting in place a 14-day limit for research on embryos and the requirement that consent be obtained from those from whose gametes the embryo had been created before any research could begin. It is perhaps the case that the visible potential of such a quasi-legal framework, within which research on embryos could continue within defined permissible boundaries, helped progress the debate. A further Unborn Children (Protection) Bill was introduced to Parliament in 1986, by Ken Hargreaves MP. While also ultimately unsuccessful, this served to keep the debates alive and maintained the need for concerted lobbying from interested individuals, organisations and pressure groups. Responding to the demands for action, the government published draft legislation in the form of a White Paper in 1987.[2]

Much debate – both outside and inside Parliament – ensued. While the framework for legislation was largely sound, the devil was in the detail, and various amendments were attempted to be made to the legislation as it passed through Parliament, some of which were accepted, some of which nearly made it, very nearly making the tenor of the whole legislation completely different from the way it started out.[3] The 1990 Act was, however, eventually passed through both Houses of Parliament (having been initially, and unusually, first presented in the House of Lords) and gained Royal Assent on 1 November 1990. The regulatory body dealing with the underlying policy of the Act and granted inspection and licence-issuing powers – the Human Fertilisation and Embryology Authority (HFEA) – was established by section 5 of the Act, and started its operations on 1 August 1991, replacing the ILA.

There is no doubt that the 1990 Act was a benchmark piece of legislation. However, by the early part of the twenty-first century, it was becoming increasingly clear that some aspects of it were outdated, either in the sense of having been outgrown by scientific development or potential, or in cultural and societal terms. While IVF and related aspects of the treatment such as the use of donor gametes, or even the form of IVF known as intracytoplasmic sperm injection (ICSI) were becoming ever more commonplace and were almost universally socially accepted, other developments raised different and often novel issues, many of which the Act was ill-equipped to answer. For one thing, in 1990 there was obviously no notion of the ways in which the growth of the internet might impact on the delivery of and access to fertility treatment services. There had also been no Human Genome Project, nor was there the knowledge and understanding that we now have – largely as a result of the kinds of research permitted by the Act – about a vast number of genetic conditions and how we might prevent these from being passed from one generation to the next. Some of this knowledge led to the development of

2 *Human Fertilisation and Embryology: A Framework for Legislation* (1987) Cm 259 (London: HMSO).

3 For example the attempt by Lady Saltoun of Abernethy to limit the availability of IVF to married couples only as what became the 1990 Act passed through the Committee Stage of the House of Lords (Hansard HL-Deb 6 February 1990, vol. 515, col. 788). The proposed amendment was defeated by a single vote.

preimplantation genetic diagnosis (PGD), in order to be able to select embryos free from disease to be used in IVF, but as more and more conditions were understood, the limits of what PGD could – and should – be authorised for came into question (these debates do not go away: see both Karpin and Gavaghan and Snelling, this volume). Thus, we had debates on tissue typing and 'saviour siblings', and on the deliberate selection of a condition (deafness) by parents for their prospective child. Embryonic stem cells had not yet been discovered, so the potential of these cells in treatments for all kinds of degenerative diseases and other conditions had not then been explored and/or harnessed. No mammal was cloned until Dolly the sheep in 1997, so the prospect of human cloning, reproductive or otherwise, had also not been contemplated in 1990 (as is indicated by the fact that the 1990 Act would not have covered the cell nuclear replacement technique used to create Dolly and that human embryos created would not have been recognised as embryos under the Act).[4] Neither had the rights of same-sex couples to have children using these technologies (indeed it was lucky that the amendment proposing that IVF be limited to married couples had been – albeit narrowly – defeated), yet progressive court decisions both domestically and from the European Court of Human Rights – and not necessarily about anything regulated by the Act – began to call into question some of the assumptions on which the 1990 Act may be said to have rested. The same could be said about developments in adoption law. While there was never a direct prohibition on same-sex couples receiving licensed treatment, in the early days it was only the most progressive clinics who would treat lesbian couples with either donor insemination or IVF, given the restrictiveness of interpretations of the 'welfare of the child' assessment that had to be carried out before treatment was allowed to proceed (then found in section 13), including the consideration of that child's 'need for a father'.

Throughout the 1990s and the early 2000s, then, there had been a growing swell of academic and other criticisms of various aspects of the legislation,[5] including legal challenges, some of which reached the highest courts in the land.[6]

4 Hence *R v Secretary of State for Health ex parte Quintavalle (on behalf of Pro-Life Alliance)* [2003] 2 WLR 692, challenging the authority of the HFEA to license research with regard to human cloning. The House of Lords eventually found that cloned embryos were embryos within the meaning of the 1990 Act (which defined them as embryos 'where fertilisation is complete') with a very purposive interpretation of the statute. The Human Reproductive Cloning Act 2001 banned the use of cloned human embryos in fertility treatments (now repealed, though the ban is incorporated in the 2008 Act).

5 See, for example, amongst many other examples, Brazier (1999), Jackson (2001, 2002, 2007), Lee (2002) and Warnock (2002).

6 See for example *R v HFEA ex parte Blood* [1997] 2 WLR 806, on a widow's right to undergo fertility treatment using sperm taken from her dead husband; *Rose & Another v Secretary of State for Health and Human Fertilisation and Embryology Authority* [2002] EWHC 1593 (Admin); *R v Secretary of State for Health ex parte Quintavalle (on behalf of Pro-Life Alliance)* [2003] 2 WLR 692 (above); *The Leeds Teaching Hospitals NHS Trust v Mr A, Mrs A and others* [2003] EWCH 259 (QBD), on the legal parenthood of twins born following a mix-up at a fertility clinic; *Evans v Amicus Healthcare Ltd and others* [2004] EWCA Civ 727 (later *Evans v UK* (application no. 6339/05), on the nature and extent of consent to treatment and its withdrawal by one party; *Quintavalle (on behalf of Comment on Reproductive Ethics) v HFEA* [2005] UKHL 28, on the use of 'saviour siblings'; *In Re D* [2005] *(A Child appearing by*

Difficult and contentious decisions had to be made by the HFEA,[7] and others were pushed through by the Department of Health, including the (controversial for some, but certainly unilateral) removal of anonymity for gamete donors in 2004/5 (*BioNews*, 2004). Furthermore, there had been various pieces of related legislation passed in relation to either legal challenges or scientific development, amending the 1990 Act's terms.[8] In 2004, the Government announced that the legislation would undergo a comprehensive review. In the same year, the cross-party House of Commons Science and Technology Committee (STC) began its own inquiry into the law, reporting its findings and recommendations for change in 2005.[9] It advocated more liberal regulation, giving more choice and control to patients. Around the same time, the HFEA reviewed and publicly consulted on a number of policy issues, including the contentious 'welfare of the child' provisions in the Act and as reflected in the HFEA's *Code of Practice*, as well as the law surrounding the donation of sperm, eggs and embryos. The Department of Health announced its own public consultation looking at ways the legislation could/should be improved for the future, stating that its aim in reviewing the Act was 'to ensure that the law remains effective and fit for purpose in the early 21st century' and that the consultation was 'part of a process of re-establishing a framework that is broadly acceptable to society'.[10] The consultation, which closed in November 2005, sought views on potential changes to the law and how it might be updated, given the 'rise of new technologies, changes in societal attitudes, international development and the need to ensure effective regulation'.[11] Draft legislation was published and put before Parliament in 2007.

The 2008 Act

Following a year of parliamentary debate, a new piece of amending legislation – the Human Fertilisation and Embryology Act 2008 (hereafter 'the 2008 Act')

her Guardian Ad Litem) (Respondent) UKHL 33, on the denial of paternity based on the meaning of 'treatment together' under the Act; *L v Human Fertilisation & Embryology Authority & Secretary of State for Health* [2008] EWHC 2149 (Fam), on the compatibility with Article 8 European Convention on Human Rights on the HFEA's absolute requirement for consent for continued use of storage of sperm after a man's death; *Quintavalle & Another, R (on the application of) v Human Fertilisation & Embryology Authority (HFEA)* [2008] EWHC 3395 (Admin), on the legitimacy of the HFEA's granting of licences for research into human admixed embryos.

7 A number of examples include decisions in relation to (among others) Zain Hashmi <http://www.hfea.gov.uk/844.html>; Charlie Whitaker <http://www.bionews.org.uk/page_12478.asp>; Alan and Louise Masterton <http://www.bionews.org.uk/page_11041.asp>; and Natallie Evans <http://www.hfea.gov.uk/766.html>.

8 For example the Human Reproductive Cloning Act 2001; the Human Fertilisation and Embryology (Deceased Fathers) Act 2003.

9 House of Commons Science and Technology Committee (2005) *Human Reproductive Technologies and the Law*, fifth report of session 2004–5, HC 7–1.

10 Department of Health (2005) *Review of the Human Fertilisation and Embryology Act: A public consultation* (London: Department of Health), 1.4.

11 Ibid, in foreword by Caroline Flint MP, then Parliament Under Secretary of State for Public Health.

was passed, receiving Royal Assent on 13 November 2008. According to the Department of Health, the key provisions of the 2008 Act were included to:

- ensure that all human embryos outside the body – whatever the process used in their creation – are subject to regulation;
- ensure regulation of 'human-admixed' embryos created from a combination of human and animal genetic material for research;
- ban sex selection of offspring for non-medical reasons;[12]
- recognise same-sex couples as legal parents of children conceived through the use of donated sperm, eggs or embryos;
- retain a duty to take account of the welfare of the child in providing fertility treatment, but replace the reference to 'the need for a father' with 'the need for supportive parenting' – hence valuing the role of all parents;
- alter the restrictions on the use of HFEA-collected data to help enable follow-up research of infertility treatment.[13]

The provisions of the 2008 Act came into force in three stages: first, the Act's revised definitions of parenthood, including a new ability for couples in same-sex relationships and unmarried couples in 'enduring family relationships' to be recognised as the legal parents of a child born via ART; second, amendments to the 1990 Act including the regulation of research on human admixed embryos and removal of the need to consider a putative child's 'need for a father' when undertaking a welfare assessment; and the final stage relating to commissioning parents' eligibility to obtain a Parental Order following a surrogacy arrangement.[14] Despite its relative infancy, it too has not been without its critics, many of whom consider that it does not represent a wholesale review of regulation, but just some 'tinkering at the margins' (Fox, 2009; also see McCandless and Sheldon, 2010a) or that it contains a less than adequate consideration of particular issues (e.g. McCandless and Sheldon 2010b; Horsey, 2010; Horsey and Sheldon, 2012; Lee et al., 2013, 2014).

This book represents a snapshot of opinions on various aspects of the 2008 Act and comparative legislation, analysing and considering whether its provisions go far enough (or even too far) and meet the aim of bringing and keeping the law up to date. It first considers the revised 'welfare of the child' clause (Blyth, chapter 2), which mandates that clinics must consider the welfare of any putative child before offering any fertility treatment. The clause in itself has always been contentious since its introduction in 1990 (see e.g. Jackson, 2002, 2007), but nevertheless it

12 This puts into statute a ban on non-medical sex selection which was already in place as a matter of HFEA policy. Sex selection (of embryos) is allowed for medical reasons – for example to avoid a serious disease that affects only boys.

13 Department of Health archive 'Human Fertilisation and Embryology Act 2008' <http://webarchive.nationalarchives.gov.uk/20130107105354/http://www.dh.gov.uk/en/Publicationsandstatistics/Legislation/Actsandbills/DH_080211>.

14 Including surrogacy, although this would not be automatic as with other types of treatment and would still require an application to be made for a Parental Order, previously outlined in section 30 of the 1990 Act, now as section 54 of the 2008 Act.

provoked a great deal of heated debate in Parliament and in the press when the new Act was being debated, largely due to the proposed removal of the terminology requiring clinics to consider the putative child's 'need for a father' as part of this welfare assessment, and replace it with a consideration of children's need 'for supportive parenting'. As has been stated and critiqued elsewhere, this point alone (billed as the fact that fathers were no longer needed) made up eight of the 80 hours in total in which the Act was debated in Parliament (McCandless and Sheldon, 2010b), highlighting its controversial nature and the potential cultural significance of the fatherhood notion.

In chapter 3, Emily Jackson considers the largely unstudied modern phenomenon of 'DIY assisted conception', analysing not only the law's failure to reach those – not illegal – private arrangements whereby one man may provide sperm for a woman or couple outside the confines of a licensed clinic and the dangers this may pose, but also the increased dangers of 'internet-assisted conception'. Jackson contends that DIY assisted conception – including the ability to travel abroad to receive treatments that perhaps are not easily available at home – can now be said to 'coexist' with strictly regulated fertility treatments, meaning that regulation both before and since cannot be said to be comprehensive, and then considers whether or not these gaps in the regulatory framework matter.

Helen Codd (chapter 4) looks at prisoners' access to fertility treatments. She argues that different questions arise when prisoners and their partners seek access to fertility services, leading to different problems and potentially different legal outcomes, and that these issues are marginalised within the larger debates on access, welfare and rights. Up to now, case law and scholarship looking at prisoners' rights in this respect have focused on access to assisted insemination services rather than IVF, thus highlighting the injustices that might be done to the partners of imprisoned people who may suffer disproportionately as a result of decisions not to allow for example a prisoner's sperm to be taken out of prison for use in clinical IVF treatment where it is the prisoner's female *partner* who needs the fertility assistance. Similarly, there are questions about who makes the decisions when it comes to prisoners seeking fertility services in the sense that it would be politicians rather than clinicians who do so, thus placing them in a category of their own and making decisions in relation to them – and again particularly for female *partners* – subject to different rules and procedures.

In chapter 5, Karen Devine thinks outside the box and considers the idea of 'benefits in kind' in relation to fertility treatments in a novel way. While IVF with egg-sharing schemes (a reduction in the cost of one's treatment in return for the contribution of ova for someone else) have been around for some time, they are not without controversy. Some define them as a 'win-win' situation, while others express reservation about the potential coerciveness of such an arrangement as well as the potential psychological consequences that might be felt if the sharer fails to conceive while the woman who also used her eggs did (see e.g. Gurtin-Broadbent, 2012). Devine, meanwhile, illustrates that while egg sharing provides both parties some benefits, the process may leave non-affluent women what she calls 'doubly disadvantaged'. To counter this, she proposes that the potential for use and exchange of a different material – umbilical cord blood (UCB) stem cells rather than eggs – might lead to both more equitable access to fertility treatment whilst also increasing the provision of a much-needed medical resource (UCB stem cells). This would require a necessary merge of the regulatory functions and oversight of the HFEA and the Human Tissue Authority (for this particular process at least), an idea seemingly off the agenda at present.

Jeanne Snelling and Colin Gavaghan then consider, in chapter 6, whether the 2008 Act is 'fit for purpose' in terms of the regulation of PGD. This is later mirrored by the chapter from Isabel Karpin (chapter 12), who compares the Australian PGD regulatory model against that of the UK. Snelling and Gavaghan outline the history of PGD's regulation and contend that the technique was one of the larger driving forces behind the introduction and the form of comprehensive legislation in the first instance (the 1990 Act). They then go on to critically analyse the approach to PGD taken by the HFEA in the years between the two Acts, followed by an analysis of the statutory parameters that govern the provision of IVF with PGD today. Comparing two examples (use of PDG to determine rhesus antibody status and to enable sex selection in conditions which are not X-chromosome linked but do have unequal sex incidence – e.g. autism), they suggest that the new regulatory regime is no clearer than it was previously. Moreover, they question the role the state has in regulating these kinds of decisions in the first place, rather than patients in conjunction with their doctors. Isabel Karpin, while comparing the approach to PGD in Australia with that in the UK, does not focus on the more usual debates regarding whether and, if so, in what circumstances, non-medical sex selection should be a permissible use of PGD. Instead, her focus is on the currently permissible *medical* sex selection or sex selection to avoid the birth of a child with a sex- or gender-related disorder. In particular, she argues that legal facilitation of this form of sex selection raises important and under-examined questions regarding the significance of the gendering of disability.

Laura Riley's chapter (chapter 7) provides a very topical overview of novel cell reconstruction techniques not yet used in humans which following Parliamentary assent in February 2015 can now be licensed under Regulations to the 2008 Act for use in fertility treatments in the UK. 'Maternal spindle transfer' and 'pronuclear transfer' are both variations of ordinary IVF currently being researched both in the UK and the US, which allow for the embryo to be created without mitochondrial DNA disorders that may result in any children born being affected by an incurable condition. The techniques are considered by many to be controversial as the resulting embryos contain the nuclear genetic material from one woman and mitochondrial DNA from another woman, creating the novel category of 'mitochondrial donor', who has donated an egg for this purpose. This has led to some commentators dubbing the technique the creation of '3-parent babies' (see e.g. Macrae, 2014) or the children who might be born as a result having 'two mothers'; Riley argues it is wrong to view it this way. While controversial, there are those who, like Riley, clearly believe that the UK is the best place to 'consider taking the next brave steps' (Flinter, 2014), given the supportive framework of the legislation and the experience of the regulatory authority (the HFEA). Others, including backbench Members of Parliament led by conservative Fiona Bruce MP, have attempted to delay the process of laying Regulations before Parliament, in the interests of 'public safety' (Hansard, 1 September 2014; col 93), saying that 'to allow these procedures at present would be tantamount to experimentation'. The issue generated a sharply polarised media and parliamentary debate, but if the yea-sayers are proved right, further uses of the techniques may be proposed, meaning that further changes need to be made to the law in the future.

In a first look at surrogacy for this volume, in chapter 8, Katia Neofytou and I first consider the failings of the 2008 Act to have touched on the sheer number of aspects of the current regulation of surrogacy that need to be addressed. While the Act does bring into line the availability of Parental Orders to same-sex couples and unmarried couples (same-sex or heterosexual) in 'enduring family relationships' with the more automatic allocation of parenthood following use of other forms of fertility treatment, it has not questioned the assumption that the Parental Order mechanism is the best (or only?) way to determine legal parenthood following surrogacy arrangements. Looking to the way surrogacy arrangements are regulated in Greece and Israel, we consider what alternative methods might be preferable. While these regulatory models have their own imperfections and their own limits, they each show the potential for pre-birth allocation of parenthood and for state-sanctioned surrogacy contracts. With the inexorably increasing wealth of internet information about surrogacy in other jurisdictions, where it is both legal (or unregulated) and easy to access (perhaps because surrogates are allowed to be paid for their services) comes increasing danger for those seeking surrogacy from the UK.

We argue that it is imperative that UK surrogacy law is fully reviewed, particularly given the failure to do so when the opportunity arose in 2005–2008, and especially if we wish to avoid the harms that may come with internationalised surrogacy arrangements. In this respect, we welcome the activities of some interest groups and within Parliament in late 2014 which seem to point towards surrogacy potentially re-entering the political agenda some time in 2015. The law has become more out of date than it ever was, and rests on assumptions that are no longer true, if they ever were. Better and more facilitative domestic regulation, including honesty about payments and better recognition of what parenthood means in this context, might mean that fewer people seek surrogates overseas. It may also mean that our judges would not be forced to find ways around existing legislative parameters in order to provide just solutions (Rozenberg, 2014), as is illustrated in both the UK and Australian context (where surrogacy is potentially even more controversial) by Anita Stuhmcke in chapter 13. Stuhmcke argues that judicial creativity in both jurisdictions is borne out of necessity, due to prohibitive domestic policies in the light of internationalised surrogacy. One answer to this, she contends, has been the creation of the notion of 'altruistic commerce' (see also Millbank, 2014), a concept that allows courts in the UK to bridge the gap between profit and morality, and judges to retrospectively authorise payments that in technical terms they otherwise ought not to, while in the Australian context the lines between family law and criminal sanctions have been blurred.

In chapter 9, Eric Blyth and Lucy Frith consider the rights of those born following the use of donated gametes or embryos to access their genetic and biographical histories. The extent to which access should be granted, and the extent of the information that may be received, has been a major focus of debate and policy in many different jurisdictions. This chapter provides a comparative overview of what is available where, noting that over the past few decades, professional practice has moved towards favouring disclosure of donor conception and this has in many instances been mirrored by legal developments. The chapter looks at the similarities and differences between the approaches of different legal regimes and considers the current UK law in this context, highlighting ways in which the law could be improved in order to promote the ability of donor-conceived individuals to discover their genetic and biographical history.

Antony Blackburn-Starza, in chapter 10, considers whether mechanisms for redress when there is a failure in the provision of a fertility service could be put on a statutory footing and/or be better recognised in the common law. He contends that although definition and categorisation of the harms that might arise in the fertility context might be difficult, this is no reason to ignore them, as they are clearly harms deeply felt by those affected (and often their families). In a detailed and philosophical reflection on the nature of fertility treatment-based harms and the kind of normative framework in which actionable damage might sit, he argues for the provision of redress to bring fertility treatments into line with other aspects of medicine and with contemporary trends in bioethics more generally.

Finally, Canada's difficulties in regulating reproduction are the subject of chapter 11. Pamela White critically analyses Canada's Assisted Human Reproduction Act 2004, a 'less than perfect law', much of which was struck down by a decision of the Supreme Court of Canada in 2010. The legislation had taken as its inspiration the framework and ideologies of the Human Fertilisation and Embryology Act 1990, and had been a long time in the making. Unfortunately, the Supreme Court felt that the 2004 Act exceeded federal powers under the Canadian constitution, raising interesting issues of governance of subjects deemed ethically and politically sensitive. White concludes by looking at future potential directions for legislation in Canada.

References

BioNews (2004) 'Donor anonymity to be removed in UK' *BioNews* 242 (21 January 2004, Progress Educational Trust).

Brazier, M. (1999) 'Regulating the reproduction business' 7 *Medical Law Review* 166.

Department of Health (2005) *Review of the Human Fertilisation and Embryology Act: A public consultation* (London: Department of Health).

Flinter, F. (2014) 'Mitochondrial donation as a clinical option: a response to Ted Morrow' *BioNews* 773 (29 September 2014, Progress Educational Trust).

Fox, M. (2009) 'The Human Fertilisation and Embryology Act 2008: Tinkering at the margins' 17(3) *Feminist Legal Studies* 333.

Gurtin-Broadbent, Z. (2012) 'Evaluating egg-sharing: new findings on old debates' *BioNews* 653 (23 April 2012, Progress Educational Trust).

Horsey, K. (2010) 'Challenging presumptions: Legal parenthood and surrogacy arrangements' 4(22) *Child and Family Law Quarterly* 449.

Horsey, K. and Sheldon, S. (2012) 'Still hazy after all these years: The law regulating surrogacy' 20(1) *Medical Law Review* 67.

House of Commons Science and Technology Committee (2005) *Human Reproductive Technologies and the Law*, fifth report of session 2004–5, HC 7–1.

Jackson, E. (2001) *Regulating reproduction: Law, technology and reproductive autonomy* (Oxford: Hart Publishing).

Jackson, E. (2002) 'Consent and the irrelevance of the welfare principle' 65 *Modern Law Review* 176.

Jackson, E. (2007) 'Rethinking the pre-conception welfare principle' in Horsey, K. and Biggs, H. (eds) *Human fertilisation and embryology: Reproducing regulation* (Abingdon: Routledge-Cavendish).

Lee, E. (ed) (2002) *Designer babies: Where should we draw the line?* (London: Hodder and Stoughton).

Lee, E., Macvarish, J. and Sheldon, S. (2013) 'The role of counsellors in infertility clinics' *BioNews* 691 (4 February 2013, Progress Educational Trust).

Lee, E., Macvarish, J. and Sheldon, S. (2014) 'Assessing child welfare under the Human Fertilisation and Embryology Act 2008: A case study in medicalisation' 36 *Sociology of Health and Illness* 500.

Macrae, F. (2014) 'Three-parent babies "could be a reality within two years" after report finds controversial IVF techniques are "not unsafe"' *The Daily Mail* 3 June 2014.

McCandless, J. and Sheldon, S. (2010a) 'The Human Fertilisation and Embryology Act (2008) and the tenacity of the sexual family model' 73(2) *Modern Law Review* 175.

McCandless, J. and Sheldon, S. (2010b) '"No father required"? The welfare assessment in the Human Fertilisation and Embryology Act 2008' 18 *Feminist Legal Studies* 201.

Millbank, J. (2014) 'Rethinking "commercial" surrogacy in Australia' *Journal of Bioethical Inquiry* (July 2014).

Rozenberg, J. (2014) 'High Court put justice before statutory requirements in surrogacy case' *The Guardian* 9 October 2014.

Warnock Committee Report (1984) *Committee of Inquiry into Human Fertilisation and Embryology*, Report. London: HMSO, Cmnd 9314.

Warnock, M. (2002) *Making babies: Is there a right to have children?* (Oxford: Oxford University Press).

2 From need 'for a father' to need 'for supportive parenting': Changing conceptualisations of the welfare of the child following assisted reproductive technology in the United Kingdom

Eric Blyth

Introduction

In previous work I have discussed the inception of the requirement to take account of the welfare of children to be born as a result of assisted reproductive technology (ART) in the United Kingdom and related policy developments up to 2006 (Blyth, 2007). This chapter continues that account, providing a critical review of policy debates and regulatory and legislative shifts up to the present time.

The principal sources of review and reform emanate from temporally overlapping and, at times, antagonistic, parliamentary, government and regulatory body initiatives – as outlined in Table 2.1:

- A Department of Health consultation on whether genetic and biographical information should be made available to a donor-conceived person (Department of Health, 2001, 2003), resulting in: (1) standardisation of collection of non-identifying donor information by the regulatory body, the Human Fertilisation and Embryology Authority (HFEA); (2) a requirement that from April 2005 all donors had to agree to disclosure of their identity to adult donor offspring (Human Fertilisation and Embryology Authority (Disclosure of Donor Information) Regulations 2004); (3) creation of a voluntary contact register for individuals conceived by donor conception prior to implementation of the 1990 Human Fertilisation and Embryology Act (hereafter 'the 1990 Act'), their donors and other genetic relatives;
- A consultation by the HFEA on the operation of the welfare of the child requirement (Human Fertilisation and Embryology Authority, 2005a), resulting: in (1) liberalisation of the child welfare provisions (Human Fertilisation and Embryology Authority, 2007); (2) advocacy of early parental disclosure of donor conception to their donor-conceived children (Human Fertilisation and Embryology Authority, 2005b);
- An *Inquiry into Human Reproductive Technologies and the Law* undertaken by the House of Commons Science and Technology Select Committee between 2004 and 2005 that advocated abolition of the welfare of the child provision

'in its current form' (House of Commons Science and Technology Committee, 2005a: 107) and criticised the removal of donor anonymity (House of Commons Science and Technology Committee, 2005a: 158);

- A Department of Health review of the 1990 Act, resulting in the replacement of the obligation on fertility clinics to take account of the child's need for 'a father' with that for 'supportive parenting' (a complex process taking place between November 2005 and November 2009 involving: (1) a public consultation (Department of Health, 2005); (2) a White Paper (Department of Health, 2006); (3) a draft Human Tissue and Embryos Bill that was subject to pre-legislative scrutiny by a Committee from both Houses of Parliament that itself involved further extra-parliamentary consultation (House of Lords/House of Commons, 2007a, 2007b); (4) a revised Human Fertilisation and Embryology Bill, which became the Human Fertilisation and Embryology Act 2008 (hereafter 'the 2008 Act'). Parliamentary debate provided further opportunity for discussion of legislative provisions regarding the welfare of children born following ARTs. Indeed, this single topic accounted for 10 per cent of the time legislators debated the Bill, before it completed its parliamentary passage in November 2008 to take effect from 1 October 2009 (McCandless and Sheldon, 2010). This was remarkable in the light of, first, the serendipitous manner in which the requirement to take account of the welfare of the child found its way into the legislation in the first place (Blyth, 2007); second, Baroness Warnock's (2007) perceptive and accurate comment (in the view of this writer) that 'it has always been a pretty ineffective bit of legislation', and third, the eventual outcome – the removal of two words, 'a father', from section 13(5) of the 1990 Act, and their replacement by two more, 'supportive parenting', as indicated below:

> A woman shall not be provided with [infertility] treatment services unless account has been taken of the welfare of any child who may be born as a result of the treatment (including the need of that child for *a father*), and of any other child who may be affected by the birth.
>
> (Human Fertilisation and Embryology Act 1990, s 13(5) – my emphasis)

> A woman shall not be provided with treatment services unless account has been taken of the welfare of any child who may be born as a result of the treatment (including the need of that child for *supportive parenting*), and of any other child who may be affected by the birth.
>
> (Human Fertilisation and Embryology Act 1990, s 13(5) (as amended) – my emphasis)

In addition, as an eventual compromise regarding divergent views on how best to promote disclosure of their genetic and biographical history to donor-conceived people, the 2008 Act gave statutory backing to the HFEA's existing guidance on early parental disclosure (Human Fertilisation and Embryology Act 1990, s 13(6C) – as amended) (see also Blyth and Frith, this volume).

Table 2.1 Welfare of the Child: UK legislative and policy review 2004–2009

June 2004	House of Commons Science and Technology Select Committee *Inquiry into Human Reproductive Technologies and the Law* launched
January 2005	HFEA *Tomorrow's Children* (welfare of the child) consultation launched
March 2005	House of Commons Science and Technology Select Committee *Inquiry into Human Reproductive Technologies and the Law* report published
April 2005	Commencement of Human Fertilisation and Embryology Authority (Disclosure of Donor Information) Regulations 2004 requiring all new gamete and embryo donors to agree to their identity being disclosed to any donor-conceived individual aged at least 18 years requesting this information from the HFEA
August 2005	Department of Health *Review of the Human Fertilisation and Embryology Act: A Public Consultation* launched
November 2005	HFEA *Tomorrow's Children* (report following welfare of the child consultation) published
November 2005	Department of Health *Review of the Human Fertilisation and Embryology Act: A public consultation* – end of consultation
December 2006	*White Paper Review of the Human Fertilisation and Embryology Act: Proposals for revised legislation* (including establishment of the Regulatory Authority for Tissue and Embryos) published
May 2007	Draft Human Tissue and Embryology Bill published for pre-legislative scrutiny by Joint Parliamentary Scrutiny Committee
August 2007	Joint Parliamentary Scrutiny Committee report on Draft Human Tissue and Embryology Bill published
October 2007	Government response to Joint Parliamentary Scrutiny Committee report published
December 2007	Human Fertilisation and Embryology Bill introduced in House of Lords
November 2008	Human Fertilisation and Embryology Act 2008 received Royal Assent
November 2009	Eighth edition of HFEA *Code of Practice* published (further revisions April 2010, April 2011, October 2011, April 2012, October 2012)

The welfare of the child in ART: 1991–2005

Legislation regulating the fast-moving world of medical technology is always going to have difficulty keeping up with the pace of change. Thus future reform of the 1990 Act was inevitable from the outset and in at least one respect review was inherent as regards the welfare of children born as a result of donor conception. The 1990 Act endorsed contemporaneous practice in donor conception in which anonymity between donor and recipient was accepted as a given. Section 31 of the Act made provision for a donor-conceived individual reaching the age of 18 years to request information about his or her donor held by the HFEA. This information was to be specified in subsequent regulations, but explicitly excluded the donor's identity. The management of requests for this information was seen as especially sensitive and pertinent to 'child welfare'; arguably, the 1990 Act militated against the welfare of donor-conceived individuals who considered knowledge of their donor to be integral to their sense of their own welfare. Following implementation of the Act, interested stakeholders who had campaigned for the abolition of donor anonymity from the outset lobbied the government to ensure a timely clarification of this information and suitable systems for its disclosure to young donor-conceived people, the first of whom to become eligible to take advantage of this provision would come of age in 2010 (Wincott and Crawshaw, 2006).

The government eventually acceded to these requests in 2001–2002 and in January 2003, the then Minister of Health, Hazel Blears MP, stated the government's position, while also making her own opinion clear:

> I think there is a strong argument in principle that donor conceived children are able to find out the identity of their donor.
>
> (Blears, 2003)

However, mindful of opposition to such a move, especially from fertility clinics, primarily concerned about the possible adverse impact on donor supply and potential conflict between the interests of different parties involved in donor conception, she proposed a 'wider debate' to elicit more information from clinics and donors, and draw on the experiences of jurisdictions that had already prohibited donor anonymity, and indicated that she intended making a final decision within six months. Meanwhile, two specific measures were agreed. First, the standardisation of non-identifying donor information collected by the HFEA to be made available to a donor-conceived person and, second, funding for a pilot voluntary contact register to enable individuals conceived before implementation of the 1990 Act, their donors, and any half siblings to establish their donor links through DNA testing and to make contact by mutual consent. (This subsequently became UK Donorlink (Crawshaw and Marshall, 2008; Crawshaw et al., 2013).)

There was, indeed, extensive and impassioned debate regarding the removal of donor anonymity and its presumed consequences. Opposition was largely presented in terms of anticipated *practical* consequences rather than as a matter of *principle*, although some critics contended that any measure likely to reduce the number of children born as a result of donor conception could hardly advance the cause of child welfare (Cohen, 2012; Harris, 2004; Jackson, 2002; Savulescu, 2004; Wilkinson, 2003). Two key adverse outcomes were anticipated – a reduction in the number of donors and a reduced likelihood of parents telling their donor-conceived children about their conception because of fears they might contact their donor.

The major professional medical bodies representing physicians working in ART voiced opposition to the proposed policy change on the grounds of its anticipated adverse impact on donor recruitment (British Fertility Society, 2004; British

Medical Association, 2004; Royal College of Obstetricians and Gynaecologists, 2004). However, the British Medical Association highlighted conflicts of opinion between the organisation's Medical Ethics Committee, which supported the abolition of anonymity, and its Representative Body. Some critics forecast a cataclysmic effect on donor conception, including the emasculation of egg sharing and oocyte donation (Henderson, 2004), while Pennings (2001: 617) predicted a loss of 'about 80%' of donors.

In the event, Blears' proposed timescale fell victim to political exigencies and it was left to her successor, Melanie Johnson, to take forward this work. Virtually one year later, Johnson announced that, despite the overwhelming opposition of clinics and mixed responses from donors whose views had been secured, the government would seek parliamentary approval for the abolition of donor anonymity with effect from 1 April 2005. The principles on which this decision was based were unambiguous:

> I believe that in an increasingly-open society, donor-conceived people born in the coming years will want as much information as possible [...] I believe they have a strong case. Is it reasonable for information about genetic origins that is held on a national database to be withheld from them? [...] It has not been an easy decision to make. We have concluded that the interests of the child are paramount [...] We believe that it is right that people conceived by future donations should be able to obtain identifying information about their donor.
>
> (Johnson, 2004)

Subsequently, two overlapping processes involving exploration and debate on child welfare issues took place during 2004 and 2005. In June 2004, the House of Commons Science and Technology Select Committee launched its *Inquiry into Human Reproductive Technologies and the Law,* reporting in March 2005 (House of Commons Science and Technology Committee, 2005a, 2005b). During 2005, the HFEA undertook consultations on the 1990 Act's welfare of the child provisions (HFEA, 2005a, 2005b). Both exercises evinced divergent views held by various interested parties who were sufficiently motivated to make known their opinions.

House of Commons Science and Technology Select Committee Inquiry into Human Reproductive Technologies and the Law

The 1990 Act's welfare of the child provisions, the government's continuing support for these and the abolition of donor anonymity were severely criticised by the Committee, although half of its members formally distanced themselves from the libertarian partisanship evident in its report, which was approved only with the chair's casting vote (House of Commons Science and Technology Committee, 2005c). The Committee proposed abolition of the child welfare provision 'in its current form' because it 'discriminat[es] against the infertile and some sections of society, [is] impossible to implement and [...] of questionable practical value in protecting the interests of children born as a result of assisted reproduction' (House of Commons Science and Technology Committee, 2005a: 107). The Committee specifically slated articulation of the 'need for a father' for being 'too open to interpretation and unjustifiably offensive to many' (House of Commons Science and Technology Committee, 2005a: 101). Nevertheless, acknowledging that there might be occasions when valid child welfare issues might be raised as a result of providing ART services to particular individuals, the Committee's proposed solution implausibly advocated increasing the workloads of already overstretched child safeguarding agencies:

> The State employs social services to protect children from harm. If it has reason to believe that children born as a result of assisted reproduction are at increased risk then healthcare professionals can alert social services at an early stage.
>
> (House of Commons Science and Technology Committee, 2005a: 103)

The Committee voiced its objection to the removal of donor anonymity not only on the anticipated adverse impact on donor supply,[1] but also because of the possibility that parents would be less inclined to tell their donor-conceived children about their conception in the first place, a proposition initially floated by the British Medical Association (2004: 228). In her evidence to the Committee, Professor Susan Golombok (2004: 136) asserted that empirical evidence on this matter was largely anecdotal. Despite the manifestly thin evidence base, the Committee nevertheless concluded:

> there is a *powerful* argument that the ending of such anonymity would result in a greater likelihood of parents not telling the child because the fear (rational or not) of rejection in favour of an identifiable biological parent outweighs the advantage of having identifying information to transmit.
>
> (House of Commons Science and Technology Committee, 2005a: 157 – my emphasis)

A more circumspect conclusion would suggest that while the jury is still out, there is some emerging evidence to contradict the Committee's conclusion, in which

1 Continuing criticism of the removal of donor anonymity from other interested parties followed implementation of the legislation, augmented by legendary fertility specialist Lord Winston (2006), and two former chairs of the HFEA, Sir Colin Campbell (2006) and Baroness Deech (2006). Dr Evan Harris MP, a member of the House of Commons Science and Technology Committee, described the abandonment of anonymity as 'stupid and misguided' (cited in Woolf, 2006) and in June 2008 claimed: 'There was no good reason for removing anonymity, which has led to a catastrophic drop in the number of patients treated by donor insemination. There was always a huge risk that this would happen, diminishing the capacity of both the NHS and private clinics to treat infertility. There are probably now thousands of untreated couples who may be forced abroad, or into the unregulated sector' (cited in Henderson, 2008).

encouragement and facilitation of increased transparency, whether through regulation, legislation or professional practice, appear to contribute to a climate of increased parental disclosure.

Further, as official HFEA data illustrate (Table 2.2), the impact of the legislative change to remove donor anonymity on donor recruitment has been significantly less draconian than feared by opponents. The number of new semen donor registrations dropped to an all-time low in 2004, coinciding with the removal of donor anonymity. Subsequently, modest increases were recorded each year until 2012. However, a slight fall-back was recorded in 2013 and about one-third of new sperm donor registrations are of foreign imports that fulfil UK regulatory requirements (the most recent available data) (HFEA, 2014). HFEA data show a steady increase in new oocyte donor registrations between 1992 and 2001, followed by reductions until 2006 (where a significant fall was recorded). In the years since 2006, however, modest continuous increases have been sustained.

HFEA Review: Tomorrow's Children

In January 2005, the HFEA initiated a public consultation on the operation of section 13(5) (Human Fertilisation and Embryology Authority, 2005a). Unlike

Table 2.2 All new donors registered 1992–2013

Year	*Semen donors*	*Oocyte donors*
1992	375	451
1993	426	528
1994	417	732
1995	414	749
1996	419	806
1997	343	910
1998	256	943
1999	302	1,120
2000	323	1,241
2001	327	1,302
2002	288	1,174
2003	257	1,032
2004	237	1,106
2005	285	1,025
2006	307	812
2007	355	1,016
2008	403	1,157
2009	438	1,191
2010	492	1,261
2011	541	1,523
2012	631	1,634
2013	586	1,636

Source: 1992–2003 (Human Fertilisation and Embryology Authority, 2013); 2004–2013 (Human Fertilisation and Embryology Authority, 2014).

the House of Commons Science and Technology Select Committee inquiry, the HFEA review focused merely on the welfare of the child requirement within the terms of the 1990 Act and therefore could neither invite nor consider proposals for legislative change nor advocate itself for this, although the consultation provided further evidence of the controversial nature of section 13(5) (Human Fertilisation and Embryology Authority, 2005b; Jackson, 2002). Following the consultation, several key changes were made to the guidance given to clinics (HFEA, 2005c), which took effect from 1 January 2006 and which was later incorporated into the seventh edition of the HFEA *Code of Practice* (HFEA, 2007).

The new guidance was designed to:

> focus [...] more clearly on the risk factors that could lead to serious harm, [provide] … a system that is fairer for patients and more proportionate for doctors whilst still protecting children's interests, which should be predicated in a presumption to provide services to an individual or couple except where there was evidence of a risk of serious medical, physical or psychological harm to any child born (or any existing child of their family).
>
> (HFEA, 2005d)

The new focus on risk of serious harm represented further liberalisation of provisions relating to the child's 'need for a father' that the HFEA had initiated in its sixth edition of the Code of Practice (HFEA, 2004a).

Where the child will have no legal father, the fifth edition of the Code of Practice 'required':

> centres […] to have regard to the child's need for a father and [to] pay particular attention to the prospective mother's ability to meet the child's needs *throughout their childhood.* Where appropriate, centres should consider particularly whether there is anyone else within the prospective mother's family and social circle willing and able to share the responsibility for meeting those needs, *and for bringing up, maintaining and caring for the child.*
>
> (HFEA, 2001: 3.15 – my emphasis)

In the sixth edition, centres were 'expected':

> to assess the prospective mother's ability to meet the child's/children's needs and the ability of other persons within the family or social circle willing to share responsibility for those needs.
>
> (HFEA, 2004a: 3.14)

While the wording of this obligation remained substantially the same in the seventh edition, save for substituting the phrase 'is expected to assess' with 'should assess' (HFEA, 2007: G.3.3.3), the ability of a clinic to use it to justify withholding treatment was significantly reduced. Henceforth it was to be considered only in determining the child's potential exposure to risk of 'serious harm'. The guidance further warned against 'unfair discrimination on grounds of gender, race, disability, sexual orientation, religious belief or age' (HFEA, 2007: G.3.3.2), replacing a more generalised requirement to undertake a 'fair assessment', which should be conducted 'with skill and care' and with due regard 'to the wishes and sensitivities of all involved' (HFEA, 2004a: 3.12).

In response to criticism regarding the HFEA's previous requirement for a patient's GP to be contacted as a matter of routine, the new guidance specified that enquiries of 'any individuals, agencies or authorities for [...] further factual information' should be undertaken only where the clinic suspected a risk of serious harm to the child, or where the information gathered was incomplete, inconsistent or deception was suspected (HFEA, 2007). Once further information was obtained, treatment should be refused only if this indicated that either the child to be born or any existing child of the family is likely to experience 'serious harm' or where the clinic *still had insufficient information 'to conclude that there is no significant risk'* (HFEA, 2007: G.3.4.5 – my emphasis). This replaced previous guidance that a clinic 'may refuse treatment where it is unable to obtain sufficient information or advice on which to make a proper assessment' (HFEA, 2004a: 3.23(iii)).

As had been the case previously, further enquiries should not be undertaken without the individual's consent and the clinic should still take account of a refusal to consent. However, in a departure from previous policy, the HFEA stated that this 'should not itself be grounds for refusing treatment' (HFEA, 2007: G.3.4.4).

Parental disclosure of donor conception

Prior to the *Tomorrow's Children* review, the HFEA had required centres to take account of 'a child's potential need to know about their origins and whether or not the prospective parents are prepared for the questions which may arise while the child is growing up' (HFEA, 2001: 3.14a). Following the review, however, the HFEA adopted a radically proactive stance:

> There is evidence that finding out suddenly, later in life, about donor origins can be emotionally damaging to children and to family relations. Therefore, it should be made clear to individuals seeking treatment with donor gametes or embryos that telling their child/children about their origins early in childhood is in their welfare interests. Clinics should encourage and prepare patients to be open with their children from an early age about the circumstances of their conception
>
> (HFEA, 2005c: 5.6; 2007: G.5.4.6)[2]

2 However, the HFEA did not specifically cite the source of this evidence.

Promotion of increased transparency was part of a new approach pursued by the HFEA, which had – separately – seen the encouragement of clinics to 'respond as fully as possible to patients' requests for non-identifying information about the donor or donors used in their treatment' (Human Fertilisation and Embryology Authority, 2004b) – later encapsulated in the eighth edition of the *Code of Practice* (HFEA, 2009: 30.16(d)) – and what transpired to be a short-term measure, to provide parents of donor-conceived children with details of their children's donor codes (Blyth, 2012).

Department of Health Review of the 1990 Act

As part of its review of the 1990 Act, the government initiated a further round of public consultation (Department of Health, 2005). Notwithstanding the Science and Technology Committee's criticism of the removal of donor anonymity, the government made clear that this decision would not be revisited. Indeed, views on the question: 'what measures would be appropriate, if any, to *ensure* that parents tell children conceived through gamete or embryo donation that they are donor-conceived?' were specifically invited (Department of Health, 2005: 6.31 – my emphasis), as were comments on the welfare of the child provisions.

Respondents to the consultation proposed a range of possible options regarding parental disclosure, from parent-directed approaches as to whether and when to tell child(ren), to a legal obligation to do so. Some of those favouring a legal mandate suggested using birth certificates to indicate the individual's donor conception status, although this was rejected by others (People Science & Policy, 2006: 48–49). In the event, neither the White Paper (Department of Health, 2006: 2.58) nor the Human Tissue and Embryos (Draft) Bill 2007 made any reference either to parental obligations to tell their donor-conceived children about their conception or to the potential role of birth certificates in facilitating disclosure, although it was intended that provisions would be made to help donor-conceived people to ascertain if they had half-siblings as a result of donor conception.

As regards the welfare of the child provisions, members of the public who responded to the consultation generally favoured retention of a reference to the child's 'need for a father', with some recommending that reference be made to a need 'for both a mother and a father' (Department of Health, 2006: 2.25). The government, however, announced its intention to remove reference to the 'need for a father', taking into consideration recent legislation relating to civil partnerships, and its failure to be 'convinced that the retention of this provision could be justified in terms of evidence of harm, particularly when weighed against the potential harms arising from the consequences of encouraging some women who wish to conceive to make private arrangements for insemination rather than use licensed treatment services' (Department of Health, 2006: 2.26) (see also Emily Jackson in this volume).

The Human Tissue and Embryos (Draft) Bill 2007 (Department of Health, 2007a: 21(2)(b)) proposed the streamlined requirement that:

> A woman shall not be provided with treatment services, unless account has been taken of the welfare of any child who may be born as a result of the treatment, and of any other child who may be affected by the birth.

In line with new provisions regarding the introduction of proposed legislation, the draft Bill was sent for review by a joint parliamentary committee comprising members of the House of Lords and the House of Commons, in which the Committee called for both oral and written evidence (House of Lords/House of Commons, 2007a, 2007b). The Committee received evidence that largely replicated that obtained previously by the Department of Health, although it reached somewhat different conclusions. As regards disclosure of donor-conception status, the Committee was concerned that the benefit of removing donor anonymity was 'illusory if the fact of donor conception is not known' (House of Lords/House of Commons, 2007b: 272), and:

> [r]ecognise[d] the force of the argument that the fact of donor conception should be registered on a person's birth certificate. This would create the incentive for the parent(s) to tell the child of the fact of his or her donor conception and would go some way to address the value of knowledge of genetic history for medical purposes… [A]ssisted conception by its nature involves the authorities and we are deeply concerned about the idea that the authorities may be colluding in a deception. However, we also recognise that this is a complicated area involving the important issue of privacy, as well as issues of human rights and data protection. We therefore recommend that, as a matter of urgency, the Government should give this matter further consideration.
>
> (House of Lords/House of Commons, 2007a: Recommendation 28)

The Committee was also perturbed by the government's proposals to remove all reference to a child's parenting needs and the potential adverse implications of single parenting that eradication of the 'need for a father' requirement would presage. It observed that:

> a loving, supportive family network is more important for a child's development than the gender of the second parent and we note the provisions on parenthood in the draft Bill [….] in which a reference to a 'father' would no longer simply refer to a child's male parent, but would also refer to a woman who is a child's parent […] In an area such as this, the law has symbolic value. Ultimately, however, the issue is one of what is in the best interests of the child.
>
> (House of Lords/House of Commons, 2007b: 242)

And went on to recommend that:

> the current provision … including the 'need of that child for a father' should be retained but in an amended form in a way that makes clear it is capable of being interpreted as the 'need for a second parent'.
>
> (House of Lords/House of Commons, 2007b: 243)

In responding to the Committee's recommendations, the Department of Health acknowledged the sensitivity of birth certificate annotation but indicated its preference for educational rather than legislative measures to promote parental disclosure (Department of Health, 2007b: 69). However, it did promise to 'keep the matter under review' and to engage in 'constructive dialogue with stakeholders' (Department of Health, 2007b: 70). It also rejected the Committee's proposition to include reference to a 'second parent', even if this could be done without compromising single women's access to ART services, on the grounds that this would contribute nothing of significance to the existing proposal (Department of Health, 2007b: 57).

The government subsequently withdrew the draft Bill and a new Bill, the Human Fertilisation and Embryology Bill 2007, was introduced to the House of Lords in November 2007. As expected, this contained no specific measures regarding parental disclosure of donor conception and no reference to birth certificates, but included a revised child welfare requirement, that:

> a woman shall not be provided with treatment services unless account has been taken of the welfare of any child who may be born as a result of treatment *(including the need of that child for supportive parenting)*, and of any other child who may be affected by the birth.
>
> (Human Fertilisation and Embryology Act 1990, s 13(5) as amended – my emphasis)

During debate on the Bill in both the House of Lords and the House of Commons, further attempts were made to instate into the legislation provisions to use birth certification to record donor conception (Earl Howe, 2007; Baronesses Barker and Warnock and Earl Howe, 2007; Lord Jenkin, 2008; Robert Key, 2008). While none of these was supported, Parliament did agree to statutory backing of the HFEA's existing guidance regarding:

> (a) the importance of informing any resulting child at an early age that the child results from the gametes of a person who is not a parent of the child, and
> (b) suitable methods of informing such a child of that fact.
>
> (Human Fertilisation and Embryology Act 1990, s 13(6C) – as amended)

In addition, government ministers highlighted a previously announced agreement to work with the Donor Conception Network to explore 'ways in which current and potential parents of donor-conceived children can be encouraged to tell the children about their origins' (Royall, 2007) and gave a 'firm commitment' to 'carry out a review of practices in informing donor-conceived children of the fact of their donor conception and whether there is a need for a change in the law to best ensure that donor-conceived children are informed of their donor conception' within four years of the Act coming into force (Primarolo, 2008a, 2008b, 2008c, 2008d; Royall, 2008).[3] Similarly, members of both Houses sought to amend the welfare of the child requirement (see McCandless and Sheldon (2010) for a detailed review and discussion, especially the removal of the 'need for a father' requirements), although the government's original formulation prevailed.

Subsequent to the enactment of the Human Fertilisation and Embryology Act 2008 in 2009, the HFEA revised its *Code of Practice* that provides a definition of 'supportive parenting' as follows, extending the liberalising trend regarding the welfare clause evident in previous editions of the *Code*:

> Supportive parenting is a commitment to the health, well-being and development of the child. It is presumed that all prospective parents will be supportive parents, in the absence of any reasonable cause for concern that any child who may be born, or any other child, may be at risk of significant harm or neglect. Where centres have concern as to whether this commitment exists, they may wish to take account of wider family and social networks within which the child will be raised.
>
> (HFEA, 2009: 8.11)

Conclusions

Just over five years following implementation of the 2008 Act, it might be pertinent to ask whether it has made any difference either to professional or parental behaviour. An absence of evidence militates against a conclusive response at this point in time.

As regards parental disclosure, contrary to the fears of the Science and Technology Select Committee and others, such evidence as there is (from studies undertaken in the UK, Finland and Sweden) suggests increasing levels of parental disclosure over time. In 2008, Crawshaw published the results of a survey of counsellors in UK fertility clinics that was undertaken after the law on donor anonymity was changed in 2005. Counsellors reported that, compared with past experiences, more patients who were planning to build their family by means of donor conception were indicating their intention to tell their child about the nature of his or her conception. Whether or not such intentions translated to actual practice remain, of course, open to speculation in the absence of follow-up studies. Although no research has yet been published involving donor-conceived children born since anonymity was removed, a study of parents of children born

3 This commitment fell victim to the change of government following the general election of 2010 – since which time there has been no evidence that the government considers any such review to be sufficiently pressing.

following oocyte donation in 2000 who were interviewed when the children were one year old (Golombok *et al.*, 2004) and again when the children were aged seven years (Readings *et al.*, 2011) indicates increased levels of parental disclosure, albeit 'reflected more in [....] intentions than in actual disclosure patterns' (Readings *et al.*, 2011: 492), as well as illustrating parental discrimination in what to reveal (such as divulging recourse to IVF but not to oocyte donation). In the first phase of the study, in which 51 families participated, 29 (56%) parents stated their intention to tell their child about the circumstances of her or his conception, 11 (22%) were uncertain and 11 (22%) had decided not to tell. By the time of the second phase, 19 families had dropped out. Of the 32 families remaining in the study when their child was aged seven years (62.8% of the original group), 13 (40.6%) reported that they had already told their child, 10 (31.3%) were intending to tell, four (12.5%) were uncertain and five (15.6%) had decided not to tell. Unfortunately, the authors neither enumerate the dropout rates from each of the three initial disclosure groups nor pair participants' initial and later disclosure plans; this would have made it possible to generate specific decision-making trajectories for these parents and provide more helpful information to guide future policy and professional practice. Similar trends regarding increased parental inclinations have been observed in Sweden, where donor anonymity was removed in 1985 (Gottlieb *et al.*, 2000; Isaksson *et al.*, 2012; Lalos *et al.*, 2007; Milsom and Bergman, 1982) and in Finland, where donor anonymity was removed in 2007 (Söderström-Anttila *et al.*, 2010).

Lee, Macvarish and Sheldon (2012, 2014) have undertaken the first – and so far only – empirical study of practice in fertility clinics since implementation of the 2008 Act. The study highlighted a strong presumption by clinics to provide treatment in the absence of serious concerns about the welfare of the child, virtually universal support for taking account of children's welfare, concerns to avoid discriminating against potential patients, especially lesbian couples, and clinics' limited experiences of actually refusing to provide treatment on welfare grounds, although where such 'extreme cases' occurred they were usually 'complex and idiosyncratic'. At the same time, however, research participants reported their underlying awareness that, despite appearances, 'you can never know':

> the spectre of the paedophile shapes perceptions, as a person hardly ever encountered but whose threat nevertheless creates a powerful rationale for pre-emptive action.
>
> (Lee *et al.*, 2012)

Ironically, given the history of section 13(5), lesbian couples were often perceived within clinics as 'ideal parents' – although this was not especially surprising, given similar findings reported nearly two decades previously (Blyth, 1995). Concerns were, however, evident regarding the motivations of single women and their ability to be effective 'supportive' parents. As family form *per se* seemed to have retreated as a source of potential welfare concerns, these were found to be more directed towards the quality of future parent–child relationships, emotional and psychological issues, and disclosure to children where a family had been built using donor conception. The study provided evidence of confusion among at least some respondents about the meaning of 'supportive parenting'; some interpreted it as just a new way of referring to 'need for a father' especially in relation to treating single women, while others misinterpreted it as '*supported* parenting'.

However, what is perhaps the most revealing of the study's findings, given the time, energy and expense surrounding the legislative and regulatory changes, is that 'the new law appears to have had a relatively limited impact on clinics' previous practice' (Lee *et al.*, 2012), echoing a conclusion drawn by Douglas almost two decades previously following analysis of the impact of the then new Human Fertilisation and Embryology Act 1990:

> On the basis of this study s13(5) does not appear to have forced or even encouraged clinics to alter their approach to whom they will treat.
>
> (Douglas, 1993: 68)

This invites the hopefully not-too-flippant question 'What was the point?' In this case it was hardly to demonstrate the instrumental role of law or its impact in actual practice or on people's behaviour. Rather, if it serves any purpose at all, it is a symbolic one:

> whether or not legislation is implemented may be less important than the fact that the legislation has been introduced.
>
> (Stolz, 2007: 313)

The original formulation of the welfare requirement, especially including the reference to a child's 'need for a father' can be seen in this light, as an indication of concerns about the path taken by reproductive technology and the potential implications for family life as we know it or would like it to be (McCandless and Sheldon, 2010).

The past two decades have brought us increasing familiarity with ARTs – and perhaps some measure of desensitivisation regarding their more radical manifestations. The contribution of the revised welfare provisions requiring ART providers to take account of the needs of children born following ART for 'supportive parenting' towards 'ensur[ing] that the law is both effective and fit for purpose in the early 21st century' may be seen as little more than a symbolic gesture reflecting rather than shaping contemporary practice. A more rounded assessment of UK law affecting the interests of children born following ART may be made by taking account of provisions enabling donor-conceived adults to learn about their biographical and genetic heritage. Here – as Blyth and Frith (this volume) show – although there is scope for further development, the UK has emerged as a world leader.

Acknowledgement

I wish to thank Michelle Morelli for undertaking documentary research for this chapter, which was funded by an Innovations Grant from the University of Huddersfield School of Human and Health Sciences.

References

Barker, Baroness, Warnock, Baroness and Howe, Earl (2007) *Hansard* HL (Amendment 68B), 10 December, cols 91–108).

Blears, H. (2003) Speech to HFEA Annual Conference. 28 January. http://webarchive.nationalarchives.gov.uk/+/www.dh.gov.uk/en/MediaCentre/Speeches/Speecheslist/DH_4031642.

Blyth, E. (1995) 'The United Kingdom's Human Fertilisation and Embryology Act 1990 and the welfare of the child: a critique' 3 *International Journal of Children's Rights* 417.

Blyth, E. (2007) 'Conceptions of welfare' in Horsey, K. and Biggs, H. (eds) *Human fertilisation and embryology: Reproducing regulation* (London: Routledge-Cavendish) pp.17–45.

Blyth, E. (2012) 'Access to genetic and birth origins information for people conceived following third party assisted conception in the United Kingdom' 20 *International Journal of Children's Rights* 300.

British Fertility Society (2004) Memorandum from the British Fertility Society, Appendix 9. Ev 216 in House of Commons Science and Technology Committee (2005) *Human Reproductive Technologies and the Law: Fifth Report of Session 2004–05. Vol II: Oral and Written Evidence.* http://www.publications.parliament.uk/pa/cm200405/cmselect/cmsctech/7/7ii.pdf.

British Medical Association (2004) Memorandum from the British Medical Association, Appendix 12. Ev 228 in House of Commons Science and Technology Committee (2005) *Human Reproductive Technologies and the Law: Fifth Report of Session 2004–05. Vol II: Oral and Written Evidence.* http://www.publications.parliament.uk/pa/cm200405/cmselect/cmsctech/7/7ii.pdf.

Campbell, C. (2006) 'Donor identity rules and IVF' *The Times* 21 September. http://www.timesonline.co.uk/tol/comment/letters/article645747.ece.

Cohen, I.G. (2012) 'Response: rethinking sperm-donor anonymity: of changed selves, nonidentity, and one-night stands' 100 *The Georgetown Law Journal* 431.

Crawshaw, M., Gunter, C., Tidy, C. and Atherton, F. (2013) 'Working with previously anonymous gamete donors and donor-conceived adults: Recent practice experiences of running the DNA-based voluntary information exchange and contact register, UK Donorlink' 16 *Human Fertility* 26.

Crawshaw, M. and Marshall, L. (2008) 'Practice experiences of running UK Donorlink, a voluntary information exchange and contact register for adults related through donor conception' 11 *Human Fertility* 231.

Deech, Baroness (2006) 'Competing interests in sperm donor secrecy' *The Times* 23 September. http://www.timesonline.co.uk/tol/comment/letters/article1074373.ece.

Department of Health (2001) *Providing information about sperm, egg and embryo donors: Consultation document* (London: Department of Health).

Department of Health (2003) *Donor information: Providing information about gamete or embryo donors: Responses to consultation* (London: Department of Health).

Department of Health (2005) *Review of the Human Fertilisation and Embryology Act: A public consultation* (London: Department of Health).

Department of Health (2006) *Review of the Human Fertilisation and Embryology Act: Proposals for revised legislation (including establishment of the regulatory authority for tissue and embryos)* Cm 6989 (London: Department of Health).

Department of Health (2007a) *Human Tissue and Embryos (Draft) Bill 2007* Cm 7087 (London: HMSO).

Department of Health (2007b) *Government Response to the Report from the Joint Committee on the Human Tissue and Embryos (Draft) Bill* Cm 7209 (London: HMSO).

Douglas, G. (1993) 'Assisted reproduction and the welfare of the child' 5 *Current Legal Problems* 53.

Golombok, S. (2004) Evidence 136 in House of Commons Science and Technology Committee (2005) *Human Reproductive Technologies and the Law: Fifth Report of Session 2004–05. Vol II: Oral and Written Evidence.* http://www.publications.parliament.uk/pa/cm200405/cmselect/cmsctech/7/7ii.pdf.

Golombok, S., Lycett, E., MacCallum, F., Jadva, V., Murray, C. and Rust, J. (2004) 'Parenting infants conceived by gamete donation' 18 *Journal of Family Psychology* 443.

Gottlieb, C., Lalos, O. and Lindblad, F. (2000) 'Disclosure of donor insemination to the child: The impact of Swedish legislation on couples' attitudes' 15 *Human Reproduction* 2052.

Harris, J. (2004) *On cloning: Thinking in action* (London: Routledge).

Henderson, M. (2004) 'Egg shortage threatens baby hopes of thousands' *The Times* 22 January.

Henderson, M (2008) 'Childless couples denied as anonymity loss scares egg and sperm donors' *The Times* 26 June.

House of Commons Science and Technology Committee (2005a) *Human Reproductive Technologies and the Law. Fifth Report of Session 2004–05.* Vol I (London: The Stationery Office).

House of Commons Science and Technology Committee (2005b) *Human Reproductive Technologies and the Law. Fifth Report of Session 2004–05.* Vol II (London: The Stationery Office).

House of Commons Science and Technology Committee (2005c) *Inquiry into Human Reproductive Technologies and the Law. Eighth Special Report of Session 2004–05* (London: The Stationery Office).

House of Lords/House of Commons (2007a) *Joint Committee on the Human Tissue and Embryos (Draft) Bill.* Vol 1: Report (London: The Stationery Office).

House of Lords/House of Commons (2007b) *Joint Committee on the Human Tissue and Embryos (Draft) Bill.* Vol 2: Evidence (London: The Stationery Office).

Howe, Earl (2007) *Hansard* HL (Amendment 63) 10 December, cols. 91–108.

Human Fertilisation and Embryology Authority (2001) *Code of Practice*, 5th edition (London: HFEA).

Human Fertilisation and Embryology Authority (2004a) *Code of Practice*, 6th edition (London: HFEA).

Human Fertilisation and Embryology Authority (2004b) *Disclosure of information relating to gamete donation* CH(04)07. 28 October (London: HFEA).

Human Fertilisation and Embryology Authority (2005a) *Tomorrow's children: A consultation on guidance to licensed fertility clinics on taking in account the welfare of children to be born of assisted conception treatment* (London: HFEA).

Human Fertilisation and Embryology Authority (2005b) *Tomorrow's children: HFEA report of the policy review of welfare of the child assessments in licensed assisted conception clinics* (London: HFEA).

Human Fertilisation and Embryology Authority (2005c) *New guidance on welfare of the child assessments* (London: HFEA).

Human Fertilisation and Embryology Authority (2005d) 'Improved welfare checks system will be better, fairer and clearer for fertility patients, GPs and clinics', Human Fertilisation and Embryology Authority Press release, 2 November (London: HFEA).

Human Fertilisation and Embryology Authority (2007) *Code of practice*, 7th edition (London: HFEA).

Human Fertilisation and Embryology Authority (2009) *Code of practice*, 8th edition (London: HFEA).

Human Fertilisation and Embryology Authority (2013) *New sperm and egg donor registrations: UK 1992–2010*. http://www.hfea.gov.uk/3411.html.

Human Fertilisation and Embryology Authority (2014) Egg and sperm donation 2012–2013 datasheet. http://www.hfea.gov.uk/docs/Egg_and_sperm_donation_2012-2013_datasheet.xls.

Isaksson, S., Skoog Svanberg, A., Sydsjö, G., Thurin-Kjellberg, A., Karlström, P.O., Solensten, N.G. and Lampic, C. (2011) 'Two decades after legislation on identifiable donors in Sweden: are recipient couples ready to be open about using gamete donation?' 26 *Human Reproduction* 853.

Jackson, E. (2002) 'Consent and the irrelevance of the welfare principle' 65 *Modern Law Review* 176.

Jenkin, Lord (2008) *Hansard* HL (Amendment 146), 28 January, cols. 501–513.

Johnson, M. (2004) Speech to HFEA Annual Conference: Donor Anonymity and Review 21 January. http://webarchive.nationalarchives.gov.uk/+/www.dh.gov.uk/en/MediaCentre/speeches/speecheslist/dh_4071490.

Key, R. (2008) *Hansard* HC, 12 May, col. 114.

Lalos, A., Gottlieb, C. and Lalos, O. (2007) 'Legislated right for donor-insemination children to know their genetic origin: A study of parental thinking' 22 *Human Reproduction* 1759.

Lee, E., Macvarish, J. and Sheldon, S. (2012) *Assessing child welfare under the Human Fertilisation and Embryology Act: The New Law*. University of Kent. http://blogs.kent.ac.uk/parentingculturestudies/research-themes/pregnancy/wo/.

Lee, E., Macvarish, J. and Sheldon, S. (2014) 'Assessing child welfare under the Human Fertilisation and Embryology Act 2008: A case study in medicalization' 36 *Sociology of Health and Illness* 500.

McCandless, J. and Sheldon, S. (2010) '"No father required"? The welfare assessment in the Human Fertilisation and Embryology Act 2008' 18 *Feminist Legal Studies* 201.

Milsom, I. and Bergman, P. (1982) 'A study of parental attitudes after donor insemination' 61 *Acta Obstetrica et Gynecologica Scandinavia* 125.

People Science & Policy Ltd (2006) *Report on the Consultation on the Review of the Human Fertilisation & Embryology Act 1990* (London: People Science & Policy Ltd).

Pennings, G. (2001) 'The reduction of sperm donor candidates due to the abolition of the anonymity rule: Analysis of an argument' 18 *Journal of Assisted Reproduction and Genetics* 617.

Primarolo, D. (2008a) 'Human Fertilisation and Embryology Bill'. Letter from the Rt Hon Dawn Primarolo MP, Minister of State, Department of Health, 1 May. Appendix 4 in Joint Committee on Human Rights (2008) *Legislative Scrutiny* (London: The Stationery Office).

Primarolo, D. (2008b) *Hansard* HC, 12 May, col. 1160.

Primarolo, D. (2008c) *Hansard* HC, 12 June , cols. 259–260.

Primarolo, D. (2008d) *Hansard* HC, 12 June, cols. 264–265.

Readings, J., Blake, L., Casey, P., Jadva, V. and Golombok, S. (2011) 'Secrecy, disclosure and everything in-between: decisions of parents of children conceived by donor insemination, egg donation and surrogacy' 22 *Reproductive Biomedicine Online* 485.

Royal College of Obstetricians and Gynaecologists (2004) Memorandum from the Royal College of Obstetricians and Gynaecologists in House of Commons Science and Technology Select Committee (2005) *Human Reproductive Technologies and the Law: Fifth Report of Session 2004–05* Vol II, Appendix 26. Ev 283.

Royall, Baroness (2007) *Hansard* HL, 10 December, col. 104.

Royall, Baroness (2008) *Hansard* HL, 4 February, col. 904.

Savulescu, J (2004) *Memorandum from Professor Julian Savulescu to the House of Commons Science and Technology Committee: Human Reproductive Technologies and the Law*, Appendix 62. Ev. 359 in House of Commons Science and Technology Committee (2005).

Söderström-Anttila, V., Sälevaara, M. and Suikkari, A.M. (2010) 'Disclosure decisions in families with oocyte donation children born during a 15-year period' 25 *Human Reproduction* 2535.

Stolz, B.A. (2007) 'Interpreting the US human trafficking debate through the lens of symbolic politics' 29 *Law and Policy* 311.

Warnock, Baroness (2007) *Hansard* HL, 19 November, col. 720.

Wilkinson, S. (2003) *Bodies for sale: Ethics and exploitation in the human body trade* (London: Routledge).

Wincott, E. and Crawshaw, M. (2006) 'From a social issue to policy: Social work's advocacy for the rights of donor conceived people to genetic origins information in the United Kingdom' 43 *Social Work in Health Care* 53.

Winston, R. (2006) 'Sperm donors and secrecy' *The Times* 22 September. http://www.timesonline.co.uk/article/0,,59-2368771,00.html

Woolf, M. (2006) Sperm: 'Your country needs you' *Independent* 30 July. http://news.independent.co.uk/uk/health_medical/article1204521.ece

3 The law and DIY assisted conception

Emily Jackson

Introduction

In the UK, fertility treatment services have been the subject of intensive regulation for 25 years. When the Human Fertilisation and Embryology Authority (HFEA) was set up in 1991, it was largely taken for granted that British citizens with a need for fertility treatment would seek treatment in a licensed centre in the UK, normally following referral from their GP. When the original Human Fertilisation and Embryology Bill was debated in both Houses of Parliament, the assumption was that the activities governed by the resulting Act could not and would not take place in the UK without a licence from the HFEA. In defending the Bill, Lord Hailsham explained that:

> The road which I believe is right to pursue is that responsible people with a responsible licensing system should be allowed to proceed with responsible activities with which some people do not agree but which others regard to be necessary or desirable.[1]

If treatment were to take place only in licensed centres, it could be subject to a wide array of controls: age limits for sperm and egg donors, for example, and restrictions on the number of embryos that can be put back in one IVF cycle. The outcomes of treatment could also be recorded, giving the HFEA a comprehensive overview of the provision of fertility treatment in the UK and enabling it to monitor success rates and to track trends (such as donor insemination's replacement by intra-cytoplasmic sperm injection (ICSI) as the preferred treatment for men with reduced fertility).

Largely as a result of the internet, the picture is now rather different. It is now straightforward for prospective patients to find out about services offered by clinics in other countries, where regulation may be absent or patchy. Within the UK, 'introduction' websites, where potential gamete donors and surrogate mothers make contact with would-be parents, have emerged. On these websites, 'members' make private arrangements that are intended to lead to the birth of a child, but they do so in a regulatory vacuum. Opting out of regulation may raise

1 HL Deb 8 February 1990 vol 515 cc950–1000, 967.

safety concerns, in the case of unscreened sperm, and it also means that there is very little information about the incidence and outcomes of these arrangements. When the Human Fertilisation and Embryology Act 1990 was amended in 2008, it was assumed that the regulation would continue to be comprehensive. As a result, strictly regulated fertility treatment in the UK now coexists with almost completely unregulated DIY assisted conception. Whether or not this matters is the subject of this chapter.

Regulated reproduction

In 1982, the Committee of Inquiry into Human Fertilisation and Embryology, chaired by Mary Warnock, an academic philosopher, was commissioned to make recommendations on the regulation of fertility treatment and embryo research.[2] Published in 1984, the Warnock Report's principal focus was the moral status of the human embryo and the acceptability, or otherwise, of using embryos created by IVF in research. When the government finally introduced a Bill to implement the recommendations of the Warnock Report, in 1989, unsurprisingly parliamentary debates were also dominated by the question of whether and in what circumstances embryo research should be permitted, under licence.

Insofar as there was debate over the rules governing access to fertility treatment, it was assumed by many parliamentarians that most fertility treatment would be provided by the NHS, alongside a handful of private clinics. Some parliamentarians were concerned about the costs of IVF, believing that it would be better to spend the money on research into the causes of infertility. Lord Kennet, for example, asked:

> Why are all these people infertile in the first place? The reasons are known in general but no particular attempt is made to address them. Some of the reasons are environmental – toxins in the environment – some social, the use of unsafe contraceptive methods, the transmission of infectious diseases by sex, and even stress. There is a condition called athletic amenorrhea, which sounds fairly curable. … It seems fairly likely that the number of infertile couples could be reduced by attention to these problems far more expeditiously than by spending £25,000 per birth on IVF.[3]

But although the costs of treatment might have caused some disquiet even then, the legislation which was intended to create a 'comprehensive' regulatory framework did not attempt to regulate what has become a market in fertility treatment. Most fertility treatment in the UK is in fact provided privately, but the Act gives the HFEA no powers over the prices clinics charge, their marketing materials or the practice of recommending additional, expensive interventions after a couple

2 *Report of the Committee of Enquiry into Human Fertilisation and Embryology* (Warnock Committee Report, 1984).

3 HL Deb 7 December 1989 vol 513, c1028.

has embarked on a cycle of IVF, when they may feel under considerable pressure to agree to anything that might increase their chance of success. Any concerns over sharp practices can be addressed by the regulator only tangentially, through its jurisdiction over the Person Responsible's duty to ensure 'that suitable practices are used in the course of the activities' carried out at their centre.[4]

In addition to assumptions that treatment would take place within the NHS, it was also assumed that it would be relatively straightforward for the regulator to be able to exercise comprehensive control over fertility treatment, backed up by criminal sanctions if anyone did anything set out in the Act without first obtaining a licence from the HFEA. Kenneth Clarke MP, then Secretary of State for Health explained that:

> the Bill is the first comprehensive measure dealing with all the issues addressed by the Warnock committee concerning the legal, social and ethical implications of new methods of assisted reproduction attempted anywhere in the world.[5]

The comprehensiveness of the regulatory scheme was widely welcomed by parliamentarians in both Houses. Lord Walton, for example, said:

> I welcome warmly the proposal to establish a statutory human fertilisation and embryology authority with functions as clearly defined, and the proposal that all such work in the United Kingdom may be conducted only in centres approved for the purpose and open to regular inspection with the individual scientists concerned being licensed to conduct that work, subject always to the provision that such licences may be revoked or varied, given due cause.[6]

For many years, it was taken for granted that, aside from its inability to control prices, the UK's regulatory system was capable of exercising almost complete control over the treatment of infertility in the UK. Indeed the UK's regulatory regime served as a model for regulation worldwide.

Through its licensing and inspection functions, the HFEA monitors and regulates practices in fertility clinics. In addition to an initial inspection before a licence is issued for the first time, thereafter centres are subject to a programme of regular, scheduled inspections, with additional unannounced inspections, which can be random but are also sometimes targeted at centres where there are particular concerns. At these inspections, consent forms and patient information sheets are checked for compliance with the Act and the HFEA's *Code of Practice*; labels on the 'straws' containing embryos are audited for errors and low nitrogen alarms are monitored.[7] Patients are interviewed, and the clinic's standard operating

4 Human Fertilisation and Embryology Act 1990, section 17(1)(d).
5 HC Deb 2 April 1990 vol 170, c917.
6 Lord Walton of Detchant, Hansard HL Deb 7 December 1989 vol 513, c1052.
7 On clinical errors and what should be done about 'reproductive harms', see Blackburn-Starza, this volume.

procedures and patient records will be scrutinised. Inspection reports are then considered by the HFEA's Executive Licensing Panel or Licence Committee and, if anything gives cause for concern, the Licence Committee has a range of powers at its disposal including, in extreme cases, revoking the clinic's licence.

Because all treatments and their outcomes have to be reported and recorded on the HFEA's Register, the HFEA holds a very large dataset about the practice of fertility treatment in the UK. Data are produced and published about every clinic in the UK, enabling success rates to be compared. Although used by the media to produce crude and misleading 'league tables',[8] the HFEA has employed sophisticated data analysis to demonstrate that, in fact, clinics' success rates vary very little. Aside from a handful of outliers, which can often be explained by the characteristics of the patients rather than the practices in the clinics, most apparent differences between licensed clinics in the UK are not statistically significant.

Of course there have always been a few types of fertility treatment that happen outside of this tight regulatory regime. Informal sperm donation, not uncommonly involving a lesbian couple asking a friend to act as a sperm donor, does not require treatment in a licensed centre and hence the sort of controls that would be exercised within a clinic – testing the sperm first to make sure that it was suitable for use in treatment and quarantining it to eliminate the risk of HIV infection, for example – are absent. There were always also some aspects of a patient's treatment cycle that did not require a licence from the HFEA, perhaps most notably the prescription of super-ovulatory drugs, with their obvious risks for patients. Nevertheless, insofar as gaps existed in the regulatory framework, they affected relatively few people. They certainly did not cast doubt on the HFEA's ability to exercise almost complete control over the provision of treatment using sperm, eggs and embryos outside of a woman's body in the UK.

Gaps in the regulatory framework

In 1999, Margaret Brazier presciently remarked upon the HFEA's inability not only to control the market in reproduction, but also to exercise any control over cross-border reproductive treatment:

> Another nightmare awaits the HFEA and its counterparts in continental Europe. Each national jurisdiction has sought to fashion a scheme of regulation acceptable to its own culture and community. However those wealthy enough to participate in reproduction markets can readily evade their domestic constraints. If I can order sperm on the internet, or hire a surrogate mother from Bolivia, are British regulators wasting their time? The international ramifications of the reproductive business may prove to be a more stringent

8 See, for example, 'League table highlights best and worst fertility clinics' *Daily Mail* 10 January 2007 (http://www.dailymail.co.uk/home/article-427863/League-table-highlights-best-worst-fertility-clinics.html).

> test of the strength of British law than all of the difficult ethical dilemmas that have gone before.
>
> (1999: 193)

Fifteen years ago, evading national regulation by seeking treatment abroad was an unusual step to take, principally because navigating access to healthcare services in another country was much more difficult than it is today. Now clinics worldwide directly target their online materials at overseas patients. There is no shortage of Spanish fertility centres with websites in English: the *Instituto Murciano de Fertilidad* (Imfer)'s website, for example, explains that:

> Every year Imfer assists many foreign patients who want to undergo an assisted reproduction treatment. In order to serve them better, Imfer offers a department devoted exclusively to foreign patients.

Its website also offers foreign visitors information about its location:

> Located in the southeast of Spain, the Region of Murcia is characterized by its mild temperatures and its many hours of sun. Here, as in a small continent, a variety of environments and landscapes offer countless possibilities to the visitor. Beaches, rural environments, cities, traditions, folklore, culture, sports and health mix together in a dynamic and active touristic offer.[9]

Typing 'surrogacy in India' into Google returns over one million 'hits', many of which are from clinics clearly keen to attract Western customers. The website of *Surrogacy Centre India*, for example, features dozens of pictures of happy couples and smiling babies, almost all of whom are white.[10] The market in cross-border reproductive treatment enables thousands of UK couples each year to completely bypass the UK's regulatory scheme.

Another growing gap in the regulatory framework in the UK is internet-assisted conception, mainly but not exclusively involving sperm donation. An HFEA licence is only necessary if sperm is 'procured'. In 2010, Ricky Gage and Nigel Woodforth received suspended jail sentences for procuring sperm without a licence (*The Guardian*, 2010). Their service, from which they had made £250,000, had involved using couriers to deliver sperm to purchasers. This was held to involve 'procuring' sperm, and since they were unlicensed, they had committed a criminal offence.

'Introduction' websites, which operate similarly to dating websites, do not involve procuring and therefore are both lawful and unregulated. These are websites on which would-be donors and would-be recipients give a short description of themselves and their motivations. Only those who pay a subscription fee (one

9 www.ivfeggdonation.es.

10 www.surrogacycentreindia.com.

such site, coparents.co.uk, charges members £22 for one month and £54 for six months) may contact each other. Members then get in touch directly in order to work out if they wish to proceed, and the terms on which they plan to do so. Coparents.co.uk claims to have helped 'thousands' of people in the UK to find sperm donors, but its only records of outcomes are the testimonials on its site, such as 'I've found a sperm Donner [sic]. Thank u so much for helping me and my wife finding a daddy for our child'. There is no systematic data collection, and the site offers no screening services at all.

Finally, the regulation of surrogacy was never within the HFEA's powers, although where an IVF cycle is involved, that would clearly have to happen in a licensed clinic. The HFEA's *Code of Practice* contains guidance on the information that should be provided to all those involved in IVF surrogacy arrangements. They should, for example, receive information about legal parenthood and Parental Orders (HFEA *Code of Practice*, paras 14.2–14.6). The *Code of Practice* also specifies that all those involved in the arrangement should be subject to a welfare of the child assessment (para 14.1). The HFEA can exercise no control at all over 'partial' surrogacy arrangements, where the surrogate is artificially inseminated at home. Nor does it have jurisdiction over the increasingly common practice of employing a surrogate mother in another country, such as India or the US.

Taken together, it is clear that the HFEA's almost watertight regulatory umbrella is now rather full of holes, even after the legislation was updated in 2008 in order to render it 'fit for purpose'. In what follows, I consider the significance of cross-border reproductive treatment, internet-assisted conception and surrogacy for the future of the regulation of reproduction.

Cross-border reproductive treatment

There are a variety of reasons why people seek reproductive treatment in another country. Worldwide, the most common reason is that the treatment is not available in one's home country (Ferraretti et al., 2010). Within Europe, for example, gamete donation is illegal in several countries, and it is therefore routine for couples and individuals to travel to other European countries with more liberal regimes in order to access treatment with donated eggs or sperm (Ferraretti et al., 2010). The UK's liberal regulatory framework means that there are not many illegal treatments that UK couples might seek overseas. One example would be sex selection for social reasons, for which anyone willing to pay at least $18,000 per cycle might travel to the US.

It is more common for British people to seek treatment abroad in order to avoid waiting lists or because they perceive that treatment might be 'better' or cheaper overseas. The shortage of egg donors in the UK, and the resulting waiting times, has meant that people seeking treatment with donated eggs might travel to Spain or Cyprus, for example, where donors are more readily available, perhaps because they are paid. People who find that they have a need for fertility treatment are often patients 'in a hurry'; anxieties about declining fertility, and the fact that a diagnosis of infertility commonly happens at least a year after people have decided to try to start a family, means that the prospect of waiting another year to find an egg donor will often prompt people to investigate more immediately available options. First or second generation immigrants have reported difficulties in finding ethnically matched donors in the UK, and some express a preference for being treated in their country of origin (Inhorn, 2011).

When people seek treatment abroad because they perceive it to be better than treatment at home, this may be because of dissatisfaction with the treatment that they have received in the UK, perhaps because they feel that they have run out of options and need to 'try something new' (Culley et al., 2011). In their study of the motivations of people seeking treatment abroad, Culley et al. found that 29 per cent mentioned better success rates. Dutch patients seeking treatment in Belgium believe that treatment there is more patient-centred and, as a result, more likely to succeed, even though there is, in fact, no difference in success rates between the two countries (Van Hoof et al., 2013). There is also evidence that some patients are willing to try anything in order to increase the chance of pregnancy, regardless of the risks. For example, in their study of women presenting with higher order multiple pregnancies at a London hospital, McKelvey et al. (2009) found that the fact that an overseas clinic was prepared to put back more than two embryos in one cycle was regarded as a good reason for seeking treatment abroad.

The notion that having more than two embryos returned to the woman's uterus is preferable to treatment in the UK, where this ought not to happen, is troubling, however. Multiple pregnancies represent the most serious and largely avoidable health risk from IVF. Twins and triplets are much more likely to be born prematurely, and the risk of death around the time of birth is between three and six times higher for twins and nine times higher for triplets.[11] Women pregnant with twins are at higher risk of hypertension, pre-eclampsia and gestational diabetes; they are also twice as likely to die during pregnancy or childbirth.

In order to reduce the multiple pregnancy rate associated with IVF, for some years the HFEA has worked with professional bodies on its multiple birth policy. Since 2007, the HFEA has set a maximum multiple birth rate that clinics should not exceed, which has progressively dropped from 24 per cent to 10 per cent. In order to meet this target, each centre is expected to devise its own 'multiple births minimisation strategy', which essentially sets out which patients it considers suitable for elective single embryo transfer (eSET). A properly targeted eSET protocol can ensure that the risk of multiple pregnancy is virtually eliminated in those women who are most likely to become pregnant. And the HFEA's policy has been successful: the multiple pregnancy rate has dropped significantly in the UK without a corresponding drop in pregnancy rates.[12] The health gains for women and children are considerable, as are the savings to NHS neonatal services.

Of course, it is only possible for the HFEA to exercise control over embryo transfers that happen in licensed clinics in the UK. It may have had considerable

11 See further www.oneatatime.org.uk.

12 Ibid.

success in ensuring that good prognosis patients receive eSET in order to dramatically reduce the multiple pregnancy rate, but if women are regularly returning from having had IVF in India, pregnant with triplets or quadruplets (McKelvey et al., 2009), the HFEA's ability to eliminate iatrogenic higher order multiple pregnancies is clearly significantly weakened.

Facilitators of cross-border reproductive treatment sometimes emphasise the advantages to undergoing stressful and disruptive treatment at the same time as a holiday. One of Whittaker and Speier's interviewees (2011), the owner of a company called IVF Holidays, explained:

> it's bad enough when you do it in the States, you gotta go to work, there's more stress at work, you have that going against you, plus you're trying to do these shots, and you're thinking about your upcoming donor cycle. I think it really helps a lot that it's a true vacation.

It is not clear that this view is shared by patients. Blyth (2010) found no evidence that patients themselves regarded the possibility of taking a holiday at the same time as an advantage of cross-border reproductive treatment. Indeed, it appears that patients find the term 'reproductive tourism' insulting, with its implication that travelling abroad for treatment is a desirable leisure activity, rather than something they feel compelled to try after failing to become pregnant through treatment in their home country. Some have argued that the equally emotive but less positive term 'reproductive exile' would be a more accurate description of the experience of those who seek treatment in other countries (Inhorn and Patrizio, 2009).

Although clinic staff may complain about the administrative burden of submitting comprehensive data to the HFEA, the statutory requirement that it gathers a complete record of treatments, patients, donors and outcomes means that the UK has a comprehensive dataset that can be mined for invaluable information about the quality and effectiveness of treatment. It also means that, if something goes wrong, it is comparatively easy to trace the source of the problem. In contrast, we know very little about cross-border reproductive treatment and its risks and outcomes. Patient survey data are incomplete and likely to be inaccurate. In his internet survey of people who had sought treatment abroad, Eric Blyth (2010) found that over half of his respondents had 'come away with a child'. This could be evidence that for the majority of patients, treatment succeeds in the end. But it could also illustrate the reluctance of ex-patients whose treatment has failed to engage with this sort of survey.

Not only does increasing resort to cross-border reproductive treatment expose the existence of significant gaps in the regulatory scheme, but it is also almost impossible to imagine what could be done to plug those gaps. We can bemoan the lack of accurate and comprehensive data about its prevalence and outcomes, and advocate better information for would-be patients, but it is very difficult to work out what could be done, other than issuing warnings about the risks of treatment abroad.

One country has attempted to control its citizens' access to treatment overseas. Turkey strictly prohibits third party involvement in reproduction, and has tried to stop Turkish citizens receiving treatment using donor eggs, sperm or surrogacy overseas by requiring that 'the person who has conducted this procedure, the persons who have referred patients or acted as intermediaries, the impregnated person, and the donor will be reported to the state prosecutor' (Gurtin, 2011). In practice, this provision is likely to be completely unenforceable against both overseas doctors and Turkish patients who receive treatment abroad. Worse still, it is likely to be counter-productive since its chief consequence will be to make Turkish clinics reluctant to provide advice, support or preliminary treatment to couples seeking treatment with donated gametes overseas. As Zeynep Gurtin (2011) explains:

> It will effectively amount to tying the hands of professionals, thereby significantly curtailing the resources (to information, guidance and preparatory treatment at home) of men and women who are already in an extremely difficult situation. If, being afraid of repercussions, practitioners stop referring patients to trusted partners and cease providing preliminary care and information, the potential dangers and discomforts of [cross-border reproductive care] for patients will undoubtedly increase. Those intent on pursuing CBRC may have to travel further and for longer and find themselves making decisions on the basis of insufficient knowledge and incomplete information.

Ironically, then, the only country that has attempted to control its citizens' access to cross-border reproductive treatment has probably simply made it less safe for them.[13]

Internet-assisted conception

It is impossible to know how common it is for people to find gamete donors or surrogate mothers online via social media and introduction websites. The internet exercises no control over would-be donors and recipient; there is no screening and no recording of data. Judging by the profiles on introduction websites, some of the people seeking sperm donors or offering their sperm for donation are looking for a coparenting arrangement, with ongoing contact throughout childhood. In those cases, it is possible that the donor will be recorded as the father on the child's birth certificate. Others are looking for 'no contact' arrangements and in those cases, it may be that no father is recorded on the birth certificate, or, if the mother has a partner, his name might be recorded as that of the father.

Despite the apparent ease with which these arrangements can be made, it is worth spelling out the risks in seeking a sperm donor through the internet. First, unlike sperm supplied by licensed clinics, it is impossible to know if the sperm will even be capable of resulting in a pregnancy, or often even if it is from the source

13 However, several Australian *states* have also introduced criminal sanctions for their citizens' recourse to commercial surrogacy overseas. This has – of course – raised similar issues.

from which it is claimed to come. It is possible that men who are azoospermic or who have very low sperm counts will donate sperm without realising that there is very little or no chance of conception. Second, there are no age limits on donors. The upper age limit for sperm donors in licensed clinics is there for both health reasons and to increase the chance of success (Simon et al., 2012; Lewis et al., 2013). Third, the sperm will not have been screened for HIV or any common genetic conditions. Infection of the woman is then possible, as is passing on a disease to any child who is born.

Fourth, the child's ability to access information about the donor will be both variable and patchy. Unlike children conceived in licensed clinics, children conceived through informal sperm donation will not have the right to access non-identifying and, for children conceived since 2005, identifying information about their donor when they reach the age of 18 (see Blyth and Frith, this volume). It is not just the child's interest in information that is at stake. If the donor or the child is subsequently diagnosed with a genetic condition, it may be impossible to trace either offspring or donor in order to pass on information about their elevated risk. Fifth, unlike treatment in a licensed centre, there are no restrictions on how many times a man could donate, meaning that it would be possible for a man to father hundreds of children in this way, all of whom would have no way of knowing whether or not they are related to each other. Finally, there is plainly scope for these sorts of arrangements to go quite badly wrong. For obvious reasons, it is impossible to know how many informal reproductive agreements break down. We are only likely to know about the breakdown of these agreements if either the case reaches the courts, or one or other of parties chooses to publicise their situation via the media.

The most likely reason why a court might become involved in the aftermath of informal reproductive arrangements is to resolve questions of parentage. This was the case in *M v F*,[14] in which the legal fatherhood of a child, whose biological father was a donor who, in his evidence to the court, had claimed to have fathered around 30 children through both artificial insemination and sexual intercourse, depended upon whether he had been conceived through artificial insemination or sex. If conception had been achieved through artificial insemination, section 35 of the Human Fertilisation and Embryology Act 2008 would apply to recognise the mother's husband as the child's father, provided he had consented to her insemination. If, on the other hand, conception had been the result of sexual intercourse, the donor would be the child's legal father. Whether or not conception was achieved artificially or as a result of sexual intercourse was clearly a question of fact, but it was one on which the accounts of the mother and the donor differed. It was a difficult question for the judge to resolve, not only because of the obvious absence of witnesses, but because both parties were untrustworthy. According to Peter Jackson J, the mother and the donor were both:

> individuals that have over long periods of time been untruthful, devious and manipulative. In relation to contested issues, I regret that they both lied

14 [2013] EWHC 1901 (Fam).

> extensively throughout their evidence, and one of them was of course lying about the central issue of the child's conception.

The mother was 'a fluent fabricator' with 'a capacity for determined and malevolent action to achieve her ends'. She showed 'no sign of discomfort when caught in an obvious lie [and] freely stated that she is motivated by her own need for [the donor] to be punished'. The donor was a man with 'an unmistakable track record of inveigling or encouraging recipients into engaging in sexual activity with him from the very first meeting', who had once 'advertised himself in graphic terms as willing to participate in a "breeding party", i.e. a male-dominated orgy designed to get a woman pregnant'. Peter Jackson J found that he had taken 'the strategic decision to tell the truth where possible and to lie where necessary'.

Peter Jackson J's judgement starts with a remarkable timeline of events. The mother alleges that she had sex with the donor on multiple occasions and towards the end of the timeline, that this took place without her consent. The donor claims that insemination took place artificially, although he admitted to having had sexual intercourse with the mother when she was pregnant for the second time, her first pregnancy having been terminated after her husband reacted 'violently' to the news of her pregnancy. In order to take revenge on the donor, the mother was said to have adopted a number of aliases in order to publicise his activities to newspapers and to his professional body.

Peter Jackson J remarked upon the risks involved in these arrangements, as compared with regulated sperm donation:

> regulation is broadly successful in protecting participants from exploitation and from health risks, while providing some certainty about legal relationships. … In comparison, participants in informal arrangements have to judge all risks for themselves. They may not be in a good position to do so. Those seeking to conceive may be in a vulnerable state and not all donors are motivated by altruism.

Participants in these arrangements cannot rely on those behind the website to protect their interests. In *M v F*, Peter Jackson J commented that the website had charged 'not inconsiderable fees to those looking for donors while projecting a rose-tinted account of successful, problem-free conception'. And the strain he found this dispute had placed upon the participants had been considerable: 'It has taken a high toll on the well-being of each of the adults and has threatened Mr F's career. The costs are enormous. The parties have spent almost £300,000 in legal fees'.

We have no evidence of the impact of this sort of arrangement on the children born as a result. In time, it is to be hoped that the scope of researchers' interests in the children born following assisted conception is broadened out to include children conceived through DIY arrangements (see, for example, Casey et al. (2013), Golombok et al. (2013)). Of course, the child in this case may never be told about the circumstances of his conception, and so may never find out about his parents' behaviour. But it is hard to imagine what it would be like to read Peter Jackson J's judgement, in the knowledge that he was talking about one's own conception.

It is not just sperm donors who can be found online. In *Re TT (Surrogacy)*[15] Mr and Mrs W, the commissioning couple, had met the surrogate mother online. She refused to hand over the baby after birth, and although Baker J refused the father's application for a residence order, the case is notable for his criticism of all parties' behaviour, and in particular of their use of the internet. The mother had been deceitful and lied to the court, and she was, as Baker J explained, a 'heavy user of the internet':

> In one chatroom, she has chosen to use the soubriquet: 'Thongs, G-Strings, French Knickers, IT'S ALL GUD'. I am concerned that she is at risk of exposing herself to malign and possibly dangerous influences via the internet which could in turn affect the children. For the sake of her children, I advise her to adopt greater restraint in the use of the internet.

Baker J was also 'concerned about the dangerous and murky waters into which [the commissioning couple], and particularly Mrs. W, have strayed via the internet'. Before they met T's mother, Mr and Mrs W had invited a woman known as CL into their home. Although Mrs W claimed to have met her in an internet chatroom, rather than on a surrogacy introduction website, Baker J did not believe her. The Children's Guardian appointed by CAFCASS[16] to protect the child's welfare had made inquiries about CL and found that CL was:

> a prostitute, with seven children in care in Scotland. It is alleged that she is known on the internet as a surrogate parent and has claimed (to whom and in what terms is unclear) that she had 13 children. She left Edinburgh when pregnant with her sixth child and went to stay with the Ws in England, claiming that Mrs. W was her sister. When social workers visited the Ws' home, Mrs. W told her that the woman she knew as D was someone she had met over the internet. The social workers were concerned that the Ws might have arranged to take over the baby that CL was carrying. The Scottish social worker told the Guardian that CL had met the Ws on an internet surrogacy site and was going to sell her baby to the Ws.

Although it was impossible to corroborate the allegation that the Ws intended to 'buy' CL's baby, Baker J gave them a stern warning about the risks of their conduct:

> It cannot be said too strongly that it is extremely unwise to invite someone into your home whom you have only met over the internet. If the information obtained by the Guardian is correct, CL may pose a serious risk to children. It

15 [2011] EWHC 33 (Fam).
16 Children and Family Court Advisory and Support Service.

was wholly irresponsible of the Ws to invite her into their home, and the fact that they have no awareness of this risk is alarming.

Insofar as *M v F* and *Re TT* are among the first cases in which internet-assisted conception has come before the courts, they paint an unedifying picture of the sort of arrangements people make via the internet and how wrong they can go for all concerned.

Surrogacy

Anyone entering into a surrogacy arrangement in the UK or, as is becoming increasingly common, abroad, receives comparatively little protection from UK law (see Horsey and Neofytou, this volume). It is, perhaps, especially noteworthy that the government did not use the opportunity presented by reform of the Human Fertilisation and Embryology Act in 2008 to make anything more than piecemeal changes to the law relating to surrogacy. The arrangements continue to be unenforceable and hence precarious (Horsey and Sheldon, 2012), and given that it is still a criminal offence to be paid to negotiate a surrogacy contract, there continue to be obstacles to accessing professional advice. For many years, the judiciary has been warning of the dangers of unregulated surrogacy arrangements, and crucially it has been doing so in proceedings brought in order to settle the parenthood and/or residence arrangements of a child who already exists as a result of a surrogacy arrangement.

Both the Warnock Report and the Brazier Committee's 1998 report (Brazier et al., 1998) took the view that the law should not encourage surrogacy. Liberal, facilitative regulation was ruled out by both Committees on the grounds that the law should discourage people from entering surrogacy arrangements, or, at the very least, ensure they do so only as a last resort. In practice, however, far from deterring people from entering into surrogacy arrangements, the lack of legal clarity instead is resulting in more and more cases coming before the courts. Indeed there are now so many reported surrogacy cases that they follow a very familiar pattern.

The child's existence means that the court is essentially presented with a *fait accompli*: a child whose best interests will generally be served by enabling her to stay in her settled home. In most cases, the court's task will be to make decisions about the parentage and/or residence of a child who is already living with the couple or individual who employed the surrogate mother. In these circumstances, the judge effectively has no choice but to employ whatever tools he or she can to transfer legal parenthood to the person or people caring for the child. Where there is an application for a Parental Order, invariably this means retrospectively authorising payments that would ordinarily be judged to be in excess of reasonable expenses.[17] As Theis J explained in *Re W*:

17 See, for example, *Re W* [2013] EWHC 3570 (Fam); *Re C (A Child) (Parental Order)* [2013] EWHC 2408 (Fam); *J v G (Parental Orders)* [2013] EWHC 1432 (Fam).

> A Parental Order will give permanency and security to the day to day arrangements that exist at the moment. Most importantly a parental order will confer joint and equal legal parenthood and parental responsibility upon both applicants. This will provide lifelong security for the children's relationship with the applicants, which is what the welfare of each child overwhelmingly demands.

Where Parental Orders are not an option, then other family law tools such as wardship and residence orders have been employed in order to ensure that the child's carer(s) also have parental responsibility for her.[18]

Although in theory, the courts suggest that an order might be refused if the amount paid was 'an affront to public policy', in practice the child's welfare operates as a trump card. In one of the first overseas surrogacy cases to come before the courts, Hedley J was clear that he was 'most uncomfortable' with the process of retrospective authorisation, but his hands were tied:

> The difficulty is that it is almost impossible to imagine a set of circumstances in which by the time the case comes to court, the welfare of any child (particularly a foreign child) would not be gravely compromised (at the very least) by a refusal to make an order.[19]

In addition to the routine retrospective authorisation of payments to surrogate mothers, it is also now almost customary for judges to warn of the dangers of entering into surrogacy arrangements without proper legal advice. Back in 2008, Hedley J drew attention to the 'many pitfalls [which] confront the couple who consider commissioning a foreign surrogacy'.[20] Three years later, in *Re IJ (A Child)*,[21] which was, like *Re X & Y*, a surrogacy case involving a child born in the Ukraine, Hedley J once again spelled out the dangers:

> One reason for adjourning these reasons into open court is to emphasise once again the legal difficulties that overseas surrogacy agreements can create. In the experience of the court to date, all overseas jurisdictions can confer parental status on the commissioning couple but that status is not recognised in our domestic law nor (at least where a commercial agreement has been in place) could it be. Those who travel abroad to make these arrangements really should take advice from those skilled in our domestic law to be sure as to the problems that will confront them (not the least of which is immigration) and how they can be addressed. Reliance on advice from overseas agencies is dangerous as the provisions of our domestic and immigration law are often not fully understood.

18 *JP v LP* [2014] EWHC 595 (Fam).
19 *Re X & Y (Foreign Surrogacy)* [2008] EWHC 3030 (Fam).
20 *Ibid.*
21 [2011] EWHC 921 (Fam).

Two years later, in *Re W*, Theis J was yet again explaining that:

> This case is another timely reminder of the importance for intended parents embarking on surrogacy arrangements abroad to ensure they have appropriate legal advice in the jurisdiction where the surrogacy arrangement is entered into.[22]

And it is not just overseas surrogacy arrangements that can lead to difficulties. As Eleanor King J explained in *JP v LP*:[23]

> the facts of this case stand as a valuable cautionary tale of the serious legal and practical difficulties which can arise where men or women, desperate for a child of their own, enter into informal surrogacy arrangements, often in the absence of any counselling or any specialist legal advice.

Bizarrely, the law works to put obstacles in the way of specialist legal advice. The ban on commercial involvement in surrogacy arrangements was intended to prohibit baby selling, but in an echo of the counter-productive Turkish ban on receiving treatment overseas, in fact it increases the risks surrogacy poses to children. In the absence of professional advice, it is more likely that children will be handed over without any formal transfer of parenthood, with the result that the people caring for the child have no legal relationship with, or obligations towards her.

In *JP v LP*, the hospital where the child was to be born had insisted on seeing a surrogacy contract before they would allow the commissioning couple to take away the baby. An agreement was drawn up but the solicitors who had (for payment) done so were negotiating surrogacy arrangements on a commercial basis in contravention of section 2 of the Surrogacy Arrangements Act 1985 and therefore committed a criminal offence. In addition to drawing up an illegal contract, the solicitors had not advised their clients that a strict time limit applies to Parental Orders and hence the parents were out of time before their application was made. A failure to know about, or at the very least check the rules governing Parental Orders will have lifelong consequences for this child, whose parents will never be able to both have legal parenthood for him. The parents had split up which meant that adoption by the 'mother', in order to give her legal parenthood would extinguish the father's parental responsibility, and adoption together was not an option because the parents were neither married nor living in an 'enduring family relationship'.[24]

The central problem is that it seems to be the exception for people contemplating surrogacy to appreciate the complex legal ramifications of these arrangements until after the child is born. Perhaps it is time to think about subjecting surrogacy arrangements to some sort of pre-conception scrutiny, not necessarily

22 [2013] EWHC 3570 (Fam).
23 [2014] EWHC 595 (Fam).
24 Adoption and Children Act 2002, s.144(4)(b).

in order to vet participants, although that could be a possibility where the arrangements reveal family circumstances of which social services should be aware, but more commonly simply to ensure that everyone involved understands what the intended parents would have to do in order to ensure that they acquire legal parentage for their child.

Does unregulated assisted conception matter?

Of course, it could be argued that by breaking free from the tight restrictions that govern regulated assisted conception services in the UK, unregulated assisted conception is in fact going some way to equalise the positions of those who do, and those who do not need third party assistance in order to conceive. If two people are capable of conceiving through sexual intercourse, they do not need the prior approval of a clinic or regulatory body in order to have sex. They are not screened to check that they will not pass on a disease to the other person or to any child that might be born. Data about the incidence of sexual intercourse and its outcomes are not collected by a non-governmental public body. Of course, children's births must be registered, but aside from birth registration, sexual reproduction – just like internet-assisted conception – takes place relatively free from external scrutiny and data collection. It is increasingly common for people to meet their sexual partners online, so does it matter if they also find sperm donors or surrogates online?

Perhaps the best way to answer this question is to think about the purposes of regulation. While many clinicians and patients experience it as overly bureaucratic, placing obstacles in the way of doctors just 'getting on with' treating their patients, there are reasons for many of the restrictions and requirements in the HFE Act. Keeping a register of treatments and their outcomes facilitates epidemiological research into the safety and outcomes of treatments that have never been subjected to randomised controlled clinical trials. It also means that children can find out if they are related to a prospective sexual partner. Screening of sperm protects the safety of women and children, and increases the chance of a successful pregnancy.

Opting out of regulation can mean opting out of some of the benefits of regulated treatment. Where this means receiving unscreened sperm, then the risk is mainly, but not exclusively to the woman who is looking for sperm online, and since the risks of unprotected sexual intercourse are well known, perhaps it would be unduly paternalistic to seek to protect her from the foolishness of her decision to inseminate herself with a stranger's sperm. But there are other benefits of regulation, where opting out could have negative effects for people aside from the adults making arrangements for themselves, and which are not necessarily obvious to people contemplating travelling overseas for IVF treatment or surrogacy, or looking for a sperm donor online. People may not appreciate that it is in a child's interests for there to be a register of treatments, for example. It is evident from the surrogacy cases reaching the UK courts that many potential parents do not understand the rules governing legal parentage, which may leave them caring for a child with whom they have no legal relationship, and to whom they owe no legal obligations.

If there is a widespread lack of understanding about the benefits of regulation, a two-pronged strategy may be necessary. First, it might be important for the regulator to broaden the scope of its public education function. It might not only be important to have authoritative advice about the risks of opting out from regulation, but also, more positively, a clear and accessible explanation of what the benefits of regulation are, for patients and for children. For example, if it is a benefit of treatment with donated sperm in licensed centres that the sperm has been screened in order to increase the chance of the birth of a healthy child, and to minimise the risk to the mother, then this should be clearly communicated to patients. Or if there are women in the UK who believe that it is an *advantage* of treatment overseas that more than two embryos can be put back, then the message about the dangers of multiple pregnancy has not been effectively communicated.

In addition to persuading people of the advantages of seeking regulated treatment services, there may be circumstances in which it would be appropriate to provide *incentives* to seeking regulated treatment services. Certainly in relation to surrogacy, any attempt to introduce a system in which surrogate mothers and commissioning parents went through a formal approval process before embarking on a surrogate pregnancy would have to be accompanied by some sort of advantage to doing so, otherwise few people would be willing to submit themselves to a potentially intrusive process which would have no possible benefits for them. If pre-approval of the surrogacy arrangement meant pre-approval for a Parental Order, then perhaps some would-be parents might be persuaded that going through an official pre-approval procedure could make their lives easier in the long run.

Conclusion

The cases that are now reaching the courts involving unregulated assisted conception suggest that many people only become aware of the potential pitfalls of such arrangements after the event, once a child has been born. In *M v F*,[25] for example, it does not seem likely that the child's mother understood the rules governing fatherhood before becoming involved with Mr F. In *JP v LP*,[26] the parents clearly had no idea that Parental Orders following surrogacy could only be obtained within the first six months of the child's life.

Of course, there is no reason why members of the public should understand the complex set of rules governing assisted conception and parentage, but on the other hand, it is perhaps shocking that the public knows so little about infertility treatment and its legal consequences. Sex and relationships education (SRE) in schools understandably concentrates on those sex and relationships issues that are more likely to affect teenagers, such as 'puberty, menstruation, contraception, abortion, safer sex, HIV/AIDS and STIs'.[27] It is clearly important that young

25 [2013] EWHC 1901 (Fam).
26 [2014] EWHC 595 (Fam).
27 FPA Factsheet, SRE Education (FPA, 2011).

people understand the risk of pregnancy, but the unintended consequence of SRE's emphasis on avoiding unwanted pregnancy is that girls and boys grow up believing that sex will lead to pregnancy, and while this may be true for most of them, for some it will not. Infertility often comes as a profound shock to people who have spent many years strenuously trying to avoid pregnancy at all costs.

Of course, teenagers are not likely to be a receptive audience for education about infertility, its treatment and the legal pitfalls of unregulated treatment. Nevertheless, it would seem sensible for SRE in schools to at least prepare pupils for the fact that parenthood cannot always be achieved through sexual intercourse. For teenagers who know or suspect that they might be gay, it is also important for them to understand that parenthood can be achieved without heterosexual intercourse. The difference between legal and biological parenthood is clearly poorly understood but of critical importance to people who start their families in unconventional ways. As the internet increasingly becomes people's first port of call for information about almost everything, including assisted conception, it may be valuable to at least introduce the idea that there are significant risks from conceiving a child via an internet contact or overseas. Although people may not remember much that they are told in school, for SRE not to acknowledge the reality of infertility, and the existence of alternative means of conception, is to paint a misleading picture of future family life for a significant proportion of the population.

Public information about the risks of unregulated treatment and the benefits of regulated treatment should be clearer and more accessible. Although the HFEA has a role in explaining the purposes of regulation, it is not necessarily fair to expect the HFEA to play the role of public educator about treatments over which it has no control. Rather, it may be time to increase the scope of its public information function, or to give some other body responsibility for ensuring that people can readily access information that enables them to understand the potential consequences of the steps they are contemplating taking in order to have a baby. If one searches for 'find a sperm donor online', there is nothing from the HFEA on the first page of matches. Unfortunately, people are therefore more likely to click on a site like California Cryobank's *Donor Look-a-Likes*™, which carries links to pictures of celebrities that donors are said to resemble, than they are to come across clear, authoritative guidance about much more important issues like the legal parentage of any child who may be born.

References

Blyth, E., 'Fertility patients' experiences of cross-border reproductive care' (2010) 94 *Fertility and Sterility* e11.

Brazier, M., 'Regulating the reproduction business?' (1999) 7 *Medical Law Review* 166.

Brazier, M., Campbell, A. and Golombok, S., *Surrogacy: Review for Health Ministers of Current Arrangements for Payments and Regulation* (HMSO, London 1998).

Casey P., et al., 'Families created by donor insemination: Father-child relationships at age 7' (2013) 75 *Journal of Marriage and Family* 858.

Culley, L., Hudson, N., Rapport, F., Blyth, E., Norton, W. and Pacey, A., 'Crossing borders for fertility treatment: motivations, destinations and outcomes of UK fertility travellers' (2011) 26 *Human Reproduction* 2373.

Ferraretti, A.P., et al., 'Cross-border reproductive care: a phenomenon expressing the controversial aspects of reproductive technologies' (2010) 20(2) *Reproductive BioMedicine Online* 261.

Golombok, S., et al., 'Children born through reproductive donation: A longitudinal study of child adjustment' (2013) 54 *Journal of Child Psychology and Psychiatry* 653.

Guardian, 'Illegal fertility company owners given suspended prison sentence', 12 October 2010.

Gurtin, Z.B., 'Banning reproductive travel: Turkey's ART legislation and third-party assisted reproduction' (2011) 23 *Reproductive BioMedicine Online* 555.

Horsey, K. and Sheldon, S., "Still hazy after all these years: The law regulating surrogacy" (2012) 20(1) *Medical Law Review* 67.

Inhorn, M.C. and Patrizio, P., 'Rethinking reproductive "tourism" as reproductive 'exile' (2009) 92 *Fertility and Sterility* 904.

Inhorn, M., 'Diasporic dreaming: return reproductive tourism to the Middle East' (2011) 23 *Reproductive Biomedicine Online* 582.

Lewis, S., et al., 'The impact of sperm DNA damage in assisted conception and beyond: Recent advances in diagnosis and treatment' (2013) 27 *Reproductive BioMedicine Online* 325.

McKelvey, A., et al., 'The impact of cross-border reproductive care or "fertility tourism" on NHS maternity services' (2009) 116(11) *British Journal of Obstetrics & Gynaecology* 1520.

Simon, L., et al., 'Sperm DNA damage has a negative association with live-birth rates after IVF' (2012) 26 *Reproductive BioMedicine Online* 68.

Van Hoof, W., et al., 'Reflections of Dutch patients on IVF treatment in Belgium: a qualitative analysis of internet forums' (2013) 28 *Human Reproduction* 1013.

Warnock Committee Report, Committee of Inquiry into Human Fertilisation and Embryology, Report (London: HMSO) Cmnd 9314 (1984).

Whittaker, A. and Speier, A., '"Cycling overseas": Care, commodification, and stratification in cross-border reproductive travel' (2011) 29(4) *Medical Anthropology: Cross-Cultural Studies in Health and Illness* 363.

4 Prisoners' access to fertility services

Helen Codd

Introduction

In the last three decades a number of cases in the United Kingdom (UK) and American courts have challenged penal policies and practices in relation to prisoners' access to fertility services.[1] Since the Human Fertilisation and Embryology Act 2008 (hereafter 'the 2008 Act'), the Human Fertilisation and Embryology Authority (HFEA) has consulted on a range of topics, in the context of the Act's stated aim that 'the law remains effective and fit for purpose in the early 21st century'. However, the questions, problems and legal ramifications which arise when prisoners and their partners seek access to fertility services are still marginalised questions within legal and ethical debates around assisted reproduction.

Unlike some issues of prisoners' rights, the thorny debates surrounding the question of whether prisoners should be permitted – and possibly facilitated – to procreate involves consideration not only of issues relating to the imprisoned person but also to potential co-parents and existing children. At the same time, sperm-smuggling incidents involving both Israelis and Palestinians have become matters of media attention (Yarwood, 2012), as has the decision of an Australian Supreme Court to allow a woman to continue with her self-funded IVF treatment after she was given an eighteen-month prison sentence for fraud.[2]

In the UK, the most significant legal development has been the decision of the Grand Chamber of the European Court of Human Rights in the *Dickson* case, when in December 2007 it held that a blanket ban on prisoners' access to assisted insemination facilities was incompatible with Article 8 of the European Convention on Human Rights (ECHR).[3] It was welcomed as challenging the previous policy which John Williams (2002) referred to as 'the constructive sterilisation of prisoners' and by others such as Owen (2003) who described the previous policy as 'a particularly regressive approach to prisoners' legal rights' (Codd, 2008). Although some pointed out that many questions had been left unanswered in the judgment

1 *Goodwin v Turner* 702 F. Supp. 1452 (W.D.Mo. 1988); *Gerber v Hickman* 273 F.3d 843 (9th Cir. 2001). See also *Bozzuti* (2003) and *Roth* (2004).

2 *Castles v Secretary to the Department of Justice* [2010] VSC 310 (9 July 2010).

3 *Dickson and Another v United Kingdom* (2008) 46 EHRR 41.

(Codd, 2008), overall the case was interpreted by those working with penal reform and human rights as a positive move forward, especially for prisoners' partners. However, although this case could have prompted changes in prison policies and practices, and opened up opportunities for further challenges to law and policy in relation to broader questions of access to fertility services and questions of reproductive rights, in reality little seems to have happened in the UK, other than that the possibility of prisoners fathering children by assisted insemination has become a controversial matter of media concern and political rhetoric.

The current legal situation in the UK

Debates around whether prisoners should have access to services for assisted reproductive technologies (ART) go hand in hand with ongoing controversies about sexual behaviour in prisons, family contact and 'conjugal' or private visits in which couples are afforded sufficient privacy to engage in sexual activity. Unlike in many other jurisdictions, including some US states, such visits are not currently permitted in the UK. In jurisdictions in which private prison visits are available, the issue of access to ART may be less crucial because in most cases a partner wishing to become pregnant could, depending on the dates of the visit, have intercourse without contraception with the express aim of conceiving. However, where prisoners and their partners would need ART services from outside of the prison, then even if couples have intercourse during visits, this may not mean that the woman could conceive. Where prisoners are serving short sentences, or coming to the end of long sentences, forms of 'home leave' such as Release on Temporary Licence (ROTL) may afford couples the opportunity to become pregnant, but this possibility is not available to all inmates.

To date, the UK cases, and the published academic research literature, have focused primarily on access to assisted insemination (AI) and have not engaged with other forms of ART such as IVF. To quote the vivid title of an academic journal article in the US, it has been a 'fuss about the contents of a plastic cup' (Harrington, 2001). This invisibility of consideration of other forms of assisted reproduction is not surprising, however, as little attention has been paid in the UK medical and criminological research literature to reproductive experiences and provision in the prison setting, with the notable exception of pregnancy and birth care for imprisoned mothers and neonates, in relation to which the published literature is extensive. The published research in relation to reproductive rights and choices, including prisoner abortion, is far more extensive in relation to the US than the UK, due to the constitutional questions of abortion access, but little is known in either jurisdiction about pregnancy loss, including miscarriage and stillbirth (Codd, 2012).

In contrast with the US, where prisoners are banned from accessing AI, in the UK prisoners can apply, and the decision as to whether to grant a prisoner access to the relevant facilities is made by the Family Ties Unit of the Prison Service: 'Unlike the position in the United States, the right of prisoners to procreative freedom in the United Kingdom is not removed at the prison gates' (Sutherland,

2003). The granting of such access is discretionary. The starting point for the decision is that such requests will be carefully considered on individual merit.

In the UK, the two most important cases have been those brought by Gavin Mellor,[4] which was unsuccessful, and by Kirk and Lorraine Dickson.[5] Prior to the challenge brought by the Dicksons, access would only be granted in exceptional circumstances. This policy had previously and unsuccessfully been challenged in *Mellor*. Following *Dickson*, and as a consequence of a request by the Joint Committee on Human Rights, the Minister and Secretary of State explained that no consultation had taken place as a consequence of the decision but that he and the Secretary of State had concluded that 'only minor amendments were required to bring the former policy into line with the judgment'. Under this amended policy approach the discretion to authorise access to insemination services for prisoners would remain with the Secretary of State. Permission would not be limited to exceptional circumstances, but the Secretary of State would be free to take into account any factors or considerations which (s)he considers relevant. The policy stated that each case would be considered on its merits and no single factor would be weighed more heavily than another. A non-exhaustive list of factors that might need to be considered, provided to the Joint Committee, included:

- The welfare of the child to be born;
- The wishes, consent and medical fitness of both parties;
- The reasonableness of any delay, taking into account the prisoner's release date and his ability to assume parental responsibilities;
- Information about the offending history of the prisoner, including any risk of harm and 'other factors which suggest it would not be in the public interest' to permit him to access artificial insemination facilities;
- Whether the prisoner and his partner are in a well-established and stable relationship which is likely to continue after the prisoner's release; and
- Whether the provision of insemination facilities are the only means by which conception is likely to occur.

This list of considerations followed the existing policy, the only significant change appearing to be the removal of the express statement that permission for access to insemination services would only be granted in 'exceptional circumstances'. Although the Joint Human Rights Committee criticised this policy, especially as it included some public interest arguments which had been dismissed by the Grand Chamber of the European Court of Human Rights, this policy represents the law as it now stands.

The *Mellor* case

In *Mellor*, the Court of Appeal upheld a judgement dismissing an application for access to insemination facilities from Gavin Mellor, a prisoner serving a life

4 *The Queen on the Application of Mellor v Secretary of State for the Home Department* [2001] 3 WLR 533.
5 *Dickson and Another v United Kingdom* (2008) 46 EHRR 41.

sentence. Mellor's wife, whom he married in prison in 1997, would have been 31 years old when the tariff element of his life sentence expired, and he would have been 35. Mellor claimed that the refusal to allow him access to insemination services breached his right to respect for private and family life under Article 8 of the ECHR, as well as his right to marry and found a family under Article 12. The court rejected Mellor's claim, stating that one of the purposes of imprisonment was to punish the criminal by depriving him of certain rights and pleasures which he could only enjoy at liberty, including the enjoyment of family life, the exercise of conjugal rights and the right to found a family. In his judgement, Lord Phillips argued that a policy which generally accorded prisoners the right to conceive children by insemination would 'raise difficult ethical questions and give rise to legitimate public concern'. He also discussed the policy difficulties of creating a de facto single-parent family, contending that it is both legitimate and desirable that, when considering whether to have a general policy of facilitating insemination services for prisoners or the wives of prisoners, the State should consider the implications of children being raised in those circumstances. In this case, the applicant and his wife would still have been in their thirties at the time of release, so it could be argued that in purely practical terms this is still an early age for declining fertility to pose a significant issue if they chose to try to conceive then. However, a subsequent case involved a much clearer problem of declining or loss of fertility, as the woman in the case would have been much older.

The *Dickson* case

A challenge was brought jointly by Kirk and Lorraine Dickson, one a serving prisoner and the other an ex-prisoner, who had married in a prison ceremony in 2001. At the time of the application for access to insemination services, Lorraine Dickson had been released from prison, but her husband was not eligible to apply for release on licence until 2009, by which time she would have been 51. Mr Dickson had no children; Mrs Dickson had three children by other relationships. In October 2003, Kirk Dickson's application for access to insemination facilities was refused (*Hull Daily Mail*, 2003). In a letter, the Secretary of State set out his policy for responding to such requests, which was very close to that considered by the court in *Mellor*.

A subsequent application for leave to apply for judicial review was unsuccessful. The Dicksons then sought permission to appeal, and asked for an extension of time in which to do so. In September 2004, the Court of Appeal refused leave to apply for judicial review, stressing the validity of the Prison Service policy, and describing the Home Secretary's decision as 'an exercise of discretion and proportionality'. The Dicksons took their case to the European Court of Human Rights, arguing that the refusal of access to insemination facilities breached their right to respect for private and family life under Article 8, and again also that the refusal breached their right to found a family under Article 12. The European Court initially held that there had been no violation of either Article. The case was then referred to the Grand Chamber.

In December 2007, the Grand Chamber held that there *had* been a violation of Article 8, but that it was not necessary to examine the complaint under Article 12. Despite attempts by the UK Government to suggest otherwise, the Grand Chamber held that Article 8 was applicable in that the refusal of AI facilities concerned the applicants' private and family lives, which incorporate the right to respect for their decision to become genetic parents. Referring to *Hirst*,[6] the Grand Chamber reiterated that a person retains his or her Convention rights on imprisonment, so that any restriction on those rights must be justified in each individual case, and that this justification cannot be based solely on what would offend public opinion.

The Grand Chamber agreed with the Dicksons, stating that 'whilst the inability to beget a child might be a consequence of imprisonment, it is not an inevitable one, it not being suggested that the grant of artificial insemination facilities would involve any security issues or impose any significant administrative or financial demands on the State'. The court, as the Chamber, reiterated that there is no place under the Convention system where tolerance and broadmindedness are the acknowledged hallmarks of democratic society, for automatic forfeiture of rights by prisoners based purely on what might offend public opinion, but accepted that public opinion may have a role to play in the development of penal policy. The court also highlighted the evolution in European penal policy towards the increasing relative importance of the rehabilitative aim of imprisonment. The court accepted that considerations as to the welfare of a child to be conceived were indeed legitimate but that states 'cannot go so far as to prevent parents who so wish from attempting to conceive a child in circumstances like those of the present case, especially as the second applicant was at liberty and could have taken care of any child conceived until such time as her husband was released'. The Grand Chamber held that the policy as set out in *Mellor* placed an inordinately high 'exceptionality' burden on the applicants when requesting access to AI. It held that a fair balance between the competing public and private interests involved was not struck and that accordingly there had been a violation of Article 8.

Dickson, at first sight, appears to focus on AI and prisoners. However, in reality it has had little impact on prison policies and regime decision-making in relation to AI. The case points out that a blanket policy, particularly a blanket prohibition, would be incompatible with the ECHR, but then allows for the Secretary of State to consider each case on its merits. The only real change appears to have been the removal of the requirement that the circumstances for approval need be 'exceptional' and so this is hardly the substantial change to the law trumpeted by the news media when the case was heard. The real impact of *Dickson* is that it makes clear that the human rights of prisoners' partners are not abrogated simply by reason of that person being in a relationship with a prisoner, and thus partners of prisoners retain all their convention rights. The reason the Dicksons' application resulted in a different outcome to the other attempts to challenge

6 *Hirst v United Kingdom (No 2)* [2005] ECHR 681.

the government's position is at least in part because *Dickson* was based on a joint application by both a prisoner and non-prisoner.

The impact of *Dickson*

The *Dickson* case differed from *Mellor* in that the application and the subsequent legal decisions explicitly addressed the wife's rights as well as the prisoner's. This was applauded by academics and practitioners working on prisoners' rights and those of prisoners' families as representing a significant development in the UK context, where recognition of the specific rights of prisoners' partners had been very limited (Codd, 2008; Eijkholt, 2008).

In contrast, most of the media reporting of the decision (in the UK) focused solely on the question of prisoners' rights, and almost without exception the decision was vociferously and vehemently criticised. Wilson (2007) writing in the *Daily Mail* called it a 'perversion of human rights', referring to Kirk Dickson as a 'jail thug', a 'wicked man', 'a moron' and a 'murderous cretin'. Commentators predicted a flurry of applications from male prisoners and their female partners, and some questioned whether this would open the door to imprisoned women applying as well, including the possibility of lesbian couples in civil partnerships, but both in prison, applying to be allowed access to AI and to give birth whilst they were both incarcerated (Dunn, 2002). It is interesting to note that, since *Dickson,* even on the occasions when a prisoner has simply made an application to be allowed access to AI, as in the case of Scott Hurford, a convicted drug trafficker, the application becomes a matter of media interest and scrutiny even before any decision has been made (Wheatley, 2010). Mary Yarwood makes the point that 'the Human Rights Act applies to everyone. Human rights, including the right to found a family, are not just granted to nice people, or to people who "deserve" them. They are given to everyone, to all humans, including prisoners' (Yarwood, 2011). However, discourses of less eligibility, exclusion and approaches to imprisonment predicated on a view that prison should be a place for punishment, not punishment itself, have meant that, at least in the eyes of the editors and readers of the tabloid news media, human rights do or should not apply to prisoners.

It has proved particularly difficult to ascertain whether the decision has led to any real changes in the law, or in the numbers of prisoners being granted access to AI. In 2011 it was reported that a Freedom of Information Act request by the *Daily Mail* newspaper revealed that one prisoner had been granted permission for his partner to make use of AI whilst he was in custody. The partner was not in custody, although no other information was revealed. The response to the Freedom of Information Act request showed that five similar applications were under consideration at that time, but also that a further 16 had been rejected in the previous four years since the *Dickson* decision in December 2007 (Doyle, 2011). The then Justice Secretary, Kenneth Clarke, launched an inquiry into the circumstances by which the permission was granted, whilst other Members of Parliament castigated the prison authorities for allowing this one case. For example, Priti Patel MP said that providing 'nasty, vile criminals the right to have a family' was 'extraordinary' and called the reasons for the decision 'human rights nonsense' (Jones, 2011). Combined with the decision to allow Wayne Bishop out of prison in order to care for his children, Phil Davies MP raised a concern that a prisoner could now father a child whilst in prison, then demand to be released to care for it, and is cited as saying: 'The whole point of being in prison is that your liberties are taken away from you. What's the point of locking people up if this pseudo-court, with the help of Ken Clarke, is going to give them all their rights back?' (Jones, 2011).

It is tempting to interpret this one prisoner being granted access to AI following *Dickson* as 'a break from previous decisions' and as a 'a change in approach', as did Koomson and Flower (2011). They then go on to argue that following *Dickson* the Ministry of Justice has been obliged to 'lower the bar for granting prisoner requests'. However, in light of the situation prior to *Dickson* it does not appear that a great deal has changed, despite the over-excited reporting in some news media. This point has been made succinctly by Richard A. Edwards in a blog post prompted by the announcement in February 2013 by the Lord Chancellor, Chris Grayling, that he had recently instigated a review of the policy and practice (Edwards, 2013). Edwards calls the issue 'something of a red herring', challenging the Lord Chancellor's assertions that 'there can be no clearer example of why we need changes to the human rights framework' (Doyle, 2013).

The government responded to the decision in *Dickson* by revising the policy, but not rigorously, stating that only minor amendments were required to bring the policy in line with the judgement. The policy has remained broadly the same as it was before *Dickson*, except that permission to access insemination facilities is no longer limited to 'exceptional circumstances'. The European Court of Human Rights itself noted that before *Dickson*, since 1996, 28 applications for AI had been made. Of these, 12 were not pursued, one was withdrawn due to relationship breakdown, in one case the prisoner was released on parole, so there was no need for AI, and two were pending. Of the remaining 12, three were granted and nine refused. As explained by a HM Prison Service spokesman in relation to Scott Hurford's application, a number of factors will be considered including the age of the woman and how long the couple has been together, the main concern being the welfare of the child who might be conceived. The Secretary of State has to consider each case on its merits, with no single decision-making factor being given more weighting than any other. The response of the Ministry of Justice was criticised by the Parliamentary Joint Committee on Human Rights (Joint Committee on Human Rights, 2008), which noted that the list of factors taken into account still included some which had been criticised, or at least deprecated, by the European Court of Human Rights. Despite this, the response of the Ministry of Justice has been characterised more by inaction than action. Edwards (2013) labels Grayling's announcement, in which Grayling declared his aim to ban AI/IVF access for prisoners completely, as 'little more than an exercise in spin'. He makes the point that, as found by the judges deciding the cases, a blanket ban is disproportionate and would very likely be found to be incompatible under ECHR Art 8(2). Edwards also links this with the availability of – or lack of – conjugal/private visits for prisoners in the UK, which could provide alternative processes by which prisoners' rights to try to procreate, as encompassed in Article 8, could be maintained. Put simply, whilst the symbolic impact of the decision in *Dickson* may have been considerable, the actual impact in terms of practical change has been minimal (Lord Chancellor and Secretary of State for Justice, 2009)

Issues and challenges

Access to fertility services as a political issue

In the current penal climate it is unsurprising that the courts have chosen to interpret the rights of prisoners and their families in this way (see Scott, 2013; Pratt et al., 2005). Dilemmas about policy and practice concerning prisoners' access to assisted conception services are part of a broader spectrum of legal and rights debates around reproductive rights in prisons, including access to antenatal care for pregnant women, access to abortion, and also access to sexual health services and contraception services for both men and women. The whole topic has become politicised and a matter of political sensitivity, raising fundamental questions about crime, the family, punishment and rights. In a recent insightful article on the question of whether prisoners in the UK should be allowed the right to vote, following the decision of the European Court of Human Rights in *Hirst v UK (No 2)*,[7] Colin Murray described the problem of prisoner voting as amounting to 'a perfect storm' of competing ideological debates around penal populism, human rights and Euro-scepticism, and argued that the controversy surrounding prisoners' voting rights has strengthened anti-prisoner feeling in the UK (Murray, 2011). The vexed question of whether prisoners and their partners should be allowed access to assisted conception services is similar, incorporating as it does questions of human rights, punishment, reproduction, sexuality, fertility and a subtle form of eugenics (Sutherland, 2003), although it is noted that prisoner voting affects many more prisoners than the very small minority who seek access to such services.

The fact that only one prisoner seems to have been granted access to AI since 2007 shows that, far from the regime becoming less controlled and characterised by the opening of 'floodgates' for many further applications, the government still operates a restrictive policy, which reflects Scott's analysis of the development of prisoners' rights in the UK (Scott, 2013). However, as Edwards (2013) suggests, by focusing on 'spin' the issue represents an opportunity for government ministers to appear to be doing something to challenge the European Court of Human Rights,

7 *Hirst v United Kingdom* (74025/01) Times, April 8 2004 (ECHR). For a commentary on the case, see Foster, S. (2004) 'Prisoners and the Right to Vote – the Decision in *Hirst v UK* (NO.2)' 4 *European Human Rights Law Review* 436.

by purporting to clamp down on something which is in fact very rare and already highly regulated.

Reproductive choices, decisional liberty and the Secretary of State

The *Dickson* case highlights the fact that couples where one partner is imprisoned have to seek external approval in order for their choice to try to conceive to be facilitated. Thus the choice as to whether to attempt to procreate goes from being a private choice, of an individual or a couple, to a semi-private choice in which the application has to be approved by the relevant prison authorities and is under the oversight of the Secretary of State (although of course the semi-private and needing approval context is in place for all those who seek assisted conception services, not just prisoners). There are two relevant issues here. First, the question of why there needs to be any such external oversight and approval of the decision to procreate and, second, whether the Secretary of State or his/her delegated agents are the appropriate people/body to be making that decision.

The first issue, that of external oversight and approval of the decision to procreate, relates not only to prisoners and their partners but to assisted conception in general. Emily Jackson (2002) has argued in this regard that 'we should each have the liberty to shield certain personal decisions from public scrutiny'. The second issue relates specifically and solely to prisoners and their partners seeking assisted conception services. At present, the decision as to whether the welfare of the child test is satisfied in the context of prisoner applications is made not by medically qualified professionals acting under the guidance of the HFEA but by an administrative department of the Prison Service. That is not to say that if doctors were to make these decisions the situation would be unproblematic, and indeed the existence of the welfare principle in any context has been criticised (Jackson, 2002, 2007). However, given that the welfare principle was retained, albeit in a slightly modified form, in the 2008 Act, then we must continue to question how it is applied in a prison context. There are strong arguments that it is inappropriate for this decision to be taken by civil servants. Indeed, it is potentially more worrying for those committed to prisoners' human rights if that decision has to have the approval, either explicitly or by implication, of the Secretary of State who, after all, is an elected politician and ultimately aware of the political ramifications of any decision at an individual, party and governmental level. We have already seen the power of the Home Secretary over life sentence prisoners' release dates eroded and ultimately removed as a consequence of legal challenges, with decision making placed firmly in the hands of the judiciary.[8] But it is still the case that an elected politician retains responsibility for the decision whether to allow a prisoner and his partner a chance to try to conceive. It could be argued that the Secretary of State is mandated to reflect the wishes of society as a whole, and that it is therefore appropriate for the decision to be made by or with the oversight of

8 See *Dennis Stafford v United Kingdom* (2002) 35 EHRR 32; *R. (on the application of Anderson) v Secretary of State for the Home Department* [2002] UKHL 46.

an elected state official. However, there is a question of whether, even if we accept this to be the case, the Secretary of State is the best person to decide on questions such as the welfare of any child who could be born. For matters of family law, such as access to AI services, it could be argued that the inclusion of consideration of the welfare of any child born could be input into the Secretary of State by professionals, but there is also a question here of whether this should be a matter for the family courts, or possibly for some independent, quasi-judicial decision-making panel, comprised of legal experts and lay representatives, as lay representation has always been a visible and core element of the regulation of fertility and embryology in the UK, via the HFEA. In addition, access to the courts has provided a key foundational principle of prisoners' rights claims in the UK.

Arguments against all access

Of course, there are some who argue in favour of a blanket ban on such arrangements on the basis that prisoners who are guilty of serious offences, and thus imprisoned, should not be allowed to conceive or father children whilst imprisoned as this deprivation constitutes a core aspect of their punishment, both in terms of the punitive and also deterrent function of imprisonment. Any 'bonuses' people perceive prisoners to be obtaining may potentially lead to decreased public confidence in the penal system (Koomson and Flower, 2011). This is also linked to questions of limited public funding for assisted conception services: put simply, the costs of private attempts at AI and IVF can be extremely high, making such services inaccessible to many, and there is potentially a public perception that prisoners unfairly have easy access to fertility services for which they do not have to pay. Although the Freedom of Information Act request referred to above made it clear that in that particular prisoner's case he would be responsible for meeting the costs, this may not be known to the public and, rather as there is a perception that prisoners receive luxurious in-cell items such as games consoles, there may be a public resentment of prisoners 'having it easy' in terms of access to assisted conception services.

Associated with the view that loss of the opportunity to procreate is inherent in a prison sentence is the view that prisoners lose not only their liberty but also the privileges of citizenship. As has been pointed out (Scott, 2013), the continued refusal of the UK government to implement policies and practices which allow prisoners to vote in elections, in the face of continued rulings by the European Court of Human Rights that imprisonment does not lead to disenfranchisement, buttresses and reinforces similarly negative views of prisoners as non-people, or as people who do not possess rights. By removing the right to vote, prisoners become citizens who are not deemed worthy of democratic input. This results in a merry-go-round when intermingled with debates around prison and procreation: popular sentiment revolves around the duality of the question that, 'if they can't be trusted or permitted to vote then why should they be trusted or permitted to be parents? If they can't be permitted or be trusted to be parents then how and why could they be trusted or permitted to vote?'

The removal of the right to liberty is inherent in the prison sentence, but the decision of the House of Lords in *Raymond v Honey*[9] made it clear that prisoners do not lose *all* their rights on incarceration. In this highly significant case, which arose from the action of a prison governor who intercepted a prisoner's letter to the Crown Office, the Law Lords affirmed that 'under English law, a convicted prisoner, in spite of his imprisonment, retains all civil rights which are not taken away expressly or by necessary implication'. Further, *Dickson* makes it clear that prisoners' partners do not lose their *own* rights consequent upon the incarceration of a partner, and any interference by a state must be necessary and proportionate. Within this political debate, as Scott (2013) argues, prisoners appear to become the subject of rhetoric and soundbites, rather than considered thought.

The welfare test?

The welfare of the child test continues to be one of the grounds for decision-making following the decision in *Dickson*. The adoption of these welfare considerations in this context reflects the principle enshrined in section 13(5) of the Human Fertilisation and Embryology Act (HFEA) 1990 and now the modified version in section 14(2)(b) of the 2008 Act, which provides that, in relation to fertility services, a woman should not be provided with treatment services unless account has been taken of the welfare of any child who may be born as a result of the treatment.

In relation to prisoners' access to assisted conception services this principle has been applied to children who have not yet even been conceived. This has been vociferously challenged even in the non-prison context and less than convincingly defended (Jackson, 2002, 2007; Laing and Oderberg, 2005). Jackson (2002) argued that the inclusion of welfare considerations in the decision in *Mellor* (referring to the Court of Appeal decision in the case) was 'misguided' and that to consider the future welfare of any child a prisoner may conceive is 'too speculative a consideration' in this context. In referring to the 'best interests of the unborn child' the Court of Appeal and the European Court in *Dickson* hit a complex philosophical issue head-on, that is, the 'non-identity problem', that is, the person protected never benefits from this interpretation of their best interests because they are never born (Sutherland, 2003). As Sutherland perceptively points out, whilst it is undisputed that the state has obligations to children already born, in terms of promoting their welfare and protecting them from harm, 'in denying the opportunity to procreate it is going a great deal further by policing access to parenthood itself'. Thus, prisoners and their partners who wish to conceive have to meet a higher threshold standard of proof of potential adequacy as parents for prisoners than most putative non-imprisoned parents usually have to attain before conceiving a child, including those who cannot conceive without assistance. Whilst from the perspective of punishment and consequences for harm, imprisonment removes any right to autonomous decision-making as to conception, as the *Dickson* decision

9 *Raymond v Honey* [1983] 1 AC 1.

recognised it is philosophically and legally difficult to justify the extension of this loss of autonomy to prisoners' unconvicted partners.

This could be tenable if there were significant public resource implications, but here it is important to distinguish AI services from IVF and to consider whether, as is often argued, AI can be achieved as simply as by a prisoner handing over a filled receptacle to his partner during a visit. There is also an assumption underlying these cases, as was also visible in *Dickson* and *Mellor*, that any child born to or fathered by a prisoner would be dependent on state benefits for their upbringing, even though this was forcefully challenged by the applicants in *Dickson*, who argued that Lorraine Dickson was financially self-sufficient. It could be argued that there is more than a hint in these assumptions of genetic transmission of criminality from parent to child, which would mean that any child fathered by a prisoner and brought up by someone in a relationship with a prisoner would be bound to become an offender themselves. It is striking that it seems better in the eyes of the courts and the government to allow a child to be born after a father's death, as long as the relevant consent can be deemed to have been provided, as in cases where sperm or embryos have been frozen and utilised later, than it is for the child to have a father who is alive but imprisoned for at least some of their childhood.

Conclusions

Despite the potential impact of *Dickson*, little or nothing has changed in the UK. There has been no flurry of applications and no sudden explicit recognition of a prisoners' right to procreate (Eijkholt, 2010). There are still potential situations which could give rise to litigation and policy challenges, but these situations have not arisen in the UK. In Spain, for example, two prisoners imprisoned for terrorist activities linked to ETA, were granted access to IVF treatment whilst in prison (Blackburn-Starza, 2010). There have been no such joint applications, either for AI or IVF, brought by serving prisoners in the UK, as far as it is possible to ascertain this from the published information on applications, nor have there been any applications from women prisoners seeking AI either with a male or female partner or alone, whether the partner is imprisoned or not. That said, although it has not yet happened, a whole new set of questions would be prompted if imprisoned women sought access to AI. For example, a woman could seek AI with sperm donated by a male partner or friend who is not imprisoned, or from an unknown donor. Similarly, a female prisoner could seek to be allowed to conceive with sperm donated by her partner if he is imprisoned in a different prison, as no mixed-gender prisons exist in the UK.

Although the possibility of women prisoners seeking access to AI was first raised a long time ago (Dunn, 2002), it is not possible to determine with any degree of certainty how the prison service, and the courts, would respond to such an application. While Mother and Baby Units (MBUs) exist in a number of UK prisons, concerns have been expressed about the physical, mental, emotional and developmental impact of the prison environment on the babies and toddlers who spend their very early years in such settings, but these must be balanced against other concerns which are prompted when babies are separated from their mothers (Alejos, 2005). For example, if a female prisoner was allowed access to AI, became pregnant and gave birth, the baby could be brought up outside the prison by the father, or other relatives or carers, but it is likely that neither the prison setting nor separation from the mother represent outcomes for the child which would optimise that child's well-being, although emerging evidence suggests that it is better for the mother and child to remain together, even if this is in a prison nursery setting (Goshin et al., 2014). The concerns and practical issues regarding provision for the care of the child become even more acute in the context of women prisoners who seek AI to become pregnant independently, or with a partner who is also a prisoner, as then there is no obvious alternative carer for the child. These questions therefore pose interesting theoretical and policy challenges.

Thus there are still practical and theoretical issues which remain unsettled following *Dickson*. One such issue is of the potentially disproportionate impact of restricting access to AI dependent on the age of a prisoner and his or her partner. If, for example, a man in his forties is married to a woman in her mid-thirties and he is sent to prison for a determinate sentence of twenty years, then there is a possibility he may be released after ten years. However, in her mid-forties the woman's likelihood of conception is much lower than in her thirties, if possible at all. If, however, that same male prisoner was in a relationship with a woman aged 19 then, if he is released ten years later, there would be no concern raised as to her age and chance of conception. This takes the concept of a prisoner's partner being 'guilty by association' (Codd, 2008) one step further, as the older woman will suffer a harm not suffered by the younger woman. The same could be said of female prisoners seeking to become pregnant by male partners outside: for women the biological imperative of declining and ceasing fertility creates a situation of difference, and possibly discrimination. Of course, prison has different and varied impacts, and this may be viewed as an accepted consequence of incarceration: some prisoners may lose jobs, relationships and homes whereas others may keep homes and relationships, or have nothing or nobody to lose in any event. However, these questions still remain open for discussion, as they are 'invisible punishments' which accompany prison but are never explicitly stated as part of the sentence (Chesney-Lind and Mauer, 2002).

Some elements of rights challenges brought by prisoners, such as rights to health care and reasonable prison conditions as exemplified in *Napier v Scottish Minister*,[10] relate specifically to the individual inmate. *Dickson*, unlike the earlier decision in *Mellor*, hinged not only on the rights of the prisoner, but also on the rights of his non-imprisoned partner and whether her own rights under Article 8 could be limited or abrogated even though she was not incarcerated. The Grand Chamber of the European Court of Human Rights, faced with this intermingling of the rights of a non-imprisoned woman intersecting with those of her imprisoned partner, took the decision that Lorraine Dickson had not broken the law, and thus her Article 8 rights remained enforceable, subject to the permissible proportionate

10 *Napier v Scottish Minister* [2004] UKHRR 881.

limits given to states. *Dickson* did not alter the starting point for AI applications, that the matter is one for the Secretary of State, and that the right to attempt to conceive may be lost as a consequence of imprisonment, but it recognised the central role of the prisoner's partner, and stressed that there was no automatic loss of her own rights as a consequence of her association with a prisoner.

Ultimately, the most significant, or interesting, potential challenge could arise if a prisoner sought to challenge the role of the Secretary of State as decision-maker in this context, on the grounds that a politician may either be over-aware of electoral considerations, or may not be qualified to decide questions of the welfare of a child. Until this happens, however, in the current political climate there is likely to be little change in prisoners' access to fertility services.

References

Alejos, M., (2005) 'Babies and small children residing in prisons' *Quaker United Nations Offices* (QUNO, March 2005).

Blackburn-Starza, A., (2010) 'Spanish couple receive IVF treatment whilst in custody' *BioNews* 580 (18 October 2010, Progress Educational Trust).

Bozzuti, J., (2003) 'Judicial birth control? The Ninth Circuit's examination of the fundamental right to procreate in *Gerber v Hickman*' 77 *St. John's Law Review* 625.

Chesney-Lind, M. and Mauer, M. (eds), (2002) *Invisible Punishment: The Collateral Consequences of Mass Imprisonment* (New York: The New Press).

Codd, H., (2008) 'In the shadow of prison: Families, imprisonment and criminal justice', Cullompton, Willan.

Codd, H., (2012) '"Baby can I hold you?": Prisoners, reproductive choices and family life' 11(4) *Contemporary Issues in Law* (Special Issue on Criminal Law & Criminal Justice) 227.

Doyle, J., (2011) 'Prisoner allowed to father a child from jail because of a "human right to a family life"' *Daily Mail* (1 June 2011).

Doyle, J., (2013) 'Justice Secretary vows to take on Strasbourg judges' *Daily Mail* (27 March 2013).

Dunn, S.L., (2002) 'The "art" of procreation: Why assisted reproduction technology allows for the preservation of female prisoners' right to procreate' 70 *Fordham Law Review* 2561.

Edwards, R.A., (2013) 'Grayling's red herring- human rights, IVF and prisoners' *Euro Rights blog* (1 April 2013).

Eijkholt, M., (2008) 'The right to procreate is not aborted' 16(2) *Medical Law Review* 284.

Eijkholt, M., (2010) 'The right to found a family as a stillborn right to procreate?' 18(2) *Medical Law Review* 127.

Goshin, L., Byrne, M. and Blanchard-Lewis, B., (2014) 'Preschool outcomes of children who lived as infants in a prison nursery' 94(2) *The Prison Journal* 139.

Harrington, L.S., (2001) 'Life-term inmates' right to procreate via artificial insemination: Why so much fuss over the contents of a plastic cup?' 33 *McGeorge Law Review* 521.

Hull Daily Mail, (2003) 'Let me have killer's baby' (6 September 2003, p.2).

Jackson, E., (2002) 'Conception and the irrelevance of the welfare principle' 65(2) *Modern Law Review* 176.

Jackson, E., (2007) 'Rethinking the pre-conception welfare principle' in Horsey, K. and Biggs, H. (eds), *Human Fertilisation and Embryology: Reproducing Regulation* (Abingdon: Routledge-Cavendish), 47–68.

Joint Committee on Human Rights (2008) *Thirty-First Report* (London: HMSO).

Jones, B., (2011) 'Inquiry launched after UK prisoner given right to have child from jail' *BioNews* 610 (6 June 2011, Progress Educational Trust).

Koomson, H. and Flower, D., (2011) 'Fertility treatment for prisoners: the scope of human rights' *Lexology* (3 August 2011).

Laing, J.A. and Oderberg, D.S., (2005) 'Artificial reproduction, the "welfare principle" and the common good' 13(3) *Medical Law Review* 328.

Lord Chancellor & Secretary of State for Justice (2009) 'Responding to Human Rights Judgments: Government Response to the Joint Committee Government Response to the Joint Committee on Human Rights' Thirty-first Report of Session 2007–08' Cm 7524 (London: HMSO).

Murray, C.R.G., (2011) 'A perfect storm: Parliament and prisoner disenfranchisement' *Parliamentary Affairs* 1.

Owen, T., Livingstone, S. and Macdonald, A., (2003) *Prison Law* (3rd ed.) (Oxford: Oxford University Press).

Pratt, J., Brown, D., Hallsworth, S., Brown, M. and Morrison, W., (2005) *The New Punitiveness: Trends, Theories, Perspectives* (Cullompton: Willan Publishing).

Roth, R., (2004) '"No new babies": Gender inequality and reproductive control in the criminal justice and prison systems' 12 *American University Journal of Gender, Social Policy and Law* 391.

Scott, D., (2013) 'The politics of prisoner legal rights' 52(3) *The Howard Journal* 233.

Sutherland, E., (2003) 'Procreative freedom and convicted criminals in the United States and the United Kingdom: Is child welfare becoming the new eugenics?' 82 *Oregon Law Review* 1033.

Wheatley, G., (2010) 'Drug Dealer's Baby Dream' *Daily Star* (5 March 2010).

Williams, J., (2002) 'The queen on the application of Mellor v Secretary of State for the Home Department: Have the courts got it right?' 14(2) *Child and Family Law Quarterly* 217.

Wilson, A.N., (2007) 'The perversion of human rights as jail thug is allowed to become a dad' *Daily Mail* (6 December 2007).

Yarwood, M., (2011) 'Missing the point? Human rights, prisoners and artificial insemination', *BioNews* 612 (20 June 2011, Progress Educational Trust).

Yarwood, M., (2012) 'Sperm smuggling and fatherhood from behind bars' *BioNews* 672 (10 September 2012, Progress Educational Trust).

5 Thinking outside the (egg) box: Egg-share agreements, cord blood and 'benefits-in-kind'

Karen Devine

Introduction

In the present economic climate, it is likely that the rising costs of IVF treatment will lie as a heavy financial burden on any childless couple seeking fertility treatment. To address this difficulty, combined with the lack of available donor gametes, the Human Fertilisation and Embryology Authority (HFEA) has allowed 'benefits-in-kind' – free or discounted fertility treatment to gamete donors, such as those involved in 'egg-share agreements'. Whilst this mode of access to fertility treatment can benefit both donor and recipient, non-affluent women who are unable to produce their own oocytes are doubly disadvantaged. Not only do they lack the natural means to reproduce, but this factor also bars them from becoming an egg-share donor and consequently benefitting from the discounted treatment that provides; and the lack of necessary funds prevents them from seeking treatment via egg and embryo donation. What successful pregnancies can produce, however, is another type of bodily tissue of relative 'value': cord blood stem cells from the resultant baby's umbilical cord. It is suggested here that as cord blood stem cells have shown promise in therapeutic treatments, biological research and as a 'saviour sibling' resource – cord cells specifically produced as a means to treat a sick sibling – they too could be included as an item of 'exchange' in egg-share agreements.

What such a concept would require, however, is the implementation of a robust regulatory framework that straddles both the HFEA and the Human Tissue Authority (HTA) – an independent watchdog that regulates the removal, storage, use and disposal of bodily material – to ensure that both aspects of healthcare provision are rigorously overseen and controlled. Indeed, the Public Bodies Act 2011 empowers the Government to transfer functions of the HFEA to other bodies and in 2013, the Coalition Government commissioned an independent review of both the HFEA and HTA in a joint report with a view to merging the two regulatory bodies in an attempt to make them more streamlined and cost-effective (McCracken, 2013). Plans to do so, however, were shelved following the report's recommendations. It concluded that although significant saving could be made by combining the support services of the two bodies, the current regulatory landscape provided sufficient public confidence in dealing with the complex and delicate areas of law within their remit independently – for the time-being at least – and that a merger would risk the reduction of specialist expertise currently enjoyed. However, if the premise that umbilical cord blood (UCB) stem cells could be utilised as an item of exchange in the egg-share market place then it is exactly this type of joint expert specialism that would be required to carve out a workable legal and regulatory regime.

This chapter will argue that the inclusion of UCB stem cells as an exchange item in the provision of assisted reproductive services would be a useful new development in this field of healthcare provision, one that responds to two very different healthcare needs; and one that would represent a multifaceted and sensitive area of medical law that requires the collaboration of the HFEA and HTA working as a joint entity to ensure the careful navigation of the law and operating within existing ethical boundaries. The initial section of the chapter will provide a brief overview of the current perceived need for UCB, before tracing the reasons that underpin the current state of the law relating to egg-sharing and the ethical concerns such arrangements provoke. The chapter will then explore whether, in the interests of solidarity, reciprocity and a mutual need, the egg-share model can be extended to include a third party seeking UCB cells (research facilities, cord blood banks or families looking to produce a 'saviour sibling'), subsequently providing greater access to fertility treatment whilst simultaneously providing a donor pool of much needed UCB cells

Mapping the need for UCB and the law relating to egg-share schemes

A successful, wanted pregnancy produces not only enviable joy to new parents but also a potentially valuable biological material that is more often than not simply disposed of as waste. Despite the huge number of babies born each year – in 2013 alone this totalled just under 700,000 (ONS, 2013) – and knowledge of the ability to donate or personally store the stem cells from the resultant baby's umbilical cord increasing amongst pregnant women (Screnci *et al*, 2012), there remains a dearth of this much-needed resource. UCB stem cells have shown to be of enormous therapeutic value in treatments for leukaemia and anaemia, immunodeficiencies and inherited metabolic diseases (Blacklock *et al*, 2005), and may in the future be used in regenerative medicine (Kurtsberg, 1996). More specifically, UCB's utility for transplant purposes increases according to its high biological match between donor and recipient; and can be further enhanced by using assisted reproductive techniques such as pre-implantation genetic diagnosis (PGD) and tissue typing (TT) – techniques used to create 'matched' UCB for use in transplants to treat a sick sibling, leading the 'donors' of such cells to become colloquially referred to as 'saviour siblings'. With such potential therapeutic possibilities it is little wonder that more UCB is needed but access to publicly available UCB is restricted. There are only three public banks in the UK – The Antony Nolan, the Belfast and the NHS Cord Blood Banks – that collect from only eight delivering hospitals.[1] The lack of UCB

1 For a fuller explanation of the need for greater public reserves of UCB, see Devine, K. (2013) 'Ethics and choice in healthcare: the case of public v. private cord blood banking'. In: Priaulx, N., and Wrigley, A., (eds) 5 *Ethics, Law and Society*. Ashgate, pp. 55–68.

reserves has led the Royal College of Obstetricians and Gynaecologists (RCOG) to call for an improved funding infrastructure for public banks (RCOG, 2006) to enable society to capitalise upon this potentially valuable biological resource.

Whilst a successful pregnancy can therefore bring untold benefits to parents, for many women, the ability to achieve pregnancy is in itself a massive hurdle. However, advancements in reproductive technologies have opened up a world of possibilities for childless couples over the past four decades. In the UK, the use of gametes and embryos for both treatment and research purposes is rigorously regulated, seeing statutory force in the form of the Human Fertilisation and Embryology (HFE) Act in 1990 and later in its amendments in 2008. One of the provisions of the HFE Act 1990 (S12(e) as amended) expressly prohibits payments for gametes, embryos or human admixed embryos due to ethical concerns that payment will reduce the body to a commodity and subsequently pave in-roads into a trade in human tissues and possibly organs (Resnick, 1998), leaving the poor and vulnerable open to inducement and manipulation. Pitted against this concern is the need to procure much needed donor gametes for use in both treatment and research.

It is estimated that infertility affects one in seven couples in the UK (RCOG, 2007) with reports of the waiting time for donor eggs being in the region of 3–5 years in the UK (HFEA, 2011a). Despite clear guidance from the National Institute for Health and Care Excellence (NICE) that three full cycles of IVF treatment should be offered, access remains a postcode lottery, with Mid-Essex Clinical Commissioning Group (CCG) becoming the second CCG in England to refuse any form of funding except in 'clinically exceptional circumstances' (Chan, 2014), prompting outrage from campaigners for equal fertility access to all, such as Fertility Fairness.[2] Women typically request fertility treatment where they have difficulty in conceiving naturally, as experienced by those with physical complications, post-menopausal women, and single and lesbian women. Whilst assisted reproductive technologies (ART) can assist women from these groups, the financial costs involved are particularly high, even for those in the middle-income bracket (Garceau *et al*, 2002) and an increasing number of women and couples seek cheaper treatment options abroad (HFEA, 2014) where the waiting times for donor gametes are greatly reduced (Donnelly, 2010). In the spirit of solidarity and reciprocity, gamete donation is actively encouraged in the UK and, in 2012, the HFEA sought to increase the donor pool amidst renewed concerns about the risks involved in treatment being sought from overseas providers (HFEA, 2009). Although the European Tissues and Cells Directive (EUTCD) sets out standards of quality and safety that should be met within countries inside the European Union (EU) and the European Economic Area (EEA), not all EU/EEA countries have implemented this legislation and, unlike the role of the HFEA, clinics in other countries are not necessarily accredited by a competent body and therefore sufficient safeguards cannot be guaranteed.

2 Fertility Fairness http://www.fertilityfairness.co.uk/.

The donation of eggs is a practice whereby a woman offers between one to fifteen of her oocytes following clinical ovarian stimulation to infertile women for use in ART[3] – typically IVF – or for medical research purposes. Although this process is altruistic in nature, the giving of gametes can attract financial recompense for the donor. Section 12(e) of the HFE Act permits limited reimbursement to both egg and sperm donors in recognition of the donation, but only those authorised by its policy Directions, which allow sperm donors to receive a fixed sum of £35 per clinic visit (HFEA, 2012a: 5) and, due to the more invasive nature of the procedure, £750 per cycle to egg donors (HFEA, 2012a: 6). In addition, these payments may be exceeded where these are deemed by the HFEA to be reasonable, do not include loss of earnings and have been incurred by the donor solely in the UK, and where those expenses are directly attributed to the donation process (HFEA, 2012a: 8). However, these types of financial reward present a dichotomy with the 'no payments for gametes' rule espoused by the Act and are at odds with both the EUTCD and the European Charter of Fundamental Rights of the European Union (2000). The EUTCD states '[M]ember States shall endeavour to ensure voluntary and unpaid donations of tissues and cells',[4] whilst the EU Charter advocates 'the prohibition on making the human body and its parts as such a source of financial gain'.[5] Clearly, the notion of paying cash to women in the pursuit of attracting a greater number of available donor eggs contradicts the altruistic nature of gift-giving to someone in need and, as Blyth and Golding (2008) elucidate, 'Such payment necessarily confounds the accepted definition of "donor"'.

So, how can this be ethically reconciled? The EUTCD itself offers a subtle qualification to the no-payment rule: Article 12(2) surreptitiously circumvents a blanket prohibition by including the phrase, 'Member states shall *endeavour* that the procurement of tissues and cells *as such* is carried out on a non-profit basis' (my emphasis) with the words 'endeavour' and 'as such' implying that non-payment is not absolute. Moreover, Article 12(1) expressly allows compensation where this relates to 'making good' the inconveniences and expenses involved in the donation process. What these combined provisions appear to address is that whilst donation purely for financial gain is impermissible, there is also a strong recognition that donors should not be out of pocket for their efforts and concedes that appropriate monetary recompense should therefore be permitted. Such allowances have paved the way for compensation by way of 'benefits-in kind' to be permissible in other forms of donation, notably in egg-share arrangements.[6]

3 However, there can be no more than two recipients in each treatment cycle.

4 European Tissue and Cells Directive 2004, Art 12(1).

5 European Charter of Fundamental Rights of the EU (2000), Art 3(2). However, it is noted at Art 1(1) that the Charter does not extend the jurisdiction of any court within the EU or UK.

6 Similar schemes exist for sperm-sharing and egg-freezing (the free or discounted storage of eggs in exchange for donating some for treatment or research).

Egg-sharing, reciprocity and solidarity

An egg-share agreement is one in which a woman receiving IVF treatment agrees to donate some of her eggs for either treatment of another or for research purposes in exchange for free or discounted fertility treatment, subsidised by the recipient (HFEA, 2012a). This scheme undoubtedly proves attractive to those who have restricted access to NHS-funded treatment (either where they are subject to a 'postcode lottery' or have already utilised their funding allocation) and has increased in popularity since the first reported birth following an egg-share arrangement in 1992 (Simons and Ahuja, 2005), with egg share donations representing approximately 40 per cent of the total number of donated eggs each year (HFEA, 2011c). The only stipulation imposed is that a woman partaking in this arrangement must donate her eggs whilst undergoing treatment herself, thereby heading off fears she may undertake any additional risks to herself during ovarian stimulation and the retrieval process, a factor that has been the subject of much debate since the scheme's introduction (HFEA, 2005). Despite the donation taking place during her own treatment cycle, the donor may be at risk of ovarian hyper stimulation syndrome (OHSS) – a serious consequence of ovarian induction in IVF procedures – as attempts are made to ensure a successful conception for both parties. Furthermore, it is arguably more morally palatable that a 'benefit' is attained in the form of a discounted or free service as opposed to the prospect of direct cash payments being made for the eggs. Such practice is endorsed by the HFEA:

> The Human Fertilisation and Embryology Authority (HFEA) allows people to receive treatment services in exchange for donation of their gametes to treatment or research, the policy known as 'benefits-in-kind'[7] or, more commonly, egg sharing.
>
> (HFEA, 2011c)

What is perhaps more troubling, however, is that benefits-in-kind may benefit no one. In a far cry from acting in solidarity to meet each other's need, there is no guarantee of success for either party. In fact, the former HFEA Chair, Lisa Jardine, recently spoke publicly about the low chances of success following IVF and of her regret at not being in a position during her role as Chair to offer more words

7 It is noted here that the phrase 'benefits-in-kind' is arguably a little curious. The exchange of eggs for treatment does indeed provide a potential benefit for both parties to the agreement – the donor receives discounted IVF treatment, which may be successful, and the recipient receives the chance of pregnancy – but it is hardly an act of 'being kind' in the sense that it is commonly understood. Kind gestures are synonymous with being generous and compassionate and are altruistic in nature, yet the egg-share exchange is premised on the receipt of a mutual gain, where both women seek to capitalise on their assets (oocytes and cash, respectively) as a means to an individual end. The fact that each woman's potential gain may subsequently assist the other is simply a favourable consequence of the agreement rather than one borne from generosity and compassion – essentially, a happy coincidence.

of caution to those seeking treatment about the odds of achieving pregnancy (Connor, 2013). A donor may also reduce her own chances of conceiving by giving up some of her eggs – eggs that may later be shown to be the sole fruitful oocytes that she possesses. An additional concern centres on the psychological effects that may ensue should success be achieved for the recipient but not the egg donor (Johnson, 1999). This is particularly problematic given the changes to the law made in 2005 regarding anonymity, which affords any offspring resultant of ART, born after 1 April 2005, the right to know of their genetic origins and therefore seek contact with the donor when they reach the age of 18.[8] Whilst such contact might be welcomed, it could also prove to be emotionally challenging for all concerned and may even result in the donor regretting her decision to donate. Such fears, however, have been disputed by Gurtin *et al* who have concluded that there is little evidence to suggest potential psychological harm to donors, including those whose own treatment ends unsuccessfully (Gurtin *et al*, 2012a). Moreover, the results of one study reveal that 65 per cent of women who had engaged in egg-sharing would be willing to engage in future agreements (Ahuja *et al*, 1997). In another, 83 per cent of those surveyed expressed that they would still participate in egg-sharing if they could do so again with the benefit of hindsight, with the overall results of the study demonstrating an overwhelmingly positive attitude towards the scheme (Gurtin *et al*, 2012b).[9]

One further concern raised by critics of benefits-in-kind centres upon the issue of consent. As with any medical procedure, consent to treatment must be valid and ART is no exception. It has been argued, however, that the consent of donors in an egg-share agreement may be eschewed by their overriding pursuit of bearing a child, particularly for those who lack the financial means to undergo sole treatment. In this sense they may be vulnerable to manipulation by those seeking a donor, leaving them open to being unduly influenced into the agreement, which could render their consent invalid (English, 2005). Moreover, in an egg-share arrangement, there is no guarantee that the egg donor seeking discounted treatment is indeed financially insecure, and it may be wise to apprehend the words of Johnson (1999) who warns that the deficiency of consent may in fact be two-fold:

> There must be some doubt as to whether consent to paid egg sharing can be fully effective and freely given, if the couple feel that they have no choice in the matter due to financial distress. There also appears the possibility with paid egg sharing that some couples who could afford to pay, none the less claim not to be able to do so in order to circumvent the ban on direct payments for eggs. In these cases the payment would be acting as an inducement, which again might be considered to impair the quality of consent.

8 HFEA (Disclosure of Donor Information) Regulations 2004, SI 2004/1511.

9 For a summary of the research conducted between 2007 and 2009 by Gurtin *et al.*, see: Gurtin, Z.B., 'Evaluating egg-sharing: new findings on old debates' *BioNews* 653 (23 April 2012, Progress Educational Trust).

Clearly the opportunist type of egg donor may simply be utilising the permitted egg-share arrangement as a means of 'cashing in' on the vulnerable recipient's relative wealth.

Notwithstanding the issues raised, there may also be a class of potential recipients who are disadvantaged by egg-share agreements – those who are not only unable to naturally produce their own 'exchangeable' eggs but *also* lack the financial capacity to trade with an egg donor. In other words, the non-affluent egg recipient is 'doubly disadvantaged' by their lower financial position in addition to their reproductive physiology, and rather than adopting the role of participating actors, the lack of fiscal capital casts them as outsiders to the benefits-in-kind marketplace. This in turn prevents them from accessing the reciprocal reproductive schemes on offer; and for these women, the ability to act in solidarity is clearly in short supply. However, what they would possess, *if they were able to bear a child*, is a unit of UCB – a form of biological material of arguably equal value to gametes.[10]

The word 'solidarity' is one that promulgates the notion of supportive groups acting in cohesion with a singleness of purpose and sense of camaraderie. Indeed, the French National Consultative Ethics Committee has gone so far as to prioritise the principle of solidarity within society as a societal code 'without which no society can survive' (Comite Consultatif National d'Ethique, 2002). However, Prainsack and Buyx (2011a) criticise the nebulus nature of the concept of solidarity as it is commonly used within the bio-medical community. They argue that it is 'vague at best and anti-individualistic at worst' and advance an alternative definition based on analysed bioethical literature. In their report, *Solidarity: Reflections on an Emerging Concept in Bioethics*, commissioned by the Nuffield Council on Bioethics, they suggest that at an interpersonal level, solidarity is the 'manifestations of people's willingness to incur costs (understood as emotional investments, time and sometimes also money) in order to assist others' (Prainsack and Buyx, 2011b). They purport that expressing inner emotions such as empathy or sentiment do not satisfy a manifestation of solidarity with another if they not accompanied by an act; rather, a physical gesture is required when in pursuit of a common goal, including the sharing of risks. However, they also opine that this does not preclude an individual or group from receiving a benefit in the process.

If we apply this definition of solidarity to the UCB/Egg-share model it is arguable that both parties are demonstrating solidaristic behaviour. The exchange of eggs and UCB involve physical acts as opposed to charitable donations (where resources are gifted from one party to those without); they act towards a common, shared goal of achieving access to healthcare treatment (albeit a different type of treatment to the other) and do so either altruistically in the spirit of reciprocity or as a happy coincidence that they may assist each other; they acknowledge that the 'costs' involved in the arrangement may involve a financial outlay, and whilst accepting the risk of failure in their own aims, they do so in order to maximise their own

10 The term 'equal value to gametes' is meant here in the sense that for those who seek the use of UCB cells as a potential life source for *an existing* patient, this form of human tissue is to them as important as seeking gametes to bring a child *into existence*.

chance of success. In this sense, the inclusion of UCB in the benefits-in-kind marketplace clearly fits within the parameters of Prainsack and Buyx's vision of solidarity.

With the anticipated utility of UCB, like gametes, it too may be a sought-after biological commodity. An egg donor, for example, may wish to trade an oocyte for a UCB unit where she seeks a UCB transplant (either for herself or another) rather than securing discounted treatment and conversely, hospitals or research companies may be willing to pay for (in whole or in part with the egg share donor) the UCB donor's IVF treatment in exchange for the resultant UCB for use in treatment or research. This begs the question: if UCB cells, like gametes, are of benefit to another, is it possible to suggest that they too can be used as a resource in the 'benefits-in-kind' marketplace? This chapter now explores whether, under the existing legal regulations relating to egg-shares and the donation of human tissue, it is possible to think outside the (egg) box and include UCB stem cells as an item of 'exchange' in egg-share agreements.

Sowing the SEED for other benefits-in-kind?

In 2004, the HFEA undertook a review of donor-assisted conception in the UK, producing the SEED (Sperm, Egg and Embryo Donation) Report (HFEA, 2005) the following year. The aim of the report was to ensure that safe and effective services were on offer and that donors, recipients and any resultant offspring were adequately protected. Benefits-in-kind formed part of that review, with consideration given to other forms of benefit that were then on offer – notably, sterilisation and previously 'egg giving'. The report recommended that a free or discounted sterilisation procedure was not an appropriate form of benefit to be offered to the egg donor because it was already a freely available service; but more importantly, that there was no therapeutic reason for hyper-stimulation of her ovaries, which carries its own risks, such as OHSS. Likewise, the report concluded that egg-giving – the process of 'giving-up' an entire cycle of retrieved eggs to the recipient in exchange for free or discounted treatment on a subsequent cycle – was also an unsuitable practice, confirming its own view previously formed in December 2003. The reason given against accepting this practice as a form of benefit was that the donor would not be fulfilling her own chances of conceiving during that particular treatment cycle and would subsequently open herself up to the risk of OHSS for the sole benefit of the recipient.

Whilst sterilisation and egg-giving have therefore been rejected, what the SEED review suggested was that the HFEA was open to the idea of considering other forms of benefit-in-kind and whilst a mutual exchange of eggs for UCB was unlikely to have been envisaged in the HFEA at the time of the report, it does not appear to present a bar to such a suggestion. However, post the SEED report, public fears with regards to compensating gamete donors for their bodily material remained high and, in response to these concerns,[11] a further, fuller review

11 Wilkinson argues that egg-sharing creates inconsistencies between types of donors with egg-sharers being treated more generously in terms of 'compensation' than egg donors. See: Wilkinson, S.

was conducted by the HFEA in 2011, with Section 2 forming an evaluation of benefits-in-kind in the Authority's paper: *Donation review: Compensation of donors and benefits-in-kind* (HFEA, 2011b). The key recommendations relating to this practice were expressly communicated in the following Chair's letter, once again opening up the possibility of considering other forms of benefit:

> The Authority decided that egg sharing should continue, but, given that our current guidance focuses almost exclusively on egg sharing, we have reviewed our guidance to make it clear what other benefits might be included (such as free or reduced storage and moving up the waiting list).
>
> (HFEA, 2012b)

With discounted egg or embryo storage plans and a reduced waiting time now being cited as acceptable modes of trade for eggs, it would appear that there has been a widening of the parameters within which benefits may be viewed. Rather than restricting the benefits to be gained to the receipt of discounted treatment with the sole aim of achieving pregnancy, the HFEA appears to look beyond the end product and consider a broader interpretation of what the provision of services might include, for example access to the service (which currently entails waiting lists) and the need to make arrangements for the storage of any unused eggs destined for the donor's use at a later date (egg storage). What this in turn suggests is that as long as the 'exchange' is made whilst engaging ART provision in the pursuit of conceiving a child broadly construed – be that accessing treatment, expediting treatment or preparing for future treatment – then it is morally and ethically acceptable. Essentially, the desired result of bearing a child is a by-product of pregnancy brought about by the much sought-after service provision and if an exchange of assets facilitates that aim now or in the future, then the HFEA appears to offer no real objection.

With this premise in mind, it may be possible to go one step further. Like the egg recipient in an egg-share agreement, the non-affluent egg seeker pursues pregnancy by assisted reproductive means but akin to being placed on a 'waiting list', their lack of finances restricts access and potentially commits them to a lifelong wait for treatment while their financial situation improves. As the HFEA already recognises the need for greater expediency in waiting times for ART and accepts the use of prioritising those who offer eggs in exchange, then it may be possible to argue that the HFEA would not be averse to accepting UCB as a form of benefit-in-kind. This in turn would allow the non-affluent egg recipient to access ART services which would offer a mutual benefit to both the UCB donor/egg recipient and UCB recipient/egg donor and promote the spirit of solidarity. Moreover, the 2011 review paper offers little to bar this proposal and goes as far as to point out that, 'current HFEA guidance focuses almost exclusively on egg sharing arrangements in exchange for IVF, yet treatment services

(2013) 'Is the HFEA's policy on compensating egg donors and egg sharers defensible?' 21(2) *Medical Law Review* 1–40.

which can be offered are broader than this' (HFEA, 2011b). This implies that a far-reaching interpretation can be applied to the provision of services in the context of benefits-in-kind and could therefore include other bodily material such as UCB.

UCB in the egg-share marketplace

Given UCB's potentially life-saving capacity, it is not difficult to comprehend why an egg donor may wish to trade her spare eggs for UCB, particularly for women whose finances are not at issue but where the need for UCB is real, or indeed where an affluent UCB donor simply requires the acquisition of eggs to conceive and then facilitate the exchange. It is less obvious why a hospital or research company would consider paying the high costs involved in assisted reproductive services simply to receive a unit of stem cells in return, regardless of their potential utility. However, as previously discussed, if one considers that UCB remains in short supply in the UK due to a dearth of public banks combined with a limited number of participating UCB collection hospitals, it soon becomes clear that the UK relies heavily on the *import* of UCB, which itself carries substantial cost implications.

In 2009, a review by the Department of Health revealed that the cost of UCB imported and tested in preparation for transplant in the UK was in the region of £17,000, with the NHS Blood and Transplant Service (NHSBT) later citing an even higher figure of £25,000 per unit (NHSBT, 2010), and 85 units recorded as being imported into the UK per year (Technopolis 2009). Such cost implications therefore commits the NHS to an annual bill of just over £2 million. In contrast, a cycle of IVF treatment is a fraction of the cost, typically totalling around £5,000 per cycle (Jackson, 2013).[12] With these figures in mind, it is arguably more cost effective to allow free or discounted ART services in return for the resultant UCB, which could be utilised in a directed donation or general deposit to a public bank, reducing the burden and high costs involved in the import of units and simultaneously addressing the need for a greater supply of UCB in the UK. As the commissioned review group, Technopolis Group themselves, suggest, '[t]he high costs of importing samples…would suggest that it is economically favourable to have a bigger public bank and therefore reduce the need to import samples from abroad' (Technopolis Group, 2009). In terms of solidarity and reciprocity, UCB donation functions well as an ethical form of benefits-in-kind.

Clearly, the inclusion of UCB as an item of exchange within egg-share arrangements, with its ability to address the lack of publicly available UCB stocks and high import costs, combined with its capacity to serve as a potential life source

12 Also note that clinicians in Belgium have recently reported that a new technique in IVF has been successfully used at a treatment cost of a mere £170 per cycle. See: Gallagher, J., (2013) 'IVF as cheap as £170, doctors claim' *BBC News Online*. 8 July. http://www.bbc.co.uk/news/health-23223752.

for the UCB recipient and as a means of entering the egg-share marketplace for the donor is an idea not so far 'outside the box' as it may have first appeared. But in continuing with this line of enquiry it is also necessary to examine the current HFEA General Directions and *Code of Practice* as they relate to egg-sharing agreements, to determine whether any provisions contained within them attempt to head off the inclusion of any particular kind of exchange. Turning first to the latest version of the Directions, published in April 2012, an express definition of 'benefits-in-kind' is lacking, unlike terms such as 'clinic visit' and 'cycle of egg donation' which are afforded a definitive explanatory note. Rather, its meaning is confirmed as allowing the receipt of 'licenced services, such as treatment, storage or access to licensed services' (HFEA, 2012a: 15). Synonymous with the HFEA review paper, the Direction provides for what might be included, yet including the phrase 'such as' simply gives examples of current accepted practices and implies that others may be acceptable, leaving the possibility for UCB as a form of exchange at least open for consideration.

Finally, the HFEA's current *Code of Practice* concurs in its guidance relating to egg-share agreements and the use of benefits-in-kind but a closer reading could also carve sufficient room for the inclusion of UCB in its section dedicated to information provision. Amongst other provisions it advises at section 12.6(f) that those engaging in egg-share arrangements should receive information setting out 'available alternative treatment options'. Whilst this specific provision is likely to relate to the availability of alternative forms of assisted reproductive techniques to egg-sharing, such as individual treatment options using techniques such as gamete intra-fallopian transfer (GIFT), zygote intra-fallopian transfer (ZIFT) and intrauterine insemination (IUI), it is not beyond the realms of possibility that alternative forms of benefit-in-kind, such as UCB, could also be read into this section.

However, one major stumbling block in terms of UCB entering the egg-share marketplace presents itself in the form of the Human Tissue Authority (HTA). As earlier considered, whilst egg donation and the practice of egg-sharing fall under the jurisdiction of the HFEA, the authority's remit does not extend to UCB stem cells. Although arguably a possible 'product' of ART, the HFEA's remit is confined to the regulation of treatment and research involving the creation, storage, procurement or *ex utero* use of embryos and the storage, use, procurement, testing, processing or distribution of human gametes (other than partner-donated sperm which has been neither processed nor stored), and UCB does not fit within these criteria. As human biological cells, UCB stem cells instead fall under the statutory regulatory framework of the Human Tissue Act 2004, governed by the (EUTCD).

It would appear that the EUTCD, which was formerly adopted into UK law by the Human Tissue (Quality and Safety for Human Application) Regulations 2007, with its provisions being implemented and overseen by the HTA, offers little to prohibit the expansion of benefits-in-kind into the area of human tissues and cells so long as a mutual recompense is made rather than an express financial reward. As the HFEA (HFEA, 2011d: 2.1.2) has commented:

> Egg sharing arrangements serve to promote an over-arching objective of the EUTCD by increasing the availability of human cells and tissue for donation and fostering solidarity between donor and recipient.

Essentially, if the EUTCD could be construed to include egg-sharing on the premise that it promotes the ideology of reciprocity and solidarity, then the inclusion of UCB in this mode of mutual exchange could be a future possibility.

Conclusion

Whilst the prohibition of payment for an exchange of bodily material – perhaps more lucidly expressed in terms of cash payments – remains a fundamental and also controversial issue for medical law and ethics, it can be said that the HFEA has in fact already allowed 'payment' in the form of discounted treatment for the donation of gametes as a benefit-in-kind. Whilst these arrangements are of course beneficial to egg-seekers and those who require cheaper access to assisted reproductive services, they inadvertently disadvantage the egg-seeker who lacks the finances to enter the egg-share marketplace. As a means of redressing this imbalance, this chapter has sought to propose an ethical alternative to the current use of benefits-in-kind and has proposed that the inclusion of UCB may be a possible biological resource alternative. By mapping the current regulatory framework as it relates to both reproductive and non-reproductive material it has been possible to demonstrate that current ethical and legal provisions would present no overt objections to this proposal.

Whilst permitting UCB as a viable form of exchange would require a collaboration of both the HFEA and HTA to set the parameters of exchange to ensure the safety and quality of provision, and safeguard proper consent for those engaged in this new form of egg-sharing, such an idea has not been totally ruled out. Although the Government's joint review concluded that they should continue to exist independently, the Department of Health remained committed to achieving further efficiencies within the regulatory bodies, perhaps leaving the door open for a potential merger in the future. Indeed, the proposed sharing of support services could perhaps provide the infrastructure for collaborations on a smaller scale such as working together on projects involving the expansion of benefits-in-kind, whilst retaining each body's necessary independence on matters arising from their primary functions.

Under the suggested model, and akin to more traditional forms of egg-share arrangements, there would be no explicit exchange of cash for the cells thus circumventing the criticisms that surround the commodification of human tissue. Furthermore, as a non-reproductive material, UCB does not give rise to the same emotional attachment as do gametes, which arises from these cells' ability to create genetically-related offspring. Therefore, UCB appears attractive in its capacity to act as a biological asset without inviting additional social or legal responsibilities. Indeed, as a form of biological waste, collected at birth, UCB affords relatively few risks to either donor or the recipient and has the added advantage of providing a possible lifeline for the UCB recipient or being an ethical biological resource for researchers. Of course, donations of UCB offer no assurance of a successful cure for its patient recipient(s), nor will it necessarily provide fruitful research outcomes, but this should offer no bar to its consideration regardless of whether the item of exchange is an oocyte or UCB – based on the current permitted egg-share model, there is also no guarantee that a successful pregnancy will indeed result in these types of agreements, but the agreements are permitted none the less.

It is accepted, however, that the advanced proposal is not a perfect model. Critics of egg-share agreements may still fear the commercialisation of biological material and view the exchange of UCB as another form of potential exploitation of those within the marketplace desperate for the opportunity to access wanted eggs or UCB. Indeed, concerns regarding the validity of consent for either the egg or UCB seeker would remain. Valid consent is fundamental to the principles of medical law and ethics and if it is not given freely – as may occur where there is no other means to access treatment – then a person's consent may be compromised. It may also be argued that the non-affluent egg-seeker would still require an egg donor who runs the risk of OHSS and the acquisition of UCB would not be available until some nine months after the original treatment service, which may be too late for the UCB recipient. Moreover, if the egg donor/UCB seeker is still required to subsidise the egg recipient/UCB donor's treatment, it may be that she herself is disadvantaged in 'giving up' both her eggs *and* finances in pursuit of UCB; and of course, the psychological welfare of both parties, should their treatment be unsuccessful, would remain a problematic issue. But if a joint enterprise between the appropriate authoritative and regulatory bodies could oversee and regulate the service, providing safeguards for the vulnerable, and ensure that best practice is maintained, then the public may gain confidence in the scheme and be open to its introduction. Moreover, in the interests of solidarity, reciprocity and as a means to address the need for a greater number of available eggs, UCB stem cells and equal access to fertility treatment for all, considering UCB as an asset for mutual exchange, is – in principle at least – worthy of a note in the suggestions box.

References

Ahuja, K.K., Mostyn, B.J. and Simons, E.G., (1997) 'Egg sharing and egg domination: Attitudes of British egg donors and recipients' 12(12) *Human Reproduction* 2845.

Blacklock, H., Teague, L., Patton, N. and Browett, P., (2005) 'Volunteer cord blood banking and transplantation' 118 *New Zealand Medical Journal* 1208.

Blyth, E. and Golding, B., (2008) 'Egg sharing: a practical and ethical option to IVF?' 3(4) *Obstetrics and Gynaecology* 465.

Chan, S., (2014) 'Mid-Essex CCG cuts IVF funding' *BioNews* 773 (29 September 2014, Progress Educational Trust).

Connor, S., (2013) 'Lisa Jardine: nobody wants to runs stories about the people who go through IVF for nothing' *Independent Online*. 13 November. http://www.independent.co.uk/life-style/health-and-families/features/lisa-jardine-nobody-wants-to-run-stories-about-the-people-who-go-through-ivf-for-nothing-8919813.html

Comite Consultatif National d'Ethique, (2002) *Umbilical cord blood banks for autologous use or for research* (Report no.74 Paris CCNE, 2002).

Devine, K., (2013) 'Ethics and choice in healthcare: the case of Public v. Private cord blood banking' in Priaulx, N. and Wrigley, A., (eds) *Ethics, Law and Society* vol.5 (Farnham: Ashgate).

Donnelly, D., (2010) 'Desperate hunt for donor eggs forces couples to seek IVF from abroad' *Telegraph Online.* 3 July. http://www.telegraph.co.uk/health/healthnews/7869822/Desperate-hunt-for-donor-eggs-forces-couples-to-seek-IVF-abroad.html

English, V., (2005) 'Egg-sharing affects the validity of a woman's consent' *BioNews* 329 (5 October 2005, Progress Educational Trust).

Gallagher, J., (2013) 'IVF as cheap as £170, doctors claim' *BBC News Online.* 8 July. http://www.bbc.co.uk/news/health-23223752

Garceau, L., Henderson, J., Davis, L.J., Petrou, S., Henderson, L.R., McVeigh, E., Barlow, D.H. and Davidson, L.L., (2002) 'Economic implications of assisted reproductive techniques: a systematic review' 17 *Human Reproduction* 3090.

Gurtin, Z.B., (2012) 'Evaluating egg-sharing: new findings on old debates' *BioNews* 653 (23 April 2012, Progress Educational Trust).

Gurtin, Z.B., Ahuja, K.K. and Golombok, S., (2012a) 'Emotional and relational aspects of egg-sharing: egg share donors' and recipients' feeling about each other, each other's treatment outcome and any resulting children' 27(6) *Human Reproduction* 1.

Gurtin, Z.B., Ahuja, K.K. and Golombok, S., (2012b) 'Egg-sharing, consent and exploitation: Examining egg-share donors' and recipients' circumstances and retrospective reflections' 24(7) *Ethics, Bioscience and Life* 698.

HFEA SEED Report (2005) *A review of the HFEA's review of sperm, egg and embryo donation in the UK* (London: HFEA).

HFEA Press release (11 March 2009) *Thinking of going abroad? Think twice about going abroad for fertility treatment* http://www.hfea.gov.uk/632.html

HFEA (2011a) *A review of the HFEA's sperm and egg donation policies* http://www.hfea.gov.uk/docs/2011-01-13_Donation_review_background.pdf

HFEA (2011b) *Donation review: Compensation of donors and benefits in kind* (19 January 2011) 612.

HFEA (2011c) *Committee Paper 612* (19 October 2011) sec 2 (3.1)

HFEA (2011d) *Authority Meeting Papers* (19 October 2011, Paper 612) sec 2.1.2

HFEA (2012a) *General Directions, Gamete and Embryo Donation Ref: 0001, Version 3* (April 2012).

HFEA (2012b) Chair's Letter CH(12) 01 *Implementation of the outcomes of the donation review* http://www.hfea.gov.uk/6966.html

HFEA (2014) *Considering treatment options abroad – issues and risks* http://www.hfea.gov.uk/fertility-clinics-treatment-abroad.html

Jackson, E., (2013) *Medical law: Text, cases and materials* (3rd edition) (Oxford: Open University Press).

Johnson, M., (1999) 'The medical ethics of paid egg sharing in the UK: opinion' 14(7) *Human Reproduction* 1912.

Kurtsberg, J., Laughlin, M. and Graham, M.L. (1996) 'Placental blood as a source of haematopoietic stem cells for transplantation to unrelated recipients' 335 *New England Journal of Medicine* 157.

McCracken, J., (April 2013) *Review of the HFEA and the HTA* https://www.gov.uk/government/uploads/system/uploads/attachment_data/file/216947/Justin_McCracken_report_of_review_of_HFEA_and_HTA.pdf

NHSBT (2010) *The future of unrelated donor stem cell transplantation in the UK* (July 2010). http://www.nhsbt.nhs.uk/download/uk_stem_cell_strategic_forum_report.pdf

Office of National Statistics (2014) *Births in England and Wales by parents' country of birth, 2013* http://www.ons.gov.uk/ons/dcp171778_375070.pdf

Prainsack, B. and Buyx, A., (2011a) 'Can solidarity inform bioethics? Reflections on a concept and implications for biobanks' *BioNews* 636 (5 December 2011, Progress Educational Trust).

Prainsack, B. and Buyx A., (2011b) *'Reflections on an emerging concept on Bioethics'* Nuffield Council on Bioethics http://nuffieldbioethics.org/wp-content/uploads/2014/07/Solidarity_report_FINAL.pdf.

Resnick, D., (1998) 'The commodification of human reproductive material' 24 *Journal of Medical Ethics* 388.

Royal College of Obstetricians and Gynaecologists (2006) 'Umbilical cord blood banking' *Scientific Advisory Committee Opinion Paper 2* (London: RCOG).

Royal College of Obstetricians and Gynaecologists (2007) *Scientific Advisory Committee Opinion Paper 8* (London: RCOG).

Screnci, M., Murgi, E., Pirre, O., Valente, E., Gesuiti, P., Corona, F. and Girelli, G., (2012) 'Donating umbilical cord blood to a public bank or storing it in a private bank: knowledge and preference of blood donors and of pregnant women' 10(3) *Blood Transfusion* 331.

Simons, E.G. and Ahuja, K.K., (2005) 'Egg sharing: an evidence based solution to donor egg shortages' 7 *Obstetrics and Gynaecology* 112.

Technopolis Group (2009) *Cord blood banking in the UK: An international comparison of policy and practice* http://health.cat/open.php?url=http://www.technopolis-group.com/resources/downloads/reports/952_final_090114.pdf.

Wilkinson, S., (2013) 'Is the HFEA's policy on compensating egg donors and egg sharers defensible?' 21(2) *Medical Law Review* 1.

6 PGD past and present: Is the HFE Act 1990 now 'fit for purpose'?

Jeanne Snelling and Colin Gavaghan

Introduction

The United Kingdom provides a rich history of regulatory engagement with assisted reproductive technology and research. Since the Human Fertilisation and Embryology Act 1990 ('the HFE Act') was first introduced, it has been cited as a paradigmatic example of how to regulate contentious emerging technologies, ostensibly striking a principled balance between competing ethical considerations while remaining flexible enough to respond to new technological developments (Fox, 2009: 334).[1] Conversely, others suggested that the 1990 Act adopted a 'pragmatic compromise' that, in some instances, failed to address significant matters of principle (Brazier, 1999: 172; see also Montgomery, 1991: 529 and Morgan, 2004: 7).

In the intervening years, the regulatory regime, and the principles underpinning it have been subjected to ongoing ethical scrutiny and, on occasion, claims of regulatory 'disconnect' (Brownsword, 2008: 297). The 2008 amendments to the legislation provided an opportunity to address these perceived limitations. This chapter considers just one aspect of this regulatory regime, that of preimplantation genetic diagnosis (PGD).

Taking a broad approach, we first sketch the influence that PGD had on the form in which the HFE Act was originally enacted. We then outline the regulatory approach to PGD established two decades ago by the Human Fertilisation and Embryology Authority (HFEA) and the current statutory parameters introduced following the 2008 amendments (Human Fertilisation and Embryology Act 2008). Ultimately, we consider the extent to which this normative framework withstands critique. We suggest that the new regime may not have achieved greater clarity, or consistency, in respect of decisions made in this context. Further, we suggest that it continues to leave unaddressed an important matter of principle – which is what the legitimate role of the state is in regulating reproduction.

1 Cf Ouellette, A. et al (2005) 'Lessons across the Pond: Assisted Reproductive Technology in the United Kingdom and the United States' 31 *American Journal of Law & Medicine* 419–446.

PGD past: An overview of the history of PGD regulation

The benefit of examining a regulatory system with hindsight is that it enables identification of external factors, such as political agendas or ideologies, which influenced the adoption of a particular regulatory approach adopted. The history preceding the introduction of the HFE Act is a particularly salient example of how outside forces may be harnessed to influence a regulatory scheme, particularly in relation to PGD. While the catalyst for introducing legislation was the introduction of in vitro fertilisation (IVF) following the birth in England of Louise Brown in 1978, the world's first successful IVF birth (Johnson et al, 2010), the potential of PGD was partly responsible for the *nature* of the legislation that was subsequently introduced.

The Warnock Report, which was commissioned in 1982 and published in 1984, was largely focused on embryo research and recommended its ongoing lawfulness (Warnock Committee, 1984: [11.7]).[2] PGD, which was then only a *theoretical* possibility and in regards to which many clinicians/scientists were decidedly ambivalent, attracted a mere two paragraphs in the report (Theodosiou and Johnson, 2011: 464). Despite this, the prospect of PGD became a major 'player' in the human embryo research debates that followed the Report's release.

The political response to the Warnock Report's facilitative recommendations regarding embryo research was hostile. In a direct response, Enoch Powell MP tabled a Private Member's Bill in Parliament that would, if enacted, have criminalised the creation and use of IVF embryos for any purpose other than to achieve a pregnancy (Unborn Children (Protection) Bill 1985). Powell's Bill passed its second reading in Parliament with a significant majority. However, as a result of this attempt to narrowly restrict the scope of embryo research, a cluster of pro-research scientists immediately galvanised a lobby group in an attempt to defeat the Powell Bill and secure the ongoing permissibility of embryo research (Evans and McLaren, 1985).[3] Although the Powell Bill reached its third reading, it was deliberately 'filibustered' and its progress through Parliament successfully impeded (Mulkay, 1993: 722).

When the Human Fertilisation and Embryology Bill was finally introduced into Parliament in 1989–1990, Members of the House of Lords and the Commons were permitted to cast a conscience vote on the contentious issue of embryo research. Significantly, the relatively liberal statute that ensued, which permitted embryo research subject to specified limitations, resulted from a long – and deeply divided – legislative process.

There is now good evidence that the delay between the release of the Warnock Report and the introduction of the Human Fertilisation and Embryology

2 The Committee's terms of reference were 'to consider recent and potential developments in medicine and science related to human fertilisation and embryology'. The report also made recommendations regarding access to IVF and donor insemination.

3 The lobby group 'PROGRESS' (now known as the Progress Educational Trust) was formed in 1985 and consisted of an alliance of MPs, scientists, lawyers, doctors, charities, women's and family groups. See Johnson, M. (2008) *Real Progress – But More to Do*. [Online] Available from: www.bionews.org.uk.

legislation some six years later was a result of deliberate stalling tactics by pro-embryo research factions within the Government. This provided pro-research protagonists with an opportunity to convince/convert Members of Parliament who were ambivalent about, or initially opposed to, embryo research (Mulkay, 1995: 38 and 43). The potential of PGD played a significant role in this campaign. Michael Mulkay (1995) observes that in the crucial debates of late 1989 and early 1990:[4]

> 75% of those arguing for embryo research in Parliament made significant reference to [PGD's] potential contribution to the control of genetic disorders. Many speakers made it clear that acceptance of the connection between embryo research and control over genetic disease had been decisive in leading them to vote for such research … The opponents of embryo research gradually became less evident in the media, where their familiar moral denunciations were largely replaced by the stories about happy mothers and perfect babies through which the case for embryo research was conveyed to the mass audience ... Thus, the pro-research lobby won, after several years of sustained effort, by changing the focus of the debate; by returning to that fear of, and repugnance at, congenital abnormality.
>
> (Citations omitted) (p. 50)

Theodosious and Johnson similarly claim that the prospect of developing PGD technology was used as a 'strategic weapon' to defeat opponents of human embryo research. Indeed, they go considerably further. They provide cogent evidence that it was the need to demonstrate the importance of continuing embryo research to enable PGD to be developed that actually *kindled* scientific and clinical interest in developing PGD as an alternative to prenatal diagnosis for foetal abnormality. (Theodosiou and Johnson, 2011: 467)

PGD present

Despite its prominence in the scientific and political debates of the 1980s, PGD was not specifically mentioned in the original HFE Act, a situation that altered drastically after the 2008 amendment. The Act, both in its original form and as amended, establishes certain prohibitions regarding embryos[5] and authorises the HFEA to act as an arm's-length licensing body for the purposes specified in the Act.[6]

The HFEA may license clinics to perform approved activities in the course of providing 'treatment services'.[7] Treatment services are defined as 'medical,

4 See also Karpin, I. and Savell, K. (2012) *Perfecting Pregnancy: Law, Disability, and the Future of Reproduction* (Cambridge: Cambridge University Press), p. 169.

5 HFE Act, s3.

6 HFE Act, s5.

7 HFE Act, s11(1) states that 'The Authority may grant … (a) licences under paragraph 1 of Schedule 2 to this Act authorising activities in the course of providing treatment services …' Paragraph 1(3) of Schedule 2 provides that: 'a licence under this paragraph cannot authorise any activity unless

surgical or obstetric services provided to the public ... for the purpose of assisting women to carry children'.[8] The activities for which the HFEA may grant treatment licences are set out in paragraph 1 of Schedule 2 to the HFE Act.[9]

The HFEA initially authorised the performance of PGD under its authority to license research into the development of assisted reproductive technologies. It was not until almost ten years after the first PGD birth that the HFEA released an interim licensing guidance covering PGD, signalling its evolution from research to constituting a clinical service (HFEA, 1999, 2003i). Subsequently, PGD was licensed according to criteria formulated by the HFEA and set out in its *Code of Practice* (HFEA, 2003ii).[10]

The early years saw PGD permitted only for serious genetic disorders, with a clear line drawn between 'medical' and 'social' uses, primarily social sex selection. The HFEA originally advised clinicians in its *Code of Practice* that PGD should be consistent with clinical practice in the context of prenatal diagnosis (HFEA, 2003ii: 124). The rationale underlying this approach was that it would meet the needs of prospective parents at risk of passing on serious genetic disorders, while reassuring those concerned about runaway technology, 'designer babies' and embryos treated as disposable commodities (Gavaghan, 2007). While some stakeholders and interest groups – notably disability rights advocates and pro-life campaigners – never regarded this compromise position as remotely satisfactory, it could be argued to have succeeded at least in addressing the concerns of most observers most of the time.

The intervening years have witnessed a significant expansion of the permitted uses of PGD. These now include using PGD to diagnose mutations associated with the development of late-onset disease, such as the cancer susceptibility syndromes (HFEA, 2006). PGD may also be performed to sex select an embryo to avoid certain genetic conditions, such as haemophilia, which are sex-linked and only (or predominantly) affect male offspring. An additional permutation of PGD is 'exclusion testing'. This provides adults who are at risk of developing a serious late-onset disorder (such as Huntington Disease) but who do not wish to know whether they will in fact develop the disease, with a means to ensure that their offspring are free from the condition (Snelling, 2009: 65). Another better-known application of PGD is embryonic human leucocyte antigen (HLA) tissue typing to identify an embryo that is a tissue-match (and prospective stem cell donor) for an existing ill child/sibling in need of a stem cell transplant. All of these applications of PGD were initially facilitated by policy promulgated by the HFEA. The

it appears to the Authority to be necessary or desirable for the purpose of providing treatment services'.

8 HFE Act, s2 (as amended).

9 These activities include: bringing about the creation of embryos *in vitro* (a), procuring, keeping, testing, processing or distributing embryos (b), other practices designed to secure that embryos are in a suitable condition to be placed in a woman (d) and placing any permitted embryo in a woman (e).

10 The sixth edition of the *Code of Practice* included a chapter dedicated to PGD for the first time. See Human Fertilisation and Embryology Authority (2003ii) *HFEA Code of Practice*, 6th ed, London, HFEA.

Authority however drew a line at purely 'non-medical' uses of the technology. So, while sex selection was permitted to avoid the transmission of serious sex-linked disorders, social sex section was not permitted. Thus the HFEA firmly established a social/medical dichotomy.

The reform of the HFE Act 1990 was premised on various grounds. These included a perceived disconnection between the legislation and new or emerging technology, or indeed new applications of established technology, such as HLA tissue typing.[11] Other catalysts for reform included economic factors, in the form of a desire to reduce what was considered by some to be a bureaucratic and expensive system, as well as a perception that changing societal attitudes towards reproductive technologies had shifted.[12]

In 2005, the House of Commons Science and Technology Committee published a report on human reproductive technologies that purported to provide a 'blueprint for a legislative and regulatory system fit for purpose in the 21st century' (2005: 5). Specifically in regard to PGD the Committee stated:

> We see no reason why a regulator should seek to determine which disorders can be screened out using PGD. Nevertheless, clinical decisions should operate within clear boundaries set by Parliament and informed by ethical judgements.
>
> (p. 58)

The Government's response was less liberal, advocating what it described as a 'precautionary' approach (Department of Health, 2005: 6). Subsequently, the Human Tissue and Embryos (Draft) Bill was released for pre-legislative scrutiny by a joint Parliamentary Committee in May 2007 (Joint Committee on the Human Tissues and Embryos (Draft) Bill 2007). The Bill contained provisions that sought, for the first time, to regulate PGD and preimplantation tissue typing in primary legislation. After scrutiny by the Joint Committee and considerable debate in both Houses of Parliament – which clearly demonstrated that PGD had become no less contentious in the intervening years – the HFE Act 2008 was passed.

The HFE Act 1990 as amended and the Code of Practice (8th ed)

One of the objectives of the HFE Act 2008 was to categorically establish parliamentary authority over the indications for which PGD was permissible. Another was to achieve greater clarity and transparency in decision-making. Just as the

11 See *R (Quintavelle) v Secretary of State for Health* [2003] UKHL 692.

12 Calls for reform came from many sources. See Birk, D. (2005) 'The Reform of the Human Fertilisation and Embryology Act 1990', *Fam Law* 35, 563; Collier, S. (2004) 'Assisted Reproduction – Statutory Overhaul Overdue', *New Law Journal* 154, 1201; Mahendra, B. (2003) 'A Design for Life', *New Law Journal* 153. See also Morgan, R. (2004) 'Ethics, Economics and the Exotic: The Early Career of the HFEA', *Health Care Analysis* 12, 7.

HFEA declined to licence PGD for social sex selection, this is now specifically prohibited by the Act as amended (paragraph 1ZB of Schedule 2 to the Act), a prohibition that was not challenged in the Parliamentary debates on the Bill. Section 13 of the Act outlines standard conditions placed on licences authorised by the HFEA. Since amendment, section 13(5) now provides that a 'woman shall not be provided with treatment services unless account has been taken of the welfare of any child who may be born as a result'.

Section 13(9), also introduced by the 2008 amendments, specifically relates to PGD. It provides that embryos 'known to have a gene, chromosome or mitochondrion abnormality involving a *significant* risk that a person with the abnormality will have or develop' a serious physical or mental disability, a serious illness, or any other serious medical condition '*must not be preferred* to those that are not known to have such an abnormality' (our emphasis). Section 13(10) extends this restriction to preferring embryos with a particular gender-related risk of serious disability or illness. But although the Act seeks to prevent the *preferential* selection of an embryo with a known genetic anomaly, it stops short of imposing a full-blown prohibition on the selection of such embryos.

The primary reason for introducing section 13(9) and (10) was to prevent PGD being used to select embryos with mutations associated with disabling traits, such as deafness, a restriction that attracted criticism particularly from some sections of the disability rights community (Porter and Smith, 2013). However, the provision was also drafted with another situation in mind. This involves instances where PGD is undertaken to identify a particular mutation, but where all of the available (and otherwise viable) embryos are identified as having the particular mutation for which PGD was performed (Karpin and Savell, 2012: 186). Imagine for example a scenario in which PGD is performed to identify BRCA1 or BRCA2 mutations (which are associated with the development of breast and ovarian cancer in later life) but it indicates that all of the resulting embryos have that particular mutation. Although the HFE Act prevents PGD being performed with the *objective* of selecting an embryo with a disease or illness-related gene variant, the *Code of Practice* precludes a blanket prohibition being imposed on transferring embryos. In such a situation the HFEA *Code of Practice* (8th edition, 2009) states at 10C that section 13(9) and (10) of the Act:

> ... applies *only* where there is at least one other embryo suitable for transfer that is not known to have the characteristics. Where there is no other embryo suitable for transfer, an embryo with these characteristics may be transferred.
> (our emphasis)

This policy approach appears to be driven by something similar to the 'procreative beneficence' principle articulated by some bioethicists (Buchanan et al., 2000: 223; Savulescu and Kahane, 2009) who argue that if a specific outcome involving a child being born with a disability is avoidable by substituting another child, substitution is the morally preferable course of action. This theory is a derivative of philosopher Derek Parfit's famous 'Claim Q', which held that: 'if in either of two outcomes the same number of people would ever live, it would be bad if those who live are worse off, or have a lower quality of life, than those who would have lived' (Parfit, 1984: 360).

For Parfit, the intuition that it was morally preferable to create the 'better' life was hard to reconcile with the observation that, for the child actually created, the only alternative was never to have been born at all. Hence, the alternative decision, to create the 'less optimal' life, was not obviously worse for anyone in particular. This gave rise to the (for Parfit) counter-intuitive conclusion that it was a matter of moral indifference whether the 'better' or 'worse' life was created. A possible response to this relies on utilitarian 'non person-affecting' considerations, concerned less with preventing 'harm' to an identifiable individual, and more with maximising overall utility; the world is better off if it has more happiness in it, regardless of whether any identifiable person is better off than they would otherwise have been. While potentially offering a way around Parfit's 'non-identity problem', such an approach presents its own philosophical and practical difficulties.[13]

Whatever its merits and shortcomings, this appears to be the principle that – albeit tacitly – informed the approach adopted by the UK Parliament and the HFEA to PGD. While ostensibly eschewing the adoption of any overarching ethical or philosophical principle, at least in this instance they have chosen one particular position in a contested ethical terrain. In doing so, they have incurred criticism not only from reproductive 'liberals' (Gavaghan, 2007), but also increasingly from disability rights activists (Emery et al., 2010; Lucas, 2013). The HFEA *Code of Practice* (8th edition) imposes additional obligations on fertility service providers in these circumstances, stating that:

> The use of an embryo known to have an abnormality … should be subject to consideration of the *welfare* of any resulting child and should *normally* have approval from a clinical ethics committee.
>
> If a centre decides that it is appropriate to provide treatment services to a woman using an embryo known to have an abnormality … it should document the reason for use of that embryo. [10.17] (our emphasis)

For some commentators, instituting such a hierarchy of selection not only conveys a problematic attitude to the value of disabled persons' lives, but also codifies a particular concept of reproductive 'responsibility', one with extremely problematic overtones (Elliston, 2013: 123). Although such a decision directly implicates prospective parental interests, the HFEA clearly imposes a 'gatekeeper' role on the third parties identified: that is the fertility centre providing the service and the ethics committee.

13 For a summary of some of these, see Gavaghan, C. (2010) 'Regulating after Parfit: Welfare, Identity and the UK Embryology Law'. In: Goodwin, Koops and Leenes (eds) *Dimensions of Technology Regulation*. Oisterwijk, Wolf Legal Publishers.

The 2008 Act also inserted paragraph 1ZA into Schedule 2 to the HFE Act 1990, specifying the purposes for which embryo testing may be licensed by the HFEA.[14] Rather than introducing substantive changes, paragraph 1ZA(1)(a)-(d) broadly codifies the parameters for PGD that had previously been established by the HFEA. However the HFEA continues to determine, according to the newly introduced statutory criteria, the conditions for which PGD may be performed and continues to maintain a *Code of Practice* to inform its licensing decisions and to establish necessary standards for fertility clinics.

Paragraph 1ZA provides that the HFEA may not authorise embryo testing unless it is for one of the purposes specified in subparagraphs (1)(a)–(d). With the exception of preimplantation HLA tissue typing, which is licenced on a case-by-case basis, PGD is regulated on a condition-by-condition basis.[15] Consequently, once the HFEA reviews and approves PGD for a particular condition, that condition is placed on an official list.[16] A licensed PGD clinic may then offer testing for any of the conditions appearing on that list (Houses of Parliament Parliamentary Office of Science and Technology, 2013).

Paragraph 1ZA(1)(a) permits testing for the purposes of:

> (a) establishing whether the embryo has a gene, chromosome or mitochondrion abnormality that may affect its capacity to result in a live birth.

The overriding objective in 1ZA(1)(a) is to enable the testing and selection of embryos that have the greatest chance of successfully implanting in a woman's uterus and being carried to term. As such, it constitutes Preimplantation Genetic *Screening* (PGS) to increase the likelihood of conceiving and carrying a pregnancy, as opposed to the preimplantation genetic *diagnosis* of a specific disease or trait. Consequently, paragraph 1ZA(1)(a) encompasses screening in situations of recurrent miscarriage or advanced maternal age, where the incidence of chromosomal abnormalities is raised and fertility reduced.

In contrast, paragraph 1ZA(1)(b) permits a licence to authorise PGD when: 'there is a *particular risk* that the embryo may have *any* gene, chromosome or mitochondrion abnormality' (our emphasis) to establish 'whether it has *that abnormality* or *any other* gene, chromosome or mitochondrion abnormality'. Similarly paragraph 1ZA(1)(c) permits sex selection in the case of a 'particular' risk of a child having or developing a gender-related 'serious physical or mental disability', 'serious illness' or 'any other gender-related serious medical condition'.

14 HFE Act 1990, s11(1)(a).

15 In the past the HFEA *Code of Practice* provided that a clinic could only perform embryo testing for conditions, chromosomes or traits (or combinations of these) and specific tests listed in the Annex to their Licence, or as specifically approved by a Licence Committee on a case-by-case basis. See Snelling, J. et al (2006) 'Law and Regulation'. In: *Choosing Genes for Future Children: Regulating Preimplantation Genetic Diagnosis*. Dunedin, Human Genome Research Project at p. 283.

16 See *PGD Conditions Licensed by the HFEA*. Available at www.hfea.org.uk.

Given the absence of a statutory definition, the HFEA has provided guidance for its Licence Committee as to whether a 'particular' risk exists in any given situation for the purposes of paragraph 1ZA(1)(b). The HFEA requires the Committee to take into account whether or not the abnormality is heritable and the relevant mode of inheritance, which the HFEA describes as 'an objectively measurable criterion', such as a one in two chance or one in four chance of an embryo having that abnormality (HFEA, 2010: [4]).

While paragraph 1ZA(1)(b) authorises testing in the case of a 'particular' risk, it extends the ambit of permissible testing significantly further by permitting testing not only for that abnormality, but also for *any other* gene, chromosome or mitochondrion abnormality. Although this suggests an extremely broad scope of permissible testing, paragraph 1ZA(2) imposes some limits in this respect by providing that a licence cannot authorise testing for the purpose of paragraph 1ZA(1)(b) unless the Authority is *satisfied*:

(a) in relation to the abnormality of which there is a *particular* risk, and
(b) in relation to *any other abnormality* for which testing is to be authorised under sub-paragraph (1)(b)

> that there is a *significant* risk that a person with the abnormality will have or develop a *serious physical or mental disability*, a *serious illness* or any other *serious medical condition*. (our emphasis)

Given that the Authority must be 'satisfied' of a 'significant' risk of a 'serious' disability, illness or condition before approving a licence for embryo testing, the HFEA is clearly, in the absence of any statutory definitions, the final arbiter on the meaning of these terms. Consequently the HFEA has also provided guidance as to how the Licence Committee should determine the 'significance' of a risk as well as its 'seriousness'.

The guidance states that determining 'significance' requires an assessment of a mutation's 'penetrance', that is, the likelihood of an individual with the mutation developing the relevant condition (HFEA, 2010: [5]). However, where there is a range of penetrance (e.g. a 40–60% risk) it provides that the Licence Committee will assess it according to the *highest possible risk* (HFEA, 2010: [5.4]). The *Explanatory Note* also sets out factors to be considered regarding 'seriousness'. Again, where there may be variability in potential symptoms, the HFEA recommends that the Licence Committee base its decision on the *worst possible case-scenario*, clearly encouraging a generous interpretation of the provision and ensuring its greatest possible scope (HFEA, 2010: [5.5]).

Significantly, paragraph 1ZA(1)(b) permits multiple testing, not just of a mutation that may result in a known single gene disorder, but for any other genetic or structural chromosomal abnormality. Consequently, testing may be performed for a single gene disorder such as cystic fibrosis and additional genetic testing performed to identify the presence of any additional conditions or chromosomal aberrations such as trisomy 21 (Down syndrome). However, the extent of add-on testing is necessarily restricted, given that the amount of analysis that can be performed on one or two cells is currently limited. Further, the condition for which any embryo testing is performed has to have been expressly considered and approved by the HFEA (HFEA, 2009: T88 and T89). Nevertheless, the fact that the legislation permits multiple testing at once makes it clear that if whole genome analysis ever becomes possible at the preimplantation stage, the potential scope of preimplantation gene testing will increase exponentially (Harper and Harton, 2010; Hens et al., 2013; Human Genetics Commission, 2011).

Paragraph 1ZA(1)(d) sets out the statutory criteria for preimplantation tissue typing (PTT). Although a contentious issue in the Parliamentary debates, the provision in its final form essentially codifies the HFEA's policy prior to the reforms. The HFEA is authorised to license PTT where a prospective parent's existing child 'suffers from a serious medical condition which could be treated by umbilical cord blood stem cells, bone marrow or other tissue of any resulting child'.

In summary, the 2008 amendments largely maintained the status quo regarding the permissible scope of PGD. However, there has been an inexorable extension to PGD technology over the last decade. As of 2013, the list of conditions licensed by the HFEA extends to almost 300 (HFEA, 2013i). However, it seems that some licensing decisions demonstrate a significantly more generous interpretation of the statutory provisions than others. The following section discusses two illustrative cases.

Two decisions: Rhesus factor blood group and Autism Spectrum Disorder

The HFEA recently licensed PGD for rhesus disease, or 'haemolytic disease of the newborn' (HDN) (HFEA, 2013ii). This condition occurs because of the rhesus-negative (RhD-negative) maternal blood group, which is due to a polymorphism[17] involving an RhD gene deletion. This gene deletion results in the absence of a specific protein that is present on the surface of red blood cells in RhD-positive individuals. Although having RhD-negative blood is not a genetic 'condition/disorder' as such, it causes problems if a woman who is RhD-negative (Colin et al., 1991: 2752)[18] conceives an RhD-positive foetus with an RhD-positive partner, because the maternal and foetal blood types are 'incompatible'.

In the case of Rhesus factor incompatibility, if foetal blood cells come into contact with maternal blood cells the woman's immune system is triggered and antibodies are developed against what are recognised by her body as 'foreign' (foetal) cells.[19] This is called 'alloimmunisation' or 'sensitisation'. If this occurs, any future conception of an RhD-negative foetus is at risk because the maternal antibodies may cross the placenta and cause haemolytic disease of the foetus or

17 'A natural variation in a gene, piece of DNA, protein, or chromosome that has no apparent effect on the individual who inherits it' (*BioNews* Glossary www.bionews.org.uk/glossary.

18 Around 15–20 per cent of Caucasians are RhD-negative.

19 This may also occur in other situations including an ectopic pregnancy, chorionic villus testing or as a result of an induced abortion.

newborn. The condition may be fatal for the foetus/infant or cause permanent developmental deficits.

The administration of anti-D (RhIg–immune globulin) either during or immediately after pregnancy generally prevents alloimmunisation/sensitisation, which has reduced the incidence of HDN to as low as 0.2 per cent (Seeho et al., 2005). Given that delivering a timely injection of immune globulin to an RhD-negative woman generally prevents the occurrence of HDN, it is plausible that the invasiveness of PGD would only be indicated in the case of a woman who has previously been sensitized/alloimmunised to RhD-positive blood, or who is already undergoing PGD. In this context, PGD may be performed to identify and select an RhD-negative embryo and so avoid the risk of rhesus disease developing in the resulting offspring.

It is, however, doubtful whether testing for Rhesus status is encompassed by the statutory criteria contained in paragraph 1ZA(1)(b). First, it is debatable whether RhD-negative status constitutes a gene 'abnormality', or whether it is more accurately described as a normal human variation or 'polymorphism'. Leaving that issue aside, it is also relevant that PGD is used to positively select an RhD-negative embryo in order that it is 'compatible' with the (minority) maternal blood type. In this case, PGD involves de-selecting those embryos that are RhD-positive, which is the predominant/normal human trait. Ultimately, if a strict interpretation of the statutory language is applied, it is unlikely that this application of PGD comes within the scope of paragraph 1ZA(1)(b) which presupposes the *deselection* of an embryo with a gene 'abnormality', rather than its positive selection. (Clearly there is some irony that it is the presence of a 'normal' human trait that puts the pregnancy/foetus at risk in this context.)

Further, the RhD-negative child born as a result of PGD will similarly be at risk of conceiving an RhD incompatible pregnancy in the future. As already discussed, section 13(9) of the Act provides that an embryo known to have a gene abnormality involving a significant risk that a person with the abnormality will have or develop a serious illness must not be preferred to those that are not known to have such an abnormality. This could suggest that selecting such an embryo may be problematic if the RhD-negative embryo is indeed considered to have a gene 'abnormality'. However, due to the rhesus incompatibility, selecting the RhD-negative embryo avoids that embryo/future individual having/developing a serious illness.

Clearly the provisions governing preimplantation HLA tissue typing policy discussed above provide a precedent for the positive selection of a normal human trait, *if* it is associated with a legitimate 'medical' objective (in that case selecting an embryo that is HLA-identical to a sick sibling). In the case of rhesus incompatibility, the selection of an RhD-negative embryo is associated with ensuring the ongoing health of the actual embryo that is selected. Nevertheless, the current statutory language does not appear to encompass testing for rhesus status – which would arguably require legislative amendment to permit an RhD-negative woman to select an RhD-negative embryo.

It is certainly not our suggestion that rhesus factor testing is inappropriate, given the objective of preventing a potentially fatal condition in the offspring of an RhD-negative woman. This example merely serves to highlight a paradox and suggests that the statutory criteria are not adequate or sufficiently flexible to encompass the range of potentially applicable PGD. Consequently, the Licensing Committee has had to apply a generous (and possibly erroneous) interpretation of the statutory criteria. Despite this generous interpretation of the provisions in this respect, the Licence Committee refused another application that, at least on the face of it, appears to fall within the category of permissible sex selection under paragraph 1ZA(1)(c).

It has been widely accepted that autism is a gender-related condition in that it occurs more frequently in males, particularly in some families (Amor and Cameron, 2008: 731). However, the HFEA Licensing Committee recently refused to licence sex selection to avoid the inheritance of Autism Spectrum Disorder (Classic) (ASD) in the case of a family with two 'severely affected' male children (HFEA Statutory Approvals Committee, 2014).

Although a four-fold increase in the incidence of autism in male offspring was cited in the HFEA application, the known genetic contributor(s) to ASD are not (unlike other conditions for which PGD is performed) 'unitary' meaning there is not a single, major, explanatory factor).[20] Nevertheless, the gender-relatedness of autism has been assumed in some jurisdictions, including several Australian states, which permit sex selection of female embryos in the context of a familial history of autism in male children (Western Australian Reproductive Technology Council, 2013: 13).[21]

Paragraph 1ZA(1)(c) of Schedule 2 to the HFE Act permits sex selection to be licensed when 'there is a *particular risk* that any resulting child will have or develop:

(i) a gender-related serious physical or mental disability
(ii) a gender-related serious illness, or
(iii) any other gender-related serious medical condition'.

In this context, the Act *specifically* states that a gender-related medical condition is one that affects *only* one sex, or affects one sex *significantly more* than the other.[22] The provision does not obviously restrict its ambit to Mendelian X (chromosome)-linked disorders but, at least *prima facie*, extends to any disorder of unequal sex incidence, otherwise the legislative drafters could have referred to a 'sex-linked' or 'X-linked' disorder to make this distinction clear.

When recording its decision the Licensing Committee noted an opinion from Genetic Alliance opposing the use of PGD for ASD, although its reasons were

20 However, a recent study has identified one gene in a subtype of autism. See Bernier, R. et al. (2014) 'Disruptive CHD8 Mutations Define a Subtype of Autism Early in Development' *Cell* 158, 263–276.

21 See also Victoria Assisted Reproductive Technology Authority 'Preimplantation Genetic Diagnosis' www.varta.gov.au. It is also permitted in the Australian state of New South Wales.

22 HFE Act, Schedule 2, paragraph 1ZB(1)–(4).

not outlined in the Committee's Minutes. Of course other conditions have been licensed, despite the opposition of similar organisations (see King, 2007).[23]

The Committee accepted that the nature of the condition of the existing male children was 'serious'. However, it cited the opinions of its two peer reviewers that PGD did 'not guarantee that any female child born will be free of the disorder, or indeed that in any particular family affected in this way that a female is at any less risk than a male' (HFEA Statutory Approvals Committee, 2014: [11]) and further, that the statistics did not 'translate into a "particular" risk for any given embryo in [sic] specific family' (HFEA Statutory Approvals Committee, 2014: [15]). The reviewers also opined that the 'risk statistics and evidence within the papers are based on affected population studies combined data, and that each individual family will have different risks according to the precise (but usually unknown) genetic factors within the family' (HFEA Statutory Approvals Committee, 2014: [15]). Ultimately, the Licensing Committee was not satisfied that the application met the embryo testing criteria, because no definitive test for autism was available and there was 'therefore no way to ensure that any resulting child, in particular a female child, would be born without the disorder' (HFEA Statutory Approvals Committee, 2014: [16] and [18]).

It is certainly true that in the case of a known sex-linked disorder where no precise genetic test is available for the particular mutation, sex selection may still be legitimately performed, as it will still *guarantee* that any child born will not have the disorder. However, in the case of ASD, the risk of ASD is associated with all of the resulting embryos, regardless of sex. Ultimately, it appears that the HFEA considered that that selection for the 'purpose of possibly reducing the risk of this family having another affected child' was inadequate to justify licensing the condition (HFEA Statutory Approvals Committee, 2014: [19]). However, the issue of possible risk in these circumstances was not fully developed in the Committee's Minutes.

It is plausible that, based on a sibling recurrence risk of 25 per cent (cf Ozonoff, 2011: e6), the risk that another male child born in this family would develop ASD is probably over 25 per cent. Conversely, based on the established 1:4 gender ratio, the risk that a future female child might have the condition is likely to be less, perhaps between 5 and 10 per cent.[24] While the residual risk of a female child developing ASD is certainly not negligible, it is likely to be less than the risk associated with a male child, and this may be considered by some prospective parents to be significant. Indeed, the fact they apply for PGD at all, may be taken as an indicator that they do consider it as such, as in the case of the family cited above.

The Committee's reasoning suggests that unless it was clear that PGD would conclusively prevent a female child being born with ASD, it would not license sex selection via PGD. Of course, an inability to guarantee a particular outcome is

23 For example Human Genetics Alert opposed the licensing of congenital fibrosis of the extraocular muscles (CFEM), a hereditary eye movement disorder. Nevertheless, the HFEA considered CFEM met the statutory requirements on the basis that it was a serious condition.

24 The authors would like to acknowledge clinical geneticist Professor Stephen Robertson for providing this explanation.

clearly problematic, but the couple seeking sex selection may have been prepared to accept that risk, an issue not discussed in the Minutes. Nor was it made clear in the Minutes whether there was a greater risk of such a couple having another child with severe ASD if they were to conceive and carry a male child, rather than a female child.

If sex selection is incapable of substantially reducing the risk to offspring in this context, there are no grounds to claim that the HFEA decision was arbitrary or unreasonable. However, the issue is whether an incremental reduction in risk for a condition with unequal sex incidence is sufficient to justify PGD – which is clearly open to debate as individuals will assess the levels of risk differently. The Committee did not consider that ASD reached the threshold of a risk that would affect one sex 'significantly' more than the other. Indeed, it concluded that any future applications involving ASD could not be approved in the absence of scientific *certainty* regarding its genetic basis.

The reasoning underpinning the Committee's decision is not clear. It is possible that the HFEA were wary that sex selection for ASD was moving closer to 'social' sex selection or parental 'preference', and sought to avoid public criticism.[25] Alternatively, it is possible that the Authority may not have wanted to be involved with facilitating the conception and birth of a child that might, because of the inherent uncertainty, nevertheless be born with the ASD. Clearly a line was drawn, but in the absence of further explanation, it is unclear on what basis.

Conclusion

This chapter has described how the original HFE Act 1990 enabled the research agenda of scientists and clinicians to be facilitated, while policy promulgated by the HFEA placated the public on 'moral' issues involving embryo selection technologies. It also suggests that after the 2008 reforms, not much has changed, apart from establishing Parliament as the ultimate decision-maker in regard to these morally charged issues. When introducing the HFE Bill in the House of Lords in 2007, Lord Darzi observed that the intent of the Bill is to 'make explicit the basic parameters for screening and selecting embryos. Again the intention is that this should be undertaken only on the grounds of avoiding serious disease' (Hansard, 2007).

The moral framework originally established by the HFEA has essentially been codified by the 2008 amendments, endorsing the ethical compromise that permits (and at times requires) individuals to make selection choices to avoid the risk of disease or illness in prospective offspring, but prohibits other preference-based selection such as social sex selection. This attempt to draw a clear line between 'medical' and 'social' uses of the technology has long been controversial in principle, but the examples considered above illustrate that it is increasingly proving difficult to implement in practice or at least to implement with consistency. This

25 It is possible that the controversy regarding sex-selective abortion around the same time may have influenced this decision. See Department of Health (UK) *Department of Health Guidance in Relation to Requirements of the Abortion Act 1967* (May 2014) p. 5.

chapter has identified two decisions of the Statutory Approvals Committee that challenge whether the statutory provisions are (1) fit for purpose and (2) being consistently and appropriately applied by the HFEA.

Although licensing PGD to identify rhesus blood group is not necessarily contentious itself, the decision does not sit comfortably with the statutory criteria. Clearly one of the trade-offs with imposing legislative parameters, as opposed to regulating according to specified principles, is a loss of flexibility in responding to novel applications that might fall outside the scope of the legislation. While this has not deterred the HFEA from permitting PGD in this particular instance, it clearly leaves it open to the criticism that it has acted beyond its statutory remit.

In contrast, the Licensing Committee's refusal to license sex selection in the case of a family with two sons severely affected by Autism Spectrum Disorder appears, at least *prima facie*, to be inconsistent with the statutory parameters governing permissible sex selection. This suggests that there is not only ongoing uncertainty regarding the substantive provisions of the Act, but also the underlying moral framework, an uncertainty which strains the legitimacy of the resulting decisions and the Act itself.

Although the HFEA does not always appear consistent in its licensing decisions, it is clear that the overriding objective of the regulatory regime is to prevent the positive selection of non-disease traits, while facilitating selection choices that reduce the incidence of disability or illness. While this position is presumably justified on the basis that it promotes the welfare of *any* child born, it is also associated with a utilitarian objective of maximising positive birth outcomes. In doing so it is facilitating a particular version of maximising consequentialism and reproductive responsibility. It is also assuming a prominent role for the state regarding selection choices – problematic terrain given the history of eugenics.

Although these contentious issues have been much discussed and debated since the 1990 legislation was introduced, the 2008 reforms seem to have been implemented without any overt engagement with them or with the problems to which they give rise. Without explicitly articulating a normative agenda, Parliament – and, to an extent, the HFEA – have rejected liberal and disability rights critiques, in favour of the concept of 'procreative beneficence'. Whether it is the appropriate role for the state to impose maximising consequentialist duties on prospective parents will continue to be a point of ethical and political contention – though it is noteworthy that even some of the most high-profile advocates of such an ethical duty stop short of arguing for its imposition by law (Harris, 2007: 108; Savulescu and Kahane, 2009). Ultimately it is arguable that the 2008 reforms have firmly established that, at least with respect to PGD, the regulatory objective is less concerned with facilitating the reproductive choices of well-informed individuals, as it is with regulating choices along a particular normative axis.

References

Amor, J. and Cameron, C., (2008) 'PGD Gender Selection for Non-Mendelian Disorders with Unequal Sex Incidence' 23 *Human Reproduction* 729.

Birk, D., (2005) 'The Reform of the Human Fertilisation and Embryology Act 1990' 35 *Family Law* 563.

Brownsword, R., (2008) *Rights, Regulation, and the Technological Revolution* (Oxford: Oxford University Press).

Brazier, M., (1999) 'Regulating the Reproduction Business' 7 *Medical Law Review* 166.

Buchanan, A. et al, (2000) *From Chance to Choice: Genetics and Justice* (Cambridge: Cambridge University Press).

Colin, A. et al, (1991) 'Genetic Basis of the RhD-Positive and RhD-Negative Blood Group Polymorphism as Determined by Southern Analysis' 78 *Blood* 2747.

Collier, S., (2004) 'Assisted Reproduction – Statutory Overhaul Overdue' 154 *New Law Journal* 1201.

Department of Health, (2005) *Government Response to the Report from the House of Commons Science and Technology Committee: Human Reproductive Technologies and the Law* (London: The Stationery Office) Cm 6641.

Elliston, S., (2013) 'The Welfare of the Child Principle and the Use of PGD: Selecting for Disability' in McLean, S. and Elliston, S., (eds) *Regulating Pre-Implantation Genetic Diagnosis: A Comparative and Theoretical Analysis* (Abingdon: Routledge).

Emery, S., Middleton, A. and Turner, G., (2010) 'Whose Deaf Genes Are They Anyway? The Deaf Community's Challenge to Legislation on Embryo Selection' 10(2) *Sign Language Studies* 155.

Evans, H. and McLaren, A., (1985) 'Unborn Children (Protection) Bill', *Nature* 314, 127.

Fox, M., (2009) 'The Human Fertilisation and Embryology Act 2008: Tinkering at the Margins' 17(3) *Feminist Legal Studies* 333.

Gavaghan, C., (2007) *Defending the Genetic Supermarket: The Law and Ethics of Selecting the Next Generation* (Abingdon: Routledge-Cavendish).

Gavaghan, C., (2010) 'Regulating after Parfit: Welfare, Identity and the UK Embryology Law' in Goodwin, M., Koops, B.-J. and Leenes, R., (eds) *Dimensions of Technology Regulation* (Oisterwijk: Wolf Legal Publishers).

Hansard, 19 Nov 2007, Col 666.

Harper, J. and Harton, G., (2010) 'The Use of Arrays in Preimplantation Genetic Diagnosis Commission' 94 *Fertility and Sterility* 1173.

Harris, J., (2007) *Enhancing Evolution: The Ethical Case for Making Better People* (Princeton: Princeton University Press).

Hens, K. et al, (2013) 'Comprehensive Embryo Screening' 28(5) *Human Reproduction* 1418.

House of Commons Science and Technology Committee (2005) *Report on Human Reproductive Technologies and the Law* (London: The Stationery Office).

Houses of Parliament Parliamentary Office of Science & Technology (2013) *Preimplantation Genetic Diagnosis* (Post Note No 445). [Online] Available at www.parliament.uk/post.

Human Fertilisation and Embryology Authority (1999) HFEA Chief Executive's Letter: Preimplantation Genetic Diagnosis (London: HFEA).

Human Fertilisation and Embryology Authority (2003i) HFEA Chair's Letter (CH(03)04: Guidance on Preimplantation Testing (London: HFEA). Available at www.hfea.gov.uk.

Human Fertilisation and Embryology Authority (2003ii) *HFEA Code of Practice* (6th ed) (London: HFEA).

Human Fertilisation and Embryology Authority (2006) HFEA Authority Decision on PGD Policy, HFEA, London. [Online] Available at www.hfea.gov.uk.

Human Fertilisation and Embryology Authority (2009) HFEA Code of Practice (8th ed) (London: HFEA).

Human Fertilisation and Embryology Authority (2010) Preimplantation Diagnostic Testing ('PGD') Explanatory Note for Licence Committee. [Online] Available at www.hfea.gov.uk.

Human Fertilisation and Embryology Authority (2013i) PGD Conditions licensed by the HFEA. [Online] Available at www.hfea.gov.uk.

Human Fertilisation and Embryology Authority (2013ii) New PGD Conditions Licensed by the HFEA between 1 April 2012 and 31 March 2013. [Online] Available at hfea.gov.uk.

Human Fertilisation and Embryology Authority Statutory Approvals Committee (2014) Minutes, Item 6, 30. [Online] Available at www.hfea.gov.uk.

Human Genetics Commission (2011) *Increasing Options, Informing Choice: A Report on Preconception Genetic Testing and Screening* (London: HGC).

Johnson, M., (2008) 'Real Progress – But More To Do' *BioNews* 452 (7 April 2008, Progress Educational Trust).

Johnson, M., Franklin, S., Cottingham, M. and Hopwood, N., (2010) 'Why the Medical Research Council Refused Robert Edwards and Patrick Steptoe Support for Research on Human Conception in 1971' 25(9) *Human Reproduction* 2157.

Joint Committee on the Human Tissue and Embryos (2007) (Draft) Bill Human Tissue and Embryos (Draft) Bill Volume I: Report. TSO, London, Session 2006–2007.

Karpin, I. and Savell, K., (2012) *Perfecting Pregnancy: Law, Disability, and the Future of Reproduction* (Cambridge: Cambridge University Press).

King, D., (2007) 'Preimplantation Genetic Diagnosis and "Slippery Slopes"' *BioNews* 407 (13 May 2007, Progress Educational Trust).

Lucas, A., (2013) 'Prohibiting Preferences: Unjustifiable Discrimination against Deaf People Who Want a Deaf Child' 12 *International Journal of Disability, Community & Rehabilitation* [Online] Available at www.ijdcr.ca.

Mahendra, B., (2003) 'A Design for Life' *New Law Journal* 581, 153.

Montgomery, J., (1991) 'Rights, Restraints and Pragmatism: The Human Fertilisation and Embryology Act 1990' 54 *Modern Law Review* 524.

Morgan, D., (2004) 'Ethics, Economics and the Exotic: The Early Career of the HFEA' 12(1) *Health Care Analysis* 7.

Mulkay, M., (1993) 'Rhetorics of Hope and Fear in the Great Embryo Debate' 23 *Social Studies of Science* 721.

Mulkay, M., (1995) 'Political Parties, Parliamentary Lobbies and Embryo Research' 4 *Public Understanding of Science* 31.

Ozonoff, S., et al, (2011) 'Recurrence Risk for Autism Spectrum Disorders: A Baby Siblings Research Consortium Study' *Pediatrics* 128, e1-e9.

Parfit, D., (1984) *Reasons and Persons* (Oxford: Clarendon Press).

Porter, G. and Smith, M., (2013) 'Preventing the Selection of "Deaf Embryos" Under the Human Fertilisation and Embryology Act 2008: Problematising Disability?' 32 *New Genetics and Society* 171.

Savulescu, J. and Kahane, G., (2007) 'The Moral Obligation to Create Children With the Best Chance of the Best Life' 23(5) *Bioethics* 274.

Seeho, S.K. et al, (2005) 'The Role of Preimplantation Genetic Diagnosis in the Management of Severe Rhesus Alloimmunisation: First Unaffected Pregnancy' 20 *Human Reproduction* 697.

Snelling, J. et al, (2006) 'Law and Regulation' in *Choosing Genes for Future Children: Regulating Preimplantation Genetic Diagnosis* (Dunedin: Human Genome Research Project).

Snelling, J., (2009) 'Preimplantation Genetic Diagnosis: Slipping Through the Regulatory Net' in *Human Genome Research Project – Genes, Society and the Future: Vol III.* (Wellington: Brookers Ltd), 27–148.

Theodosiou, A. and Johnson, M., (2011) 'The Politics of Human Embryo Research on the Motivation to Achieve PGD' 22 *Reproductive BioMedicine Online* 457.

Warnock Committee (1984) *Report of the Committee of Inquiry into Human Fertilisation and Embryology* (London: HMSO) Cmnd. 9314.

Western Australian Reproductive Technology Council (2013) Annual Report: 1 July 2012 to June 2013. [Online] Available at www.parliament.wa.gov.au.

7 The 'three parent' misnomer: Mitochondrial DNA donation under the HFE Act*

Laura Riley

Introduction

At the time of writing, the UK government had recently confirmed its imminent intention to allow Parliament to vote on Regulations permitting two novel cell reconstruction techniques as licensed fertility treatments (House of Commons Science and Technology Committee, 2014; Department of Health, 2014b), namely 'maternal spindle transfer' (MST) and 'pronuclear transfer' (PNT). These variants of IVF techniques would be used to prevent the transmission of maternally inherited mitochondrial DNA (mtDNA) disorders. Such disorders are incurable and may cause illness, disability and death. Neither MST nor PNT has yet been used anywhere in the world to create children. Both techniques raise new legal, regulatory, ethical and social issues.

The government's announcement came after the Department of Health ran a public consultation on the content of draft Regulations in February 2014. This was supposed to gather views on the text of the draft, but instead received a majority of responses opposing the treatments in principle (Department of Health, 2014a).[1] Backbench Parliamentarians opposed to embryology and assisted reproduction treatments followed this result by debating the introduction of these 'experimental' treatments, primarily on 'safety' grounds, although other ethical or faith-based objections clearly underpinned these debates. However, one of the key elements of ethical objection to these new techniques – that the resulting children would supposedly have three genetic 'parents' because the mitochondrial donor should be regarded as a second 'mother' – was the subject of rebuttals from MPs of all parties. The Public Health Minister countered opponents by saying that 'we

1 The government's response stated: 'Although the consultation was about the detail of the draft regulations, not the policy as to whether to allow mitochondrial donation at all, the vast majority of these responses were one-liners either in support or opposing the introduction of the regulations, in principle. Where additional information was provided by the responder in these short responses, it was clear that opposition was informed by faith-based views. Where support was expressed this was generally informed by personal/family experience of mitochondrial disease. There was evidence of a co-ordinated campaign approach. From the total of 1,857 responses, around 700 expressed general support for the regulations and 1,152 opposed the introduction of the regulations with the remainder not expressing a view either way'.

cannot reduce parenthood to a matter of 37 genes from a donor. It is about so much more than that...' (Hansard, October 2014).

The government's belief that Parliament *should* be enabled to vote on allowing these treatments was certainly welcome in terms of furthering the interests of patients. Their interpretation of the statute is also obviously correct in that, if permitted, mitochondrial donors would *not* be regarded as mothers. Although the final Regulations had, at the time of writing, yet to be published for Parliamentary vote, this chapter aims to examine the ethical and regulatory issues arising from the draft Regulation, including the regulatory approach to the mitochondrial donor who would enable these techniques.

Why are mitochondrial donation techniques needed?

The two techniques under consideration, 'maternal spindle transfer' (Tachibana et al., 2009) and 'pronuclear transfer' (Craven, 2010), are currently being researched using human eggs or embryos and animal models in the UK and US. Each technique, in its own way, would allow embryologists to produce an egg or embryo free from affected mitochondria, for use in fertility treatments. The parents in each case (where no sperm donor was also used) would contribute the nuclear DNA, in the normal way, but each technique involves removal of affected mitochondria that comes from the mother and its replacement with mitochondria from an unaffected donor egg. As two women's eggs are required in the process, the popular press and others have (incorrectly) dubbed mtDNA transfer techniques '3-parent' or '2-mother' IVF.

Mitochondria are tiny organelles: structures inside our cells located in the jelly-like cytoplasm surrounding the nucleus. Mitochondria convert nutrients from food into cellular energy that cells need to function properly. It is likely that they originated as primitive bacteria which, billions of years ago came to live within the cytoplasm of cells of other organisms. Over thousands of generations, the primitive bacteria came to live as mitochondria within what is now human cell cytoplasm, while much of their genetic information migrated into what became human cell nuclei (Taanman, 1999).

Although mitochondria possess their own genetic system, it is usually only the comparatively massive *nuclear* genome (the 20–30,000 genes in the nucleus of a typical human cell) that many of us have in mind when we think of 'our genes' – those genes that are inherited in equal proportion from our genetic mother and father. Nuclear genes both create recognisable resemblances and traits within families, and make each of us genetically distinct (unless for example, we have a monozygotic or 'identical' twin). Nuclear genes influence every aspect of the makeup of our body, including mitochondrial activity. The mitochondrial genome is miniscule in comparison – each mitochondrion contains only 37 genes thought to be limited to governing the actions of the mitochondria (Taanman, 1999). Unlike nuclear genes, mitochondrial genes are not associated with observable shared physical traits or characteristics between people who share them, aside from characteristics of 'good' or 'poor' health arising from normal or inadequate mitochondrial functioning (HFEA, 2014a).

Sperm contain mitochondria, which help to power their movement. However, no paternal contribution of mitochondria is thought to survive the reproductive process, which is why mitochondria are inherited only from the genetic mother's egg. After a sperm enters an egg, it begins to form the male pronucleus within the fertilised egg and its mitochondria degenerate. The male pronucleus will then contribute its nuclear genetic material to the nucleus of the single-celled embryo, with the female pronucleus contributing nuclear genetic material from the egg. Only one study found paternal mitochondria to persist naturally after fertilisation, in muscle tissue only (Schwartz et al, 2002). No evidence of father-to-child transmission of an inherited mtDNA disorder has been published (Brown et al, 2006).

Mitochondria use a 'self-copying' process to replicate. Accordingly, 'our' mitochondrial genes are not individually personalised to us. The recombination of *nuclear* genes from an egg and sperm forms a unique pattern of genes in each cell nucleus. But *mitochondrial* genes taken alone, cannot usually be used to individuate a person from their genetic mother or their other close maternal relatives, such as siblings (with the same mother), uncles, aunts or grandmother, and so on. Most human cells contain from a few hundred to several thousand mitochondria. Because each tissue type requires a different amount of cellular energy to function properly, the greatest numbers of mitochondria are in the cells of the most energy-demanding tissues (St John et al, 2007). When mitochondria fail to produce the level of energy that cells or tissues need, this can cause very serious health problems.

A loss of normal energy production can be caused, for example, by mutation of the DNA within a single mitochondrion inherited from a genetic mother's egg. If a number of genes in individual mitochondria in the child's cells are mutated, or develop mutations, to the extent that a significant *proportion* of the mitochondrial population functions abnormally, this is likely to cause symptoms that together are described as an mtDNA disorder. Mitochondrial disorders can also arise from mutation of the DNA in the *nuclear* genes that influence the working of the mitochondria, in which case they may be inherited from either parent. Sometimes the precise origin of a mitochondrial disorder is uncertain.

Regardless of the locus of origin, the severity, age of onset, and range of symptoms of mitochondrial disorders vary widely, even between close relatives. Abnormally functioning mitochondria may cause no symptoms or only very mildly affect some people, while others will experience severe symptoms (or death) in infancy, childhood, adolescence or any stage of adulthood. If symptoms begin, they will progressively worsen. This is partly because mtDNA is also prone to accumulating non-inherited ('somatic') mutations during a person's lifetime and has a limited ability to repair itself, so mutations build up.

The cells of the brain, heart, kidneys and major muscle groups are very energy-demanding so are often impacted most severely by the loss of normal cellular energy production. Other symptoms caused by mtDNA mutations include miscarriage and stillbirth, poor growth, loss of muscle coordination, muscle weakness, neuromuscular problems, neurological problems, seizures, developmental delays, learning disabilities, hearing and/or vision loss, heart, liver, kidney or respiratory disease (which may progress to organ failure), gastrointestinal disorders, diabetes, thyroid and/or adrenal dysfunction, and immune system problems, amongst many others (Mito Action, 2008). There is no known cure for any mitochondrial disorders, and many symptoms are not resolved by medical treatment. This factor alone makes it imperative that the treatments available are licensed as quickly as possible.

Maternally-inherited mitochondrial DNA disorders, current and potential treatment alternatives

The draft Regulations sought to modify the HFE Act (as amended) to outline the process and circumstances in which eggs or embryos created using donated mitochondria can be used in treatment. They were narrower than the Regulation-making power permits, only exempting the prevention of *maternally inherited mitochondrial DNA disorders*, which effectively limits this exemption to MST and PNT used as treatments for this purpose.

About one in 400 people in the UK have a maternally inherited pathogenic mutation of mtDNA (Poulton and Oakeshott, 2012). These are the focus of the novel techniques proposed to undergo regulation in the UK. Here, mutations in the mitochondrial genes are (so far as we know) *not* caused by nuclear genes and are only inherited via women's eggs. Women may become aware that they are at risk of transmitting a disorder because of a diagnosed family history, or because they or their child(ren) are diagnosed. Given the risk to the health of *every* child born from their eggs, women in this group may feel that they have very difficult decisions to make around having any, or further, children. It can be impossible to predict how severely a child might be affected because the same woman can transmit different levels of mutated mtDNA to different eggs. Because the proportion of healthy mitochondria in the cells of the resulting child dictates the adequacy of cellular energy production, this partly relies on which individual mitochondria were 'copied' to populate the embryo's cells, which cannot be predicted in advance.

Currently, affected women can only completely avoid passing on mutated mitochondria to their children by not using their own eggs at all; that is, by using egg donation or adoption. If their form of mtDNA disorder is amenable, they may use their own eggs and seek to *minimise* transmission risks from among a selection of their embryos by using IVF with preimplantation genetic diagnosis (PGD), testing biopsied embryo cells to gain information about transmission risk. Alternatively women may be offered oocyte sampling to gather information about unfertilised eggs (Poulton et al, 2009).

Additionally, or alternatively, pregnant women may be offered prenatal diagnosis (PND), which may produce reliable information in the first trimester about the likely transmission of mutated mitochondria. However, PND may only produce more certain information by around seven months into pregnancy (Dean et al, 2003; Faivre et al, 2000; Steffann et al, 2007), by which point for many reasons considering the full range of reproductive choices including ending the pregnancy may be much less acceptable for many women. Additionally due to training and NHS resourcing issues, timely abortion care with a choice of method is often much more difficult to access at such an advanced stage of pregnancy, even though the relevant requirements of the Abortion Act 1967 have no time limit.[2]

However, with PGD, PND and even tissue sampling post-birth, there can be problems with gathering definitive information from cells because of the unpredictable pattern of distribution of mitochondrial populations through the different types of cells. This may complicate from which cell samples the result should be determined. Thus, in order to offer a *pre-conception* alternative for women seeking to (in theory) *prevent* rather than to *minimise* the risk that they will transmit mutated mitochondria, *and* who desire a nuclear genetic connection to their child, researchers developed the two mitochondrial transfer techniques. Each works by physically decoupling an embryo's inheritance of nuclear genes from its inheritance of mitochondrial genes. In both, the resulting child's mitochondrial genes come from an egg donor.

MST uses two unfertilised eggs – one from a healthy donor and the other egg from the intending mother seeking to avoid passing on her mitochondria. The donor's egg (egg 'A') is enucleated by removing its nuclear genetic material (which is grouped together in a spindle shape at this stage, thus giving the technique its name). The nuclear genetic material from the intending mother is then removed from her egg (egg 'B'), and placed into the donor's enucleated egg 'A'. This 'reconstructed' egg can then be fertilised with sperm from the intending father (or a donor) to create an embryo for transfer to the intending mother. The nuclear material removed from the donor's egg 'A' is discarded, along with the intending mother's enucleated egg 'B' containing her unhealthy mitochondria.

PNT is in principle very similar but instead uses two very early-stage (one-day-old) 'zygotes' or single-celled embryos. Instead of the cell nucleus that a more mature embryo would contain, at this stage the female pronucleus is still separate from the male pronucleus in the embryo. First, a healthy donor's egg is fertilised with sperm from the intending father (or a donor). The resulting embryo ('A') is then enucleated. Another embryo ('B') is created from the egg of the intending mother fertilised with sperm from the intending father (or a donor). The two pronuclei from embryo B are then removed and placed into the enucleated embryo A. The resulting 'reconstructed' embryo can then be transferred to the intending mother. Embryo A's pronuclei are discarded, as is the enucleated embryo B.

Background to the parliamentary vote

Patient groups have been urging for the necessary provision to allow these novel treatments to be offered for a long time (Progress Educational Trust, 2011). The power to put this regulation forward to Parliament was inserted into the amending

2 Section 1(1)(d) of the 1967 Abortion Act makes an abortion lawful provided 'there is a substantial risk that if the child were born it would suffer from such physical or mental abnormalities as to be seriously handicapped'.

Human Fertilisation and Embryology (HFE) Act 2008 (at section 3ZA(5) and section 35A) following lobbying by parts of the patient community affected by mitochondrial disorders, research funders and other interested groups.

The power allows Parliament to vote on future regulations that would make eggs or embryos with 'altered' DNA lawful for use in treatment, specifically and only 'to prevent the transmission of serious mitochondrial disease'. 'Serious' disease has no medical or legal meaning, but where a mitochondrial disorder requires clinical intervention, as it is progressive and unpredictable, arguably it is always potentially 'serious'.

Approving these Regulations would permit an exception to a key tenet of the HFE Act 1990 (as amended) making it currently illegal to put into a woman's body eggs or embryos that have had their nuclear or mtDNA 'altered'. This 'alteration' would be necessary, for example, to do reproductive cloning, via somatic cell nuclear transfer – the process which created Dolly the sheep (Campbell et al, 1996).[3] The regulation-making power was needed because only *research* in the UK on human embryos that alters DNA (and so generates nuclear and mitochondrial germline effects) is licensable by the Human Fertilisation and Embryology Authority (HFEA). The Newcastle Fertility Centre at Life had pioneered PNT research in human embryos since 2005 (HFEA, 2005). However, as reproductive *treatments,* PNT and MST would fall outside the HFE Act on several counts, necessitating the regulation-making power.

The Act makes it unlawful to place any gamete or embryo in a woman if the nuclear or mtDNA of any cell of the gamete or embryo has been altered (section 3(2) read with section 3ZA). MST treatment is prohibited because the reconstructed egg is not 'produced by or extracted from the ovaries of a woman' (section 3ZA(2)(a)), also because its nuclear or mtDNA have 'been altered' by substituting the nucleus of the egg, and if inadvertent carryover results in two mitochondrial populations in one egg (section 3ZA(2)(b)). As cell reconstruction treatments, *both* MST and PNT are prohibited because section 3ZA(4)(a) states that 'permitted' embryos for transfer to a woman can only have been created by the *fertilisation* of a permitted egg by permitted sperm, and because the 'nuclear or mtDNA of any cell of the embryo' has been altered (section 3ZA(4)(b)).

The existing Regulation-making powers in the Act do not specify the *process* by which the transmission of mitochondrial disorders should be prevented. So, theoretically, if a safe and effective process was developed in future to deal with mitochondrial disorders arising from mutation in the *nuclear* genes, that worked by altering or substituting a cell nucleus, this could be proposed at a later date. This freedom is given appropriately in the interests of future patients, given that mitochondrial disorders can be equally destructive regardless of the causative

3 While MST and PNT are forms of (mitochondrial) genetic modification, and share some techniques with cloning via somatic cell nuclear transfer (SCNT), they should not be conflated with reproductive cloning in technique, aim or result. Neither MST nor PNT transfer mature somatic or embryonic cell nuclei, nor create any nuclear genetic copies of any pre-existing person, nor require reprogramming of nuclear material as required in SCNT that is likely to increase the risk of abnormalities in resulting embryos.

genetic locus. However, the same powers as written in the current HFE Act would *not* permit a Secretary of State for Health to propose regulations for any *other uses* of MST and PNT, nor for any medical or 'social' purpose other than to avoid the transmission of 'serious mitochondrial disease'. Such a change would require the Act to be amended.

Since 2008, successive governments have stated that regulation would only be put forward for parliamentary assent if a proposed mitochondrial donation technique were thought to be *effective* and *safe* for use in treatment. To provide (repeated) assurance on this point, the HFEA's Expert Panel has now reviewed the efficacy and safety of the techniques under consideration three times, at the request of the Department of Health (HFEA, 2011b, 2013b, 2014b). The HFEA's Panel consistently found that the available evidence does not suggest that the techniques are unsafe and that the techniques are potentially useful for a specific and defined group of patients. It has also recommended that some further experiments be completed before the treatments are offered to patients. In addition, the Nuffield Council on Bioethics conducted the UK's first in-depth ethical review into mitochondrial donation after the HFEA's 2011 safety review, concluding that 'due to the health and social benefits to individuals and families of living free from mitochondrial disorders, and where potential parents express a preference to have genetically-related children… if… acceptably safe and effective as treatments, *it would be ethical* for families to use them, if they wish to do so and have been offered an appropriate level of information and support' (2012).

At the government's request, in 2012, the HFEA also sought public views on whether what it called 'mitochondrial replacement' should be allowed in principle as a treatment (HFEA, 2013a). Journalist Polly Toynbee, an adviser to the HFEA on this exercise, wrote that 'information was laid out with clarity and neutrality in what was an astonishingly thorough process. Public meetings were held around the country, with neutral explanation and impassioned advocates on both sides. An opinion poll, focus groups, deliberative workshops with participants selected for social balance and an interactive online collection of views cost £250,000' (Toynbee, 2014). From these results, the HFEA concluded that 'there is general support for permitting mitochondrial replacement in the UK, so long as it is safe enough to offer in a treatment setting and is done so within a regulatory framework' (HFEA 2013a; HFEA 2013c: para 1.7), Mitochondria replacement consultation: Advice to Government, Human Fertilisation and Embryology Authority, March 2013. http://www.hfea.gov.uk/docs/Mitochondria_replacement_consultation_-_advice_for_Government.pdf).

Debate on the techniques occurred at the same time in the US. In February 2014, an Advisory Committee of the Food and Drug Administration (FDA) heard two days' worth of evidence as part of a preliminary discussion in relation to FDA licensing of MST: 'oocyte modification in assisted reproduction for the reduction in transmission of mitochondrial disease or treatment of infertility' (*USA Today*, 2014; *NBC News*, 2014). In the US there is no legislation regulating assisted reproduction so no barrier to use in fertility treatments, nor is there express prohibition of the use of mitochondrial replacement techniques for mitochondrial disease.[4] Because there is no regulatory framework in the US, the FDA must therefore decide whether or not to allow a clinical trial which would, if approved, take place and presumably would find participants who wanted to use the method to have a baby. As yet, it has not done so.

Perhaps concerned about the US launching such a trial, less than two weeks after the FDA evidence session, and six years after the HFE Act was amended, the UK government published its draft Regulations for public consultation, with the commitment to put Regulations before Parliament the same year (within 2014). The discussion document says that the intended effects of this publication included to 'signal the UK's desire to be at the forefront of cutting edge [sic] of medical techniques' (Department of Health, 2014a, at Annex C). While parliamentary assent to these Regulations is necessary before mitochondrial donation techniques can be legally and accessibly offered, the enabling Regulations is not the final step needed before treatments may be offered. The government has confirmed that the Regulations will require clinics to apply for specific authorisation from the HFEA to be able to carry out treatments. The tests the HFEA must apply will be set by the Regulations, derived from the statute:

> 1) that the HFEA has determined that there is a particular risk that the egg or embryo of the patient has a mitochondrial abnormality, and
> 2) that the HFEA has determined that there is a significant risk that a person with that abnormality will have or develop a serious physical or mental disability, a serious illness or other serious medical condition.
>
> (Department of Health, 2014b)

The HFEA will decide *how* it will consider any such applications, however. When published, the HFEA's plans are therefore likely to engender further debate. Patient groups (e.g. Association of Medical Research Charities, Genetic Alliance UK) and others recommended in consultation responses that the HFEA should not award licences on a case-by-case basis after the treatments have become routine, but should move to a condition-by-condition approach (Department of Health, 2014b) as became the case with most applications of PGD in 2009, aiming to reduce unnecessary waiting times and administrative burden (POST, 2013 and see Gavaghan and Snelling; Karpin, this volume).

However, the Association of Clinical Embryologists does not believe it appropriate for the HFEA to take a case-by-case approach to mitochondrial donation treatment *at all*, citing available expertise within the licensed centres to interpret statutory criteria just 'as they would for any other patient referred for any form of licensed fertility treatment'. The Nuffield Council on Bioethics also submitted that the assessing of the risk or seriousness of the condition should

4 PNT was omitted from this preliminary consideration, perhaps for political reasons because it involves the destruction of human embryos, or perhaps because MST is a technique developed in the US.

be the role of clinician(s) with the patient, and not the HFEA (Department of Health, 2014b).

Sufficient NHS funding will also need to be secured to provide these treatments. Continuing with the example of PGD in the NHS, historically there was variable local provision, but since 2013 each UK nation has a consistent approach via centralised commissioning, albeit with some variation. England funds up to three PGD cycles, Scotland up to two (NHS England Clinical Commissioning Board, 2013). Mitochondrial donation would also likely be centrally commissioned. However, centralised commissioning has been seen as overly restrictive on financial grounds, because NHS funding can only ever be used to produce *one* healthy child via PGD, and it may be that similar debates take place with mitochondrial donation depending on the proposed arrangements (POST, 2013). Putting IVF costs at circa £5,000 and PGD costs at circa £10,000, the Department of Health estimates that each cycle of mitochondrial donation treatment will cost in the region of £20,000, with a likely success rate of 25% per cycle.

The Department of Heath states that 'Government intervention…is intended to reduce the harm to individuals born with mitochondrial disease and reduce the impact of treatment on the NHS and personal care services' (Department of Health, 2014a). Clearly, overly restrictive access to NHS-funded mitochondrial donation on the grounds of cost should be avoided in future, as the financial cost to the NHS of caring for a person conceived naturally and seriously affected by mtDNA disorder would be likely to be many times greater than (say) the cost of funding three cycles of mitochondrial donation if wanted, and which (if successful) could ensure a first (or second) child would be born unaffected by the disorder.

Crucially, egg donors willing to be mitochondrial donors will need to be recruited, and the success of this may to a large extent depend on the treatment of the donors under regulation, potentially raising issues about knowledge and information sharing (see Blyth and Frith, this volume).

Genetic links to three people = three parents?

We have no reason to think that future donors of mtDNA would do otherwise than understand and intend solely to contribute an energy source for a future child's cells, via the mitochondria remaining in their enucleated eggs. Because their nuclear DNA is not passed on, these donors would be consenting to make a materially different contribution than either an egg donor or a mother to a child, and we can only assume that their intention in donating would accord with this. Nonetheless a very commonly cited objection to the use of both PNT and MST has been that mitochondrial donation would mean children being born with 'three parents', or 'two mothers' (this concern notwithstanding that very many children already grow up considering that they have two mothers or three parents (or more) without apparent ill-effects) (for one recent analysis of this, see Nordqvist and Smart, 2014). This concern holds that: because mitochondria contain genes, and people who give children genes are *(always)* their *parents*, thus the social connection between donor and child would be *the same as* that of parent and child (The

Catholic Church in England and Wales, 2012; *Daily Mail*, 2013; *The Economist*, 2012; Collins, 2013). A further (also often religion-based) argument against the 'intrusion of a third party into the reproductive exclusivity of a couple' goes that 'more than two individuals are participating in the generation of a new life and therefore more than two people must be considered as parents' (Christian Action Research and Education, 2014). If 'participation' is all that is required to become a parent, a net result of only three parents is surely a gross underestimate, given the size of a typical clinical and laboratory team in assisted reproduction.

In many ways this 'multi-parent' concern stems from objections to gamete donation for reproduction, adding nothing new to those. However, there are obvious problems with the specific claim that a *mitochondrial* donor must be regarded as a 'mother' solely on the basis of her donation of *mitochondrial* genes. In social terms, this objection disregards the (presumed) *intention* of the donor to assist another woman's plan to become a mother. The donor intentionally gives only a *part* of her egg to be used in reproduction, in order that a) the recipient's child can be healthy and b) the intending mother's nuclear genes can be used, with all of the significance that may entail for both women.

Ascribing 'motherhood' to the donor also disregards the (presumed) intention of the *recipient* in seeking out this donation. While the adult protagonists could not fail to be aware that the child and the donor would be genetically related via mitochondria, because they contain genes, it seems likely that recipients of mitochondrial donation would only be women and couples who *particularly highly* value having a *nuclear* genetic connection with their future child. If the recipients placed no particular personal 'meaning' on the perceived difference between being related via mitochondrial genes versus nuclear genes, conventional routes are already open to them if they solely wanted a healthy child with whom they share no nuclear connection.

When the protagonists' intentions are deemed irrelevant, it becomes unclear which individual should be regarded as the 'mtDNA mother' on the basis of transmitting 'her' *mt*genes. Because healthy mtDNA isn't always individuated to the person who carries it, on this schema the second mother could equally be for example the donor's sister, mother or grandmother (or technically, all of any of the above plus possible others). If the contribution of mitochondrial DNA *in isolation* denotes parenthood, then all *fathers* become a redundant category of non-parents, because men are usually understood not to contribute any mitochondria to their (genetic) children. And by this allocation, we seem to arrive at two categories of mothers and perhaps their children – as presumably women who contributed *both* mitochondria *and* nuclear genes to their child, by virtue of the combined genetic contribution, should be seen as somehow *more* of a mother than one who shares 'only' a nuclear genetic connect – thus becoming a parent-*plus*.

It is obvious to state that at this time, unless they become incredibly important for health reasons, most of us do not tend to ascribe great cultural or social/familial meaning to our mitochondrial genes – assuming that we are even aware of their existence. Nuclear genes, are for most people what is thought of when we refer to 'our genes', and have a high cultural profile in many societies, and may often be placed in a specific category of cultural and social meaning, *specifically in relation to parenthood*, because these genes convey observable characteristics and other traits to future generations.

For many people, the category of social motherhood is also viewed as much more reliant on the context of everyday parenting – thus being evident where *no* (nuclear) genes were transmitted to the child and/or where a mother didn't give birth to her child, such as with recipients of donated eggs, in step, foster or adoptive mothering, or following surrogacy arrangements. While all reproductive donors and recipients will place their own personal meaning(s) on their actions, the generalised claim that contributing (solely) mitochondrial genes to a child must inevitably denote social – or any form of – motherhood, clearly appears incongruous. Indeed, as a key ethical examination of the issues observes:

> social significance tends to be ascribed to the donation of human tissue according to its context. Donors' and recipients' individual experiences of forming social relationships brought about by the donation of organs or tissue (or of a desire to form them) vary across and within different treatments. This is seen in the differing expectations around the subsequent social roles of, for example, blood, egg, sperm, or live kidney donors.
>
> (Nuffield Council on Bioethics, 2012)[5]

Legal parenthood, or motherhood is in any case not available to the mitochondrial donor under existing legislation, which was reflected in the draft Regulations. The HFE Act (as amended) outlines that only the woman who carries and gives birth to a child is the legal mother (section 33(1)). No legal concept of (nuclear or mitochondrial) 'genetic motherhood' is recognised. Reproductive egg donors (on that basis alone) are not legal mothers, unless they also carry the pregnancy as part of a 'genetic' or 'full' surrogacy arrangement. Accordingly it seems highly unlikely that the mitochondrial donor would ever come to be regarded as 'the' (or even 'a') legal mother by virtue of her donation alone.

While UK law does not permit two legal 'mothers', nor allow a child what would amount to three legal 'parents' (i.e., a legal mother plus two legal parents, or a legal mother and a legal father plus legal parent), the HFE Act was amended in 2008 to allow that a child can have a legal mother (the woman who gave birth to the baby) and a second female *legal parent*, provided that they are a same-sex couple who qualify for joint parenthood (note, not *mother*hood) under specific criteria. The child is not also permitted a legal father in this circumstance: the law recognises two parents and no more. A mitochondrial donor could thus

5 See, for example, the Nuffield Council's recent report on Nuffield Council on Bioethics (2011) Human bodies: donation for medicine and research, available at: http://www.nuffieldbioethics.org/sites/default/files/Donation_full_report.pdf.

technically become the second female legal parent, but only if she was also in a qualifying relationship with the child's mother.

Finally, while the two mitochondrial donation techniques under consideration in the UK have not been used to create children before, foregrounding safety and efficacy questions, the apparent ethical rubicon of a child being born with genetic links to three people was crossed some decades ago, something that those who oppose the procedures in question on moral grounds seem loath to mention. Beginning in the US in the 1990s, the technique that enables this, cytoplasmic (or 'ooplasmic') transfer (Dale et al, 2001) is a somewhat scientifically obscure fertility treatment. It 'augments' the cytoplasm in the intending mother's egg by injecting it with cytoplasm from an egg donor, intentionally *mixing* their mitochondrial populations in the hope of improving embryo development. There has been some scientific uncertainty about how the technique works. Some of the resulting children showed evidence of donor mitochondria when tested, while others did not (Connor, 2014). However, little has been published about the outcomes for these children and families (or their donors), making this also a difficult example of a relevant treatment for mitochondrial donation proponents to cite. Despite these uncertainties, the technique has become widely available outside the UK as a treatment designed to improve the chance of conception.

The status of the mitochondrial donor in regulation

The mitochondrial donor's legal status may influence the perceptions of donors, recipient families and wider society as to any social relationships created by mitochondrial donation. It may also influence the views and typical profile of egg donors or women considering receiving this treatment. The HFEA advised government that 'mitochondria donors should be thought of as kind of tissue donor: the resulting child should not have a right to identifying information about the donor, although information exchange and contact could be arranged locally by mutual consent', reflecting its findings of public views (HFEA, 2013a). Similarly, the draft Regulations discussion document states that 'mitochondrial donors should be treated more like organ donors than gamete donors in respect of information to be collected and made available' (at 2.21). Further, although the European Union Tissue and Cells Directive already requires of clinics that human tissues and cells (whether reproductive or not) and thus their donors are *traceable* from procurement to use and storage, which would apply to mitochondrial donors, non-reproductive organ and tissue donation have no statutory provision for *information-sharing* between donor and recipient/s.

With their consent, and according to local policy, *live* donors of non-reproductive tissue and organs may be given information about the outcome of the donation, or receive a letter from recipients passed via an intermediary organisation. With mutual consent, an initial meeting may be facilitated. Some families of *deceased* donors may be sent information about the outcome of the donation, or recipients' letters with their consent, but policies rarely allow them to meet and some specifically forbid this. However, under the draft Regulations (and as with reproductive gamete and embryo donors donating after 1 August 1991), a mitochondrial donor could ask the HFEA for limited, *non-identifying,* information about the number, sex and year of birth of any children produced using her egg (HFEA, 2012). This provision is a welcome part of valuing the mitochondrial donor's contribution.

The draft Regulations also propose to notify mitochondrial donors of any requests regarding their information from the resulting offspring upon reaching adulthood. Given that no contact is in prospect – as the information offered would be non-identifying only – this feels less welcome and more like a regulatory 'nudge' to encourage the mitochondrial donor to initiate, or be available for contact via an informal route, which seems beyond the HFEA's remit to seek to instigate.

Information about the mitochondrial donor

Under the HFE Act, donors of eggs, sperm or embryos (since 1 April 2005) are mandatorily identifiable to those born as a result of their donation (at adulthood, with some exceptions). It seems appropriate that the proposed Regulations would *not* require a mitochondrial donor to be identifiable to the resulting offspring. This is because she does not donate *nuclear* genes, creating neither observable shared characteristics nor (for most people, currently) expectations around kinship.

Similarly to provisions in the HFE Act regarding gamete and embryo donation, regulation 10 of the draft Regulations permits a person aged over 16 who thinks they may have been born as the result of mitochondrial donation, to apply to the HFEA to have this question confirmed. This seems appropriate in terms of allowing people to authenticate their origins where this is important to them to do so. It is also proposed that where relevant, the HFEA could also pass on non-identifying personal and family medical history from the donor plus

> ...any description of the mitochondrial donor as a person... and any additional matter which the mitochondrial donor has provided with the intention that it be made available to a person who requests information... in a similar way to how organ donors can provide a pen picture for the organ recipient.
>
> (Department of Health, 2014a, Background, para 2.27)

Given that the donor's medical details, unless they relate to her mitochondrial function, will be largely irrelevant to a future person, this extra information is being made available purely to answer a social interest in the donor.

The facility to request 'pre-birth' information from a treatment register is imported directly from gamete donation; that is, *nuclear* genetic connectedness. No statutory equivalent specifically enables recipients of *non-reproductive* organ and tissue donations to discover that fact, reflecting that medical records are accessible to patients and often recipients were old enough to remember or consent to the procedure. 'Pen portraits' are strongly encouraged from all reproductive gamete and embryo donors and are vetted under HFEA guidelines. While these seem likely to answer a personal genealogical interest in their donor for (nuclear) donor-conceived people, they may be less relevant to those born from a mitochondrial donation where, given the nature of what is contributed to the child, their interest (if any) in the donor may be more focused on feelings of gratitude or curiosity about the gift relationship.

The HFEA also keeps a sibling registry enabling donor-conceived children to be in contact with others born via the same gamete or embryo donor, before the age (18) at which they can request the donor's identity. By contrast, draft regulation 14 does *not* allow families with children born via mitochondrial donation to obtain information from the HFEA about other children conceived via mitochondrial donations from the same donor, which is in keeping with the stated aims for the status of the donation. Informal options for this contact seem likely to emerge online in any case, as have arisen for gamete donation siblings.

However, without the unique identifiers provided by shared nuclear DNA, and given the complexities of mitochondrial inheritance, it may be impossible for some families to definitively genetically verify their child's connection to others via a specific shared mitochondrial donor. A genetic connection to a specific donor that can be confirmed would not in any case make the children genetic (half-)'siblings' in the same way as a shared gamete donor would. Seeking to apply kinship norms around 'siblinghood' or approximating parent–sibling connections to children with a shared mitochondrial donor is discordant given that the genetic connection to the donor may be identically shared with her mother, grandmother, any uncles, aunts and siblings and cousins and so on.

Under the HFE Act, people over the age of 16 can apply jointly to the HFEA to find out if they might be genetically related via gamete or embryo donation, if they say that they are considering entering into a civil partnership, marriage, or intimate physical relationship. Regulation 11 stipulates that if such applications are made in respect of mitochondrial donation, the enquirers 'will not be treated as related to anyone who shares the same mitochondrial donor as them, or to the donor themselves. This is because there is a very small (0.01%) genetic relationship between the mitochondrial donor and any child born through mitochondrial donation' (Department of Health, 2014a). While this is a sensible policy decision, the resulting person, the mitochondrial donor and her maternal family clearly *are* genetically 'related', whatever the relative proportion of the donor's contribution. A better rationale would be that while children of consanguineous parents have a known elevated risk of autosomal, recessive nuclear genetic disorders, there is *no* analogous risk from mitochondrial donation.

In reproductive gamete donation, the HFEA also specifies that no more than ten families can use the same gamete donor, and that the donor may specify a lower limit (HFEA, 2011). It would seem disproportionate to impose such limits on a mitochondrial donor in order to replicate kinship norms, and concerns about (nuclear genetic) consanguinuity at population level are irrelevant here. The draft Regulations did not speak to this point.

The regulatory status of the sperm donor for zygotic enucleation in PNT

PNT requires two eggs to be fertilised and puts each resulting embryo to different uses, each creating different genetic connections between the sperm donor and to the resulting child. The draft Regulations omit, however, one protagonist in PNT – a licensed sperm donor who for some reason fertilised *only* the egg of the mitochondrial donor to be enucleated (in order to create embryo 'A') and did not fertilise embryo B, thus *making no nuclear genetic contribution to the resulting child.* His legal status around licensed gamete donation or legal parenthood would be unclear, as he would have consented solely for his sperm to be used to create an embryo for enucleation in which his/its nuclear material is then discarded. It seems obvious that this should not be treated identically to a sperm donor making a *nuclear genetic contribution* to the resulting child, whether, for example as the donor in PNT who creates embryo B, or who fertilises a reconstructed egg after MST, or indeed in conventional reproductive sperm donation.

The existing provisions in the HFE Act would apply the statutory status quo where the same man fertilised *both* eggs used in PNT, meaning that he would be either a licensed gamete donor, or if he is the husband or partner of the woman who carries the resulting pregnancy, arrangements for legal fatherhood will apply to him as usual after licensed assisted reproduction treatment. This provision would seem equally appropriate for a man who *solely* fertilises embryo 'B', if another man has fertilised embryo A. Intuitively it might seem appropriate to create a new category of 'male nuclear genetic donor' for men whose sperm creates a pronucleus which is then transferred elsewhere, as the process they consent to will be different to conventional gamete donation, with the same rights and duties around information-sharing as apply to sperm donors, but space does not permit further discussion of this here.

Arrangements as proposed in the draft Regulations for a mitochondrial donor should apply to a sperm donor solely creating an embryo for enucleation in the PNT process. He should not be mandatorily identifiable to the resulting adults, but should be offered limited non-identifying information about the children resulting from the donation. He should not be subject to a limit on the number of families to whom he could donate for this purpose. Further, a tailored consent process is also required around men's participation in mitochondrial donation to reflect the different outcomes relating to each embryo and different rights and duties respectively applying to the gamete donor. This consent would need to be in two separable parts, each sufficient to cover the creation of embryo A or B individually.

Other uses of MST and PNT

Since long before the advent of assisted reproduction, in certain situations, families have foregrounded or minimised the actual genetic connection between 'parents' and their children according to their needs and current kinship norms. This situational prioritisation of the genetic connection might inspire future patients to request PNT or MST to be licensed for *other* purposes than avoiding the transmission of serious mitochondrial disorders. This would require revision of the HFE Act (as amended).

For example, an intending mother may request PNT or MST using a female *nuclear genetic donor* (as opposed to a whole-egg donor for reproduction) because she wishes to prevent the transmission of a serious nuclear genetic disease and to have a mitochondrial genetic connection to her child. Ethically this seems as justified as using MST or PNT to prevent mitochondrial disorders caused by *mitochondrial DNA* whilst creating a (nuclear) genetic connection to the child. If the Act were amended to permit this for non-mitochondrial genetic disorders, because a nuclear genetic connection is involved (and perhaps as with the licensed sperm donor used to create embryo B in PNT), the regulatory status of the female nuclear genetic donor should be based on that of a conventional reproductive gamete donor. If this intending mother happened to be seeking to avoid a *mitochondrial disease with a nuclear genetic origin*, while the currently proposed draft Regulations would not assist, this patient group would be likely to benefit first, as the existing HFE Act allows Regulations to allow this should a safe and effective treatment become available.

Another therapeutic use for MST and PNT that seems likely to be commercially successful in non-UK regulatory systems, would be to resolve fertility problems arising from inadequate mitochondrial function linked to the intending mother's age. A mitochondrial donation could allow women reaching the end of their natural fertility to have a baby with whom they share a *nuclear* genetic connection, unlike with conventional egg donation. Or, with no therapeutic intention, but purely for 'social reasons', a woman (for example in a same-sex relationship) might request the use of PNT or MST because she strongly desires a *mitochondrial* genetic link between herself and the resulting child (or at any rate she would like *a* genetic connection to her child and via mtDNA is the only way to achieve this), while her partner will have the nuclear genetic link to their child. This prospective parent (and her partner and child(ren)) may invest a great deal of personal social meaning in using new techniques to create a genetic link to the child via mtDNA. In common with many other parents, they may enjoy the prospect of having a genetic connection to their child and (if the child is female) of that genetic connection being passed on to her daughter's children. They may feel (as many other parents feel about nuclear DNA connection) that this mtDNA connection adds something desirable to the social role as mother or parent to her child.

However, this reading of the significance of the *mitochondrial* genetic connection (as either enhancing parental status, or creating it) is not one (yet) with any widespread cultural recognition and so is not sufficient as a foundation for regulation for all users of these techniques. These purposes may be some way off in respect of PNT or MST, but as with any technology, in future it may become acceptable to patients and clinicians to use techniques in new or unforeseen ways, and the UK Parliament may need to consider these.

Conclusion

The proposed Regulations to allow parents to have both healthy *and* (nuclear) genetically related children accords with the drive behind many other pre-conception procedures established in the UK, including with public funding via the UK's National Health Service. Any novel social relationships created or implied by such techniques have been largely already accommodated by the families that use them and by wider society. There seems to be no reason that this accommodation should not also be the case with PNT and MST if they are made available in the UK.

* Following the writing of this chapter, on 3 February 2015, the UK's House of Commons debated Regulations to allow the introduction of mitochondrial donation to prevent the transmission of serious mitochondrial disease, as envisaged in the HFE Act (as amended). MPs voted to approve the Regulations by a majority of 254 (Ayes 382, Noes 128), making the UK the first country in the world to legislate in favour of the use of these mitochondrial donation techniques in humans. Three weeks later, on 24 February 2015, the House of Lords rejected a motion attempting to block the approval on the grounds of safety and compliance with domestic and European law by a vote of 48 for and 280 against. The draft Regulations will come into force in October 2015 accordingly. This places the techniques under the regulation of the HFEA on a case-by-case application basis, also providing that mitochondrial donors and the children born following mitochondrial donation can access limited, non-identifying information about each other. The first UK patients are expected to be offered the procedure in 2017.

References

Brown, D.T., et al, (2006) 'Transmission of mitochondrial DNA disorders: possibilities for the future' *The Lancet* 368 87.

Campbell, K.H., et al, (1996) 'Sheep cloned by nuclear transfer from a cultured cell line' *Nature* 380 64.

Christian Action Research and Education (2014) 'Three parent children' <http://www.care.org.uk/advocacy/bioethics/threeparentchildren>

Collins, N., (2013) 'Three parent babies "incompatible with human dignity"' (*Daily Telegraph*, 4 October).

Connor, S., (2014) 'Three-parent babies: "As long as she's healthy, I don't care", says mother of IVF child' (*Independent*, 25 August).

Craven, L., et al, (2010) 'Pronuclear transfer in human embryos to prevent transmission of mitochondrial DNA disease' *Nature* 46582.

Daily Mail (2013) 'Babies with three parents could be born by 2015 after controversial genetic treatment gets green light' (28 June).

Dale, B., et al, (2001) 'Pregnancy after cytoplasmic transfer in a couple suffering from idiopathic infertility' 16(7) *Human Reproduction* 1469.

Dean, N.L., et al, (2003) 'Prospect of preimplantation genetic diagnosis for heritable mitochondrial DNA diseases' 9 *Molecular Human Reproduction* 631.

Department of Health (2014a) *Mitochondrial donation: A consultation on draft regulations to permit the use of new treatment techniques to prevent the transmission of a serious mitochondrial disease from mother to child* (London, gov.uk).

Department of Health (2014b) *Mitochondrial donation: Government response to the consultation on draft regulations to permit the use of new treatment techniques to prevent the transmission of a serious mitochondrial disease from mother to child* (London, gov.uk).

Expert Panel H (2014) 'Review of scientific methods to avoid mitochondrial disease 2014' <http://www.hfea.gov.uk/8807.html>

Faivre, L., et al (2000) 'Determination of enzyme activities for prenatal diagnosis of respiratory chain deficiency' 20 *Prenatal Diagnosis* 732.

Hansard (2014) Commons debates, Mitochondrial Replacement (Public Safety) 1 Sept 2014, col 121.

House of Commons Science and Technology Committee (2014) 'Mitochondrial Donation-One-off evidence session' <http://www.parliament.uk/business/committees/committees-a-z/commons-select/science-and-technology-committee/news/141016-mit-ev/>

Human Fertilisation and Embryology Authority (2005) 'Mitochondrial DNA Disorders: Is there a way to prevent transmission?' <http://www.hfea.gov.uk/1564.html>

Human Fertilisation and Embryology Authority (2011a) 'HFEA agrees new policies about family donation and the number of families one donor can create' <http://www.hfea.gov.uk/6518.html>

Human Fertilisation and Embryology Authority (2011b) 'Review of scientific methods to avoid mitochondrial disease 2011' <http://www.hfea.gov.uk/6372.html>

Human Fertilisation and Embryology Authority (2012) 'Your rights and responsibilities as a donor – apply for information' <http://www.hfea.gov.uk/1975.html>

Human Fertilisation and Embryology Authority (2013a) 'HFEA agrees advice to Government on the ethics and science of mitochondria replacement' <http://www.hfea.gov.uk/7790.html>

Human Fertilisation and Embryology Authority (2013b) 'Review of scientific methods to avoid mitochondrial disease – 2013 update' <http://www.hfea.gov.uk/8806.html>

Human Fertilisation and Embrology Authority (2013c) Mitochondria replacement consultation: Advice to Government, Human Fertilisation and Embryology Authority, March 2013. <http://www.hfea.gov.uk/docs/Mitochondria_replacement_consultation_-_advice_for_Government.pdf>

Human Fertilisation and Embryology Authority (2014a) 'Review of scientific methods to avoid mitochondrial disease – 2014 update' <http://www.hfea.gov.uk/8807.html>

Human Fertilisation and Embryology Authority (2014b) 'Third Mitochondrial Replacement Scientific Review' (2014) <http://www.hfea.gov.uk/docs/Third_Mitochondrial_replacement_scientific_review.pdf>

Mito Action (2008) 'A clinician's guide to the management of mitochondrial disease' <http://www.mitoaction.org/guide/table-contents>

NBC News (2014) 'Three parents? FDA mulls safety of embryo technique' (24 February).

NHS England Clinical Commissioning Board (2013) 'Clinical commissioning policy: Pre-implantation genetic diagnosis (PGD)' <http://www.england.nhs.uk/wp-content/uploads/2013/04/e01-p-a.pdf>

Nordqvist, P. and Smart, C. (2014) *Relative Strangers: Family Life, Genes and Donor Conception* (Basingstoke: Palgrave Macmillan).

Nuffield Council on Bioethics (2012) *Novel Techniques for the Prevention of Mitochondrial DNA Disorders: An Ethical Review* (London: Nuffield Council on Bioethics).

POST (2013) 'Pre-implantation genetic diagnosis' POST 445.

Poulton, J., et al (2009) 'Preventing transmission of maternally inherited mitochondrial DNA diseases' *British Medical Journal* 338, b94.

Poulton, J. and Oakeshott, P., (2012) 'Nuclear transfer to prevent maternal transmission of mitochondrial DNA disease' *British Medical Journal* 345, e6651.
Progress Educational Trust (2011) 'Letter to the Secretary of State for Health concerning Treatments to Avoid Transmission of Mitochondrial Disease' <http://www.progress.org.uk/mitochondrialdisease>
Schwartz, M., et al, (2002) 'Paternal inheritance of mitochondrial DNA' 347 *New England Journal of Medicine* 576.
St John, J., et al, (2007) 'Human-animal cytoplasmic hybrid embryos, mitochondria, and an energetic debate' 9 *Nature Cell Biology* 988.
Steffann, J., et al, (2007) 'Stability of the m.8993T->G mtDNA mutation load during human embryofetal development has implications for the feasibility of prenatal diagnosis in NARP syndrome' 44 *Journal of Medical Genetics* 664.
Taanman, J.-W., (1999) 'The mitochondrial genome: structure, transcription, translation and replication' 1410(2) *Biochimica et Biophysica Acta- Bioenergetics* 103.
Tachibana, M., et al, (2009) 'Mitochondrial gene replacement in primate offspring and embryonic stem cells' *Nature* 461 367.
The Catholic Church in England and Wales (2012) 'Clones and Three-Parent Babies' <http://catholicnews.org.uk/Home/News/2012/Mitochondria>
The Economist (2012) 'Hello mothers, hello father: A technique intended to eliminate mitochondrial diseases would result in people with three genetic parents' (27 October).
Toynbee, P., (2014) 'This treatment would save children's lives – so why won't the government allow it?' (*The Guardian*, 11 February).
USA Today (2014) 'FDA weighs risks of 3-person embryo fertilization' (24 February).

8 The fertility treatment time forgot: What should be done about surrogacy in the UK?

Kirsty Horsey and Katia Neofytou

Introduction

When the UK's Department of Health announced a wholesale review of the UK's Human Fertilisation and Embryology Act 1990 (hereafter 'the 1990 Act'), with the aim of making it 'fit for purpose' in the twenty-first century (Department of Health, 2005), this was welcomed by many scholars, practitioners and others who assumed – wrongly for the most part – that such a review and 'updating' of the legislation would include matters relating to surrogacy. Prior to the announcement there had been academic and other criticism of the way that the law on surrogacy operated in the UK, particularly given that it had become, by the twenty-first century if not before, a practice relatively culturally embedded and socially accepted (Horsey and Sheldon, 2012). However, when the time came, the public consultation document leading to the passage of the Human Fertilisation and Embryology Act 2008 ('the 2008 Act') asked only about extending the way legal parenthood is acquired following a surrogacy arrangement to those who were in civil partnerships or enduring relationships, mirroring legal changes elsewhere that it would seem could never have been ignored, whatever the outcome of the consultation.[1] The consultation did not question any of the assumptions on which the current law on surrogacy rests, such as by asking whether it is desirable to continue to discourage the practice by prohibiting any commercialisation of surrogacy and the payment of surrogates, or whether surrogacy arrangements should continue to be unenforceable. Nor did it ask whether assumptions about parenthood – and motherhood in particular – following surrogacy were correct, even where those who commission a surrogate may both be the resulting child's genetic (as well as intended) parents (Horsey, 2010).

This chapter considers the regulatory approach to surrogacy in the UK and some of the pitfalls of this model in the modern day. It starts by briefly looking at how we got to where we are, and why. It then looks at what we label 'twenty-first Century surrogacy problems' which stem not only from an increasing globalisation

1 Prior to the public consultation, a report from the House of Commons Science and Technology Committee (2004) had said that the regulation of surrogacy should be reviewed, including the possibility of new, separate, surrogacy legislation.

brought about by developments in technology and communication, but also from the UK's own inertia with respect to surrogacy regulation, which remains 'hazy' after 30 years (Horsey and Sheldon, 2012) and 'thoroughly confused' (Warnock, 2002). The building momentum in support of surrogacy law reform from academic commentators, practitioners, the judiciary and some parliamentarians is then noted, giving weight to the impression that something ought to have been done about surrogacy in 2008. In the final section, we look at potential models of regulation from other jurisdictions – notably Greece and Israel – that the UK might consider when deciding how to reform surrogacy law, before concluding with some recommendations for the future.

Surrogacy in the UK

Though it had a rocky past, with its emergence into the public consciousness around the early 1980s, the public image of surrogacy underwent much transformation through the latter years of the last century. Early judicial comments in surrogacy cases were acerbic, reflecting an antipathy towards the practice and a sense that surrogacy agreements were contrary to public policy.[2] The Warnock Committee, in 1984, decried surrogacy as objectionable, a 'risky undertaking' that distorts the mother–child relationship and 'the wrong way to approach pregnancy' (Warnock Committee Report, 1984: chapter 8). The Committee ultimately recommended that the use of surrogacy as a treatment for infertility should be actively discouraged and that commercial activities relating to surrogacy be criminalised.[3] Warnock's recommendations resulted in the Surrogacy Arrangements Act 1985 (hereafter 'the 1985 Act'), which remains in force today. The 1985 Act, which had dual goals of protecting vulnerable women and discouraging surrogacy (Jackson, 2001: 262), makes it a criminal offence to advertise for or as a surrogate or to facilitate surrogacy on a commercial basis.

Later legislative provisions affecting surrogacy were put in place with the 1990 Act. Section 36 of the 1990 Act inserted section 1A into the 1985 Act, rendering all surrogacy agreements wholly unenforceable (something that the Warnock Committee had originally recommended). Sections 27 and 28 of the 1990 Act designated the legal parents of children born following the use of assisted reproductive technologies (ART) which, when it was undertaken in a clinical context using IVF procedures and/or donated gametes, would also encompass surrogacy. Section 30 of the 1990 Act established the Parental Order, a legal mechanism whereby a court could transfer legal parenthood of a surrogate-born child to the commissioning parents when certain conditions were met.

In 1998, a further review of surrogacy in the UK was commissioned by the

2 In particular see *A v C* (1978) 8 Fam Law 170; [1985] FLR 445, though contrast Latey J in *Re C (a minor)* [1985] FLR 846.

3 Though notably the published report included an annex containing a dissenting opinion written by three of the Committee. In later years, Baroness Warnock changed her views on surrogacy, coming 'to think that probably [the] minority was right' (Warnock, 2002).

government, largely to look into the money aspect of surrogacy arrangements. It had by that time become apparent that some surrogates could receive quite large sums of money for their services, notionally at least in the form of expenses. The new Committee, chaired by Professor Margaret Brazier, thus focused mainly on the issue of payments to surrogates and the way in which the law should be reformed in order that it 'continued to meet public concerns' (Brazier Committee Report, 1998: [1.1]), including via making changes to the provisions of the 1985 and 1990 Acts.[4] The Brazier Committee recommended that payments to surrogates should be prohibited, with the exception of reimbursement of 'genuine and verifiable' expenses incurred by the surrogate as a direct result of the pregnancy (Brazier Committee Report, 1998: [5.25]), which should be defined in legislation. Arguably the Committee's more important recommendation was that the 1985 Act and section 30 of the 1990 Act should be repealed and a new Surrogacy Act created in their place. This new Act should continue to render surrogacy agreements unenforceable and maintain the prohibitions on commercial surrogacy, and would require the establishment of a statutory Code of Practice for non-profit surrogacy agencies that would be registered with the Department of Health. The Code would be binding on all agencies and any party entering a surrogacy arrangement (Brazier Committee Report, 1998: [7.18]–[7.19]). The Brazier Committee also envisaged that a revised Parental Order scheme would continue to operate, adding the condition that commissioning couples would only be eligible for a Parental Order if they had complied with all the provisions of the new Surrogacy Act. The Committee's concerns regarding payments to surrogates meant it also recommended that payments (other than those reimbursing 'genuine and verifiable' expenses) would not in future be able to be retrospectively authorised by a court (Brazier Committee Report, 1998: [7.22]).

However, nothing came of the Brazier Committee's recommendations and no new Surrogacy Act was passed. The practice of surrogacy continued as it had done before and very little was heard of it in the courts for some time. For a while at least, surrogacy was off the radar: it was the fertility treatment that time forgot.

As indicated above, the limited treatment of surrogacy in the public consultation leading to the 2008 Act meant that little changed in the way surrogacy is regulated, despite the Science and Technology Committee's 2005 recommendations. Empirical studies were published a little before the Department of Health's consultation document, which indicated that children and parents in families created through surrogacy fare well (Golombok et al, 2005),[5] yet this also appears not to have made the need for better regulation more pressing. Instead, the 2008

4 By this time, the medical profession, as represented by the British Medical Association (BMA) had changed its mind about surrogacy. In 1984 it had recommended that its members did not get involved in surrogacy at all. In 1990, it had said that surrogacy would be ethical as a means of treating infertility in couples where other forms of treatment had failed. But in 1996, the BMA published guidance acknowledging surrogacy as an acceptable reproductive option 'of last resort' (British Medical Association, 1996).

5 Follow-up longitudinal studies conducted when the children were older also support this: see e.g. Golombok et al (2011); Jadva et al (2012).

Act merely extended the ability to apply for a Parental Order to same-sex couples and those in an enduring family relationship,[6] rather than just married couples; none of the other Parental Order requirements changed. While this is welcome, it hardly marks wholesale reconsideration of parenthood following surrogacy (Horsey, 2010) and indeed has been criticised as simply maintaining or replicating the 'spirit' of the 1990 provisions (McCandless and Sheldon, 2010). The 2008 Act also exempted the operation of some not-for-profit surrogacy services from the criminal provisions of the 1985 Act and allowing them to recoup financial costs involved in the provision of their services,[7] though it might be said that such piece-meal reform does not go far enough and that it would be better to have surrogacy agencies working on a proper, though regulated, commercial basis, in the interests of all parties concerned. Rather than 'tinkering with the existing legal provisions' (Fox, 2009), serious consideration should be given to how surrogacy operates in reality this century and how best to facilitate those arrangements while extending the protections deemed necessary to safeguard the interests of the parties involved. This was clearly not achieved by the 2008 Act.[8]

More recently, we have seen a spate of surrogacy cases in the courts, the majority of which concern issues arising from cross-border surrogacy arrangements, which have become increasingly common in an era of easy-access online information and easy travel. In addition, impetus stirred by some of these cases has led to advancements being made in relation to the way some aspects of surrogacy are dealt with domestically, including the introduction of maternity leave rights in 2015 for those who achieve parenthood through surrogacy, in recognition that commissioning parents perform the actual role of parent from birth.[9] At the time of writing there is impetus in Parliament, supported by practitioners and interest groups, among others, towards re-regulation. The Human Fertilisation and Embryology Authority (HFEA) has also started to update the information it provides about surrogacy, but there remains a long way to go to make the law fit for the twenty-first century, which has seen a whole new set of problems emerge and likely to continue.

Twenty-first-century surrogacy problems

The biggest problem currently arising from surrogacy is that many people are travelling to other countries to engage women there as surrogates. There are a

6 Parental Order provisions now contained in section 54.

7 Section 59 inserts section 2A into the Surrogacy Arrangements Act 1985.

8 As was acknowledged by the pre-legislative scrutiny committee, which reviewed the changes proposed in the draft legislation: changes were not enough 'to protect both children born as a result of surrogacy and surrogate mothers' (House of Lords, House of Commons Joint Committee (2007), at [289]).

9 See *RKA v Secretary of State for Work and Pensions* [2012] (unreported). The Children and Families Act 2014 allows parents through surrogacy and eligible/intending to apply for a Parental Order the same rights to time off work to care for their new children as those adopting children, broadly in line with that for other parents. Regulations provide the framework in which applications can be made. It represents the first legal recognition that intended parents are responsible for their children from birth.

handful of other nations where engaging a surrogate, even across language barriers, is made easy for those from the UK, as well as from other countries from which people might travel. There are many reasons why putative parents might travel for surrogacy. It is often easier (particularly when information about the services offered can be accessed via the internet – see Jackson, this volume), cheaper (in the long run) and quicker than trying to find a surrogate at home. For some who travel for surrogacy (though not those from the UK), it is because surrogacy is prohibited at home. For others, restrictions placed on the legal operation of surrogacy in the home country might encourage commissioning couples to go elsewhere. This potentially includes some parents from the UK, where 'clinical' surrogacy using IVF procedures is heavily regulated in ways that might not suit everyone's needs, all arrangements are precarious and unenforceable, and even private arrangements may potentially fall foul of any payments made to the surrogate (though seemingly not in practice, judging from the amount of retrospectively judicially authorised payments).[10] Describing the cross-border surrogacy trend in 2013, one professional who has worked on many of the most recent international surrogacy cases to come before the UK courts, said 'it always amazes me quite the lengths people will go to, and how impossible it is to stop this happening' (Prosser, 2013). It is not only the home nation's rules or prohibitions that encourage cross-border surrogacy. In many of the destinations where those travelling for surrogacy tend to go, the practice of surrogacy is as yet, unregulated. In others, it is commercialised to the extent that those accessing surrogacy there are more like consumers. Some, such as the US (notably California and Illinois), India, Ukraine, Georgia and Thailand have become well-known as 'open' surrogacy destinations.[11] Others are emerging, including Russia, Mexico and Canada (on the latter, see White, this volume). Though each country has its own laws (which obviously vary state by state in the US) relating directly and/or indirectly to surrogacy, each allows surrogates to receive payments (making surrogates easier to find) and often there are commercial agencies or similar willing to match prospective parents with surrogates for a fee.

Whatever the reason for travelling, it would appear that cross-border surrogacy (in the same way as for many other medical and other services) is here to stay, particularly if no change is made to our domestic law. However, crossing borders to access easier, cheaper and faster surrogacy brings with it its own set of problems, as has been illustrated in case law here and abroad, alongside media

10 See as far back as *Re Q (Parental Order)* [1996] 1 FLR 369, then more recently *Re X and Y (Foreign Surrogacy)* [2008] EWHC 3030 (fam); *Re L (a minor)* [2010] EWHC 3146 (Fam) and others. It should be noted that the Human Fertilisation and Embryology (Parental Orders) Regulations 2010 confirmed that in granting orders a child's welfare must be paramount. As Hedley J pointed out in *Re X and Y*, 'it is almost impossible to imagine a set of circumstances in which by the time the case comes to court, the welfare of the child... would not be gravely compromised at the very least by a refusal to make an order' (at [24]).

11 Note, however, that the situation in Thailand has changed following a recent parliamentary vote banning commercial surrogacy, in the wake of the 'Baby Gammy' saga and other controversies. (Ahmad and Brooks, 2015; Sharpe, 2014).

representations of how surrogacy is conducted in other countries and in particular in cases where things go badly wrong.[12] While we do not and cannot know exactly how many people travel abroad from the UK to access surrogacy (Natalie Gamble Associates, 2014), we have indications that the use of surrogacy in general is increasing, for example because of the number of applications for Parental Orders being made (Crawshaw et al, 2012). Correspondingly, there have been more cases being brought before the courts, including a significant number of cases where the surrogacy has taken place overseas, as well as more anecdotal evidence about the number of people seeking legal advice on this (Prosser, 2013) and numerous reports in the media. The first of a flurry of international or cross-border surrogacy cases in the UK were decided in 2007–8.[13] These – and subsequent cases – illustrate some of the many legal problems that cross-border surrogacy can generate, not only for potential parents, but also for the children born to surrogates overseas. This is not to mention the additional practical, personal (including financial) and social problems that might be faced.[14]

Further, hidden in the subtext of any discussion of cross-border surrogacy are some unpalatable issues and difficult questions. Inevitably there is concern about which women volunteer to be surrogates in countries where payment is allowed, and indeed whether they can truly be said to have volunteered at all. Does paying women reduce them to vessels and/or amount to the commodification of pregnancy, childbirth and even children? Or, might being paid for surrogacy in some way liberate women, allowing them financial independence or gains they might otherwise not have been able to achieve? And, notwithstanding how we feel about paying the women themselves, how can we justify allowing agencies and other intermediaries to trade in the misery of infertility by sourcing women to be surrogates?

For these reasons and more, it becomes imperative that we closely examine our surrogacy laws. We argue that the careful drafting of more facilitative regulation in the UK, which better recognises the realities of modern day surrogacy, including its internationalisation and the fact that payments are made,[15] would benefit commissioning parents, surrogates and children alike. Further, it should – if done well – put an end to judicial tinkering which, though welcome in those cases where it has occurred, serves only to indicate that the law is not currently as it should be (Rozenberg, 2014).[16] Recent findings indicate

12 Perhaps most recently illustrated by the 'Baby Gammy' situation, where one of a pair of twins born to a surrogate in Thailand was rejected by the commissioning couple for having Down syndrome and left in the hands of the surrogate (Callaghan and Newson, 2014) – as well as subsequent stories in the media piggy-backing on this unfortunate case.

13 *Re G (Surrogacy: Foreign Domicile)* [2007] EWHC 2814 (fam); *Re X and Y (Foreign Surrogacy)* [2008] EWHC 3030.

14 Such as with regards to being stuck overseas, waiting for passports for the child(ren), etc.

15 Note that similar concerns have been raised elsewhere: see e.g. van Zyl and Walker (2013); Millbank (2014) and Stuhmcke, this volume.

16 See e.g. *Re D and L* (2012), where the consent of the surrogate was waived, as she could not be found and, most recently, *Re X (a child) (surrogacy: time limit)* [2014] EWHC 3135 (Fam) in which Sir Justice Mumby, President of the Family Division, criticised the rigidity of the rules governing

that the regulation of surrogacy varies significantly not only around the world but also within Europe (McCandless et al, 2013). The analysis below offers an insight into two regulatory regimes – those of Greece and Israel – regarding the practice of surrogacy. These two models provide a basis for fruitful comparison for two reasons: first, in both countries surrogacy is condoned by comprehensive legislation; secondly, in both countries surrogacy contracts are legal and enforceable.

The Greek regulatory model on surrogacy

Greece is the only European country that adopts (since 2002) a novel approach allowing for altruistic gestational surrogacy arrangements based on enforceable surrogacy contracts that are reviewed and authorised by the national courts prior to conception, and which potentially lead to automatic transfer of legal parenthood after the birth of the child. Though the Greek regulatory model for surrogacy has provided a complete response to issues concerning the relationship of the parties to a surrogacy arrangement, issues of payments and legal parentage of the surrogate-born child, its legal stipulations have been poorly explored by the international literature. Moreover, a considerable lack of sociological data is available thus far, which makes it difficult to evaluate the effectiveness of the law in Greek society.

Greece is one of the few countries that officially recognises a constitutional right to procreate and parent a child (grounded on the individual freedom of expression),[17] even through the use of ARTs. Greek society can generally be described as placing great importance on the institution of the family, and reproduction within the family – whether natural or assisted – is endorsed by the Christian Orthodox tradition, the most popular religion in the country.[18] Low birth rates, together with high rates of infertility affecting almost 15 per cent of the adult population (Ravdas, 2010) and low IVF success rates, led the Greek legislature to suggest surrogacy as an alternative way of reproduction. Fearing concerns relating to exploitation and commodification, and in order to protect the interests of the parties to a surrogacy arrangement (most importantly, of the surrogate-born child), in 2002 Law 3089/2002 on Medically Assisted Human

Parental Orders, in particular the requirement that applications for an order must be made within six months of a child's birth, and allowed a late application to be made. In a blog post commenting on the case, Natalie Gamble Associates (2014), say that it 'demonstrates yet again, just how out of date the UK's surrogacy laws are' and describes the law as 'creaking under the strain' of modern surrogacy practice.

17 Article 5(1), Greek Constitution. See also Trokanas, T. (2011) 'Human Reproduction – Personal autonomy and its limits' (in Greek), Sakkoulas Publications, Athens-Thessaloniki, Greece: 91; Kounougeri-Manoledaki, E., (2005) 'Assisted reproduction and Family Law. The Greek regime: Laws 3089/2002 and 3305/2005' (in Greek), Sakkoulas Publications, Athens-Thessaloniki, Greece: 8.

18 The Church is against donor IVF, and having children outside the marriage. Where married heterosexual couples suffer from infertility, the Church suggests adoption. However, it has not expressed any opinion against surrogacy *per se*.

Reproduction was passed by the Greek Parliament, which facilitates surrogacy. In 2005, Law 3305/2005 was passed to establish an express prohibition on payments for surrogacy (article 13(4)), and to impose criminal sanctions (article 26).[19]

The specific provisions of the Law are incorporated into the Greek Civil Code (hereafter *GCC*), and more precisely into article 1458 *GCC*, which introduces an exception to the presumption of maternity grounded on gestation and birth (article 1463 *GCC*). Thus, a woman who has been granted a pre-conception court order approving the agreement between her and another woman (the gestational carrier) can be presumed to be the legal mother of the surrogate-born child immediately after birth. Her parental right is based on her intention to have and raise the child.

Under Greek law, surrogacy is available to single or married women, or women in *de facto* relationships, who have been medically diagnosed as unable to conceive, or bring a pregnancy to term, or to women who might transmit a dangerous hereditary condition to the child (such as sickle cell anaemia, or HIV/AIDS, among others). Although article 1458 refers to women, for reasons of gender equality (guaranteed by article 4(1) of the Constitution), surrogacy might also be an option for single men.[20] However, it is not currently allowed, for same-sex couples.

The intended mother must seek approval from the national court before fertilisation of the surrogate takes place. She must submit the written surrogacy agreement, and an affidavit from a doctor affirming her inability to carry or give birth to a child, as well as the good physical health of the potential surrogate, psychiatric assessments confirming the good emotional state of both women, and consent forms signed by the two women's co-habitants or husbands, if they have one. The latter is required because in Greece paternity is determined based on the man's relationship with the legal mother of the child (article 1463 *GCC*). Consequently, the partner or husband of the legal mother of the child will be presumed to be her legal father.[21]

Furthermore, until 2014, the intended mother's application had to prove that both she and the surrogate-to-be were domiciled in Greece (article 8,

19 The criminal sanctions refer to the intended mother and the surrogate carrier, as well as the medical staff, and any paid intermediaries who will assist the performance of surrogacy against the legal provisions. Moreover, advertising for surrogacy is illegal. The penalty is the payment of a fine up to 1,500 euros and at least 2 years of imprisonment. However, there has been no case where sanctions have been imposed by the Greek courts. The importance of the 'best interests of the child' arguably makes it very unlikely for any surrogacy contract not to be approved, even in retrospect, or for any actions to be considered as willingly circumventing the law.

20 The Greek court authorised surrogacy for a single man in 2008 and 2009 (One-Member Court of First Instance of Thessaloniki decision no. 2827/2008 and 13707/2009). Nevertheless, the Appeal Court in 2010 overturned the decision deeming the first decisions illegal, since the letter of the law clearly refers to a woman. Since the judges in Greece are not bound by legal precedent, they are free to make broad interpretations of the law, and approve a future application of a single man to surrogacy based on his constitutional right to procreate and the principle of gender equality. See also Kounougeri-Manoledaki, E. (2010): 2–3 (in Greek). The single man should prove his infertility and the need for surrogacy, as a woman would have to.

21 This presumption is rebuttable.

Law 3089/2002). This requirement was supposedly included to eliminate the possibility of 'reproductive tourism' and international surrogacy arrangements, which may render the child parentless and stateless. However, in July 2014 the Greek Parliament passed a new amendment to the law allowing for non-permanent residents to come to Greece, get treatment for surrogacy and be recognised as the legal parents of the child under the Greek law. More specifically, article 17 of Law 4272/2014 provides that either the surrogate or the intended mother in a surrogacy arrangement should at minimum be temporary residents in Greece, which then leaves open the possibility for foreign couples to seek surrogacy in Greece. This amendment could obviously place Greece as yet another popular destination to those willing to travel for international surrogacy.[22]

Importantly, the law states that the egg to be fertilised for the purposes of surrogacy should not belong to the surrogate. Only gestational surrogacy is allowed in Greece and, therefore, the egg must either come from the intended mother, or a donor, meaning that in all cases the resulting child has no direct genetic relation to the surrogate. As for the sperm, it can either come from the commissioning father, if there is one, or a donor. Accordingly, Greek law accepts the case of full social parenting, since the surrogate-born child can potentially be genetically unrelated to her parent(s). Moreover, it becomes apparent that the only way to achieve a surrogate pregnancy is through IVF, which must be performed by specialised medical personnel in a hospital or fertility clinic licensed by the National Authority for Medically Assisted Reproduction (hereafter NAMAR).[23]

The intended mother must also prove that the surrogacy arrangement is altruistic, and that no payment will be made to the surrogate during pregnancy or after childbirth, except for 'reasonable expenses'. Article 13(4) of Law 3305/2005 further stipulates what these might include: expenses relating to the

22 Stéphane Kovacs, 'La Grece, L'Eldorado de la GPA' *Le Figaro* (3/10/2014) (in French) <http://www.lefigaro.fr/mon-figaro/2014/10/03/10001-20141003ARTFIG00288-en-grece-l-eldorado-de-la-gpa.php>. See also Gènéthique, 'Greece. The New Eldorado for infertile couples' (11/08/2014) <http://www.genethique.org/en/greece-new-eldorado-infertile-couples-61946.html>.

23 NAMAR started operating in 2005, but ceased functioning in 2010. Former members of NAMAR reported that it was never able to fully operate, due to the State's continuous refusal and/or tardiness in approving its decisions, as well as the lack of state funding (Kaiafa-Gbandi et al (2012): 181, 183). The new law has re-established the Greek NAMAR (the equivalent of the HFE Authority) and it re-started its operations mid-October 2014. All Greek fertility clinics (67 in total) have in the interim been working without the necessary licence from and control of NAMAR. According to recent press announcements by the newly appointed President of NAMAR, the Authority will first and foremost focus on documenting and performing stringent controls on all the Greek fertility centres (Karlatira, P., 'Without license the 67 fertility clinics in Greece' (in Greek), Newspaper Proto Thema (15/10/2014) <http://www.protothema.gr/ugeia/article/418527/horis-adeia-oi-67-monades-upovoithoumenis-anaparagogis-sti-hora-mas/>. See also Vasiliki Aggouridi, 'NAMAR has been "resurrected"' (16/10/2014) <http://www.virus.com.gr/site/index.php/health/health-and-pharma-news-reports/item/4164-anastithike-i-ethniki-arxi-iatrikos-ypovoithoymenis-anaparagogi%E2%80%A6>.

accomplishment of pregnancy through the use of ARTs, namely the costs of IVF treatment; the costs of pregnancy clothing, drugs and any other medical treatment the pregnant woman might need; the costs for childbirth and post-natal care of the surrogate and the child; as well as any wage loss that the surrogate might incur during pregnancy and immediately after birth. NAMAR had in 2008 suggested a set payment of 10,000 euros,[24] but empirical evidence shows that the amount paid might reach 12,000 euros, or even more, since the law has introduced no mechanism for state monitoring of potential 'under the table' payments (Hatzis, 2009, 2010; Ravdas, 2010).

The judge, after reviewing all the aforementioned documentation and evidence,[25] and guided by the 'best interests' of the child principle, may approve the surrogacy agreement and authorise the fertilisation of the surrogate. Any clauses that seem to unjustifiably limit the surrogate's freedom during pregnancy are deemed invalid and illegal (article 179 *GCC*). In this light, any restrictions to the surrogate's lifestyle, or any duty to conform with a certain lifestyle, or any prohibition on her right to a lawful abortion,[26] or a non-consensual obligation for the surrogate to undergo invasive medical procedures during pregnancy, such as amniocentesis, are illegal and invalid. Immediately after the birth of the child, the surrogacy contract becomes legal and enforceable. The intended mother is presumed to be the legal mother of the child. This presumption can, however, be rebutted if the surrogate, within six months after the birth of the child, presents to the court sufficient proof that the child is in fact genetically related to her and her partner/husband (article 1464(2) *GCC*).

The court-authorised surrogacy arrangement can be described as a contract for the provision of services, operating as a mandate to the surrogate to relinquish the child to the intended mother. In case the surrogate then fails to hand the child over to the intended – and now legal – mother, the latter can apply to the court and force her to adhere to the terms of the agreement (article 946, Code of Civil Procedure). The legal mother is also entitled to compensation for breach of contract.[27] On the other hand, though this is highly unlikely, the intended mother has no right to refuse to take the child up. In the twelve years that the law has been in place, however, no application to resolve parenthood following surrogacy has reached the Greek national courts.

24 NAMAR decision, no. 36/2008 – Official Government Gazette 670/B'/16.04.2008.

25 The judge has little discretional power; he/she is required to only review the validity of the agreement and determine whether the legal conditions have been met, without investigating the reasons for choosing this method. Consequently, the court approval can be depicted as more of a formal bureaucratic procedure requirement, a 'rubber stamp', rather than a process for full judicial review of surrogacy arrangements.

26 Article 304, Greek Criminal Code (*GCrimC*). However, the surrogate that has aborted the foetus has to return any money that the intended mother might have given her up to that point, and might also be liable for compensation to the intended mother due to breach of contract.

27 If the surrogate runs away with the child, she will be held criminally liable for the criminal offence of child abduction (article 324, *GCrimC*).

Within ten days of her birth, the child must be registered in the national registry under the name of the intended/legal mother, and the name of her partner or husband, if he had consented to the procedure. Law 344/1976 governing the National Birth Registry does not introduce any special requirements regarding the registration of surrogate-born children. The legal mother must submit a copy of the court decision that had authorised the surrogacy procedure to the registrar (article 20, Law 3089/2002).[28] No other legal process, such as adoption or an application for parental order, needs to be followed.

Greek law thus offers a novel approach to surrogacy. It provides for a mechanism that is relatively simple and fast. The law allows for altruistic gestational surrogacy and is available to infertile single women (and possibly single men), married women, or women co-habiting with a (male) partner. In its current state, surrogacy is not an option for same-sex couples, but many scholars have stressed the need for a relevant legal reform. State interference in the process is limited to a court authorisation of the surrogacy agreement before the fertilisation of the surrogate. The law includes requirements for the good physical and emotional state of the surrogate carrier, and declares the paramountcy of the 'best interests' of the child. It also allows for an automatic transfer, or better yet, a presumption of maternity in favour of the intended mother based on a contract that is enforceable, and functions as a 'safety net' for the interests of the parties to the agreement, as well as the interests of the child. Finally, the Greek model protects the surrogate's autonomy rights during pregnancy, and endorses a modern approach to family, one based purely on intention, rather than biology, since the surrogate-born child might not be genetically related to either of her parents. Two potential disadvantages could be said to exist: first, there is no mechanism to ensure that the relationship between the parties is indeed altruistic (Hatzis, 2009, 2010; Stoll, 2013); and second, there is no possibility to re-evaluate the arrangement, if the situation changes after it has been authorised by the court (Stoll, 2013: 318). However, in considering the Greek model as a way of guiding reform in the UK, these issues could be considered.

The Israeli regulatory model on surrogacy

Israel can be described as 'a pronatalist society whose Jewish Israeli population will try anything in order to have a child' (Schenker, 2003: 251; Teman, 2003a: 261–2). Israeli policy seems to actively foster and promote a duty for Israeli Jews to reproduce, including through the use of ARTs, which are both legal and state-funded (Birenbaum-Carmeli, 2007; Kahn, 2000; Shalev, 1998; Stoll, 2013; Teman, 2003b). The pronatalistic ideology is deeply rooted in various religious, historical and political factors, including the centrality of the biblical directive 'to be fruitful and multiply' (Sperling, 2010); the power of Judaic authorities on society and the law (Birenbaum-Carmeli, 2007: 24); the Holocaust and immigration

28 There is no requirement for the surrogate's name to be included in the registry. The identity of any gamete donors remains undisclosed (article 1460 *GCC*).

trauma; the emotional needs of a society that is in a constant war-state (Teman, 2003b: 80); and demography politics. It is, therefore, not surprising that surrogacy in Israel is legally condoned and its practice is facilitated, although with careful state monitoring.

In 1996, the Israeli Parliament (the Knesset) passed a comprehensive law entirely devoted to surrogacy, the Surrogate Motherhood Agreements Act (hereafter 'the SMA Act'). Israel became the first country in the world to allow pre-conception surrogacy arrangements that, if approved by the government-appointed Approvals Committee, are legal and enforceable and can lead to an after-the-birth transfer of parentage to the commissioning couple. The SMA Act is designed to protect the interests of the parties to such an arrangement, and the child, doing so from a religious standpoint, and, more specifically, from a Jewish standpoint (Dorner, 2000: 194). The Act is divided into two parts: one concerning the approval of the agreement and the second regarding the determination of parentage.

The SMA Act introduces a mechanism of intense state control throughout the surrogacy process (Benshushan and Schenker, 1997). The most important features of the law are: a public committee authorises and monitors each case; surrogacy, at this point, is only available to married heterosexual couples;[29] only full surrogacy, where at least the sperm of the commissioning father is used, is permitted; the agreement is altruistic, and only reasonable expenses approved by the committee can be paid to the surrogate; the surrogate must be single or divorced, of the same religion as the commissioning couple, and not a relative of one of the commissioning parents; both the surrogate and the commissioning couple must be domiciled in Israel; the surrogate retains a very limited right to withdraw from the agreement; after the birth of the child the contract becomes enforceable; the transfer of parentage to the commissioning couple is subject to the issuance of an after-birth parentage order. Between the time immediately after the birth and the issuance of the order, the child is in the custody of the commissioning couple, but a social worker holds legal guardianship of the child.

The Approvals Committee is appointed by the Health Minister and comprises of seven members, including medical professionals, one lay member, a social worker and a clergyman (SMA Act Ch 2 S.3(a)(1)–(7)). The role of the Committee is to review all applications for surrogacy, check whether all statutory requirements relating to the surrogate or the commissioning parents have been met, and that all necessary documents have been submitted and, if so, approve agreements.

29 Under the current law, single men and women and same-sex couples cannot have a child through surrogacy in Israel, and have to travel abroad. Popular destinations for Israeli gay couples seeking surrogacy are India and, until recent changes, Thailand. If they successfully have a child through a surrogate abroad, they then must face the Israeli government's reluctance to legally recognise their children as Israeli citizens, resulting in many legal hurdles concerning the return of the child to Israel and her registration in the country's birth registers (María Victoria Rivas Llanos, 2013). The Knesset is now considering the passing of a Surrogacy Bill for singles and same-sex couples (Harkov, 2014). The decision could not have been timelier, since Indian authorities have announced that surrogacy will only be available to heterosexual couples that have been married for at least two years (Vyas, 2014).

In deciding whether to approve a certain agreement, the Committee takes into consideration the future child's welfare (Ch. 2 S.5(2)–(3)). If the couple proceeds to the fertilisation of the surrogate without the Committee's approval, penalties of up to one year in prison can be incurred (Ch. 3 S.19(a)–(b)).

The requirement that the surrogate must either be single or divorced (Ch. 2 S.2(3)(a)) is for the prevention of potential adultery. As Shalev (1998: 65) explains, this requirement is based on the religious legal (*halakhic*) principle that a child born within marriage that is not genetically related to the woman's husband is a *mamzer* (a bastard). A *mamzer* will have to face the consequence to later be only able to marry a *mamzerim* or convert. However, the Act provides an exception to the requirement of the surrogate being unmarried. If the commissioning couple has made reasonable efforts to find an unmarried potential surrogate, but has failed, the Committee might still approve their agreement (Ch. 2 S.2(3)(a)). Moreover, the surrogate must not be related to either of the intended parents (Ch. 2 S.2(3)(b)). The reason for this is the prevention of coercion potentially exerted on a female relative to act as a surrogate (Schenker, 2003). Surprisingly, though, adoptive relatives are permitted to act as surrogates and, thus, there exists the danger that they might be emotionally pressured to enter into the agreement in an effort to 'repay' for the benefit of being adopted (Frenkel, 2001: 611).

Another important requirement of the Act is that the surrogate must be of the same religion as the commissioning mother. This is because Jewishness is determined matrilineally (Shalev, 1998) and, hence, a Jewish child must have been gestated by a Jewish woman. This is, again, based on *halakhic* rationale, as is the requirement for the sperm of the commissioning father to be used for the surrogate conception (Ch. 2 S.2(4)). According to Shalev, Israeli family law provides that '[p]aternity is established at conception' (1998: 68) and, therefore, the child must be genetically related to her father. Shalev contends that this also 'stems... from *halakhic* considerations as to the certainty of paternity...[b]ut at the same time it poses the genetic continuity of the man at the centre of attention' (1998: 92). Based on the *mamzerut* rule, the commissioning couple is prohibited from using the surrogate's ova for the fertilisation. As becomes apparent, the Israeli surrogacy-conception is a fully medicalised procedure necessarily involving IVF, as is the case in Greece.

Another similar feature of the Israeli law is that, together with the surrogacy agreement, the intended couple must submit medical reports proving the inability of the intended mother to achieve pregnancy or bring it to term, and the suitability of the potential surrogate. They must also submit the results of psychological assessments of the parties. The difference in Israel is that the intended parents must additionally provide a statement that they have received professional counselling, in which they explored other alternatives to parenthood.

If all requirements have been met, the Approvals Committee will authorise the agreement. It then continues to supervise the surrogacy procedure by reviewing and approving the payment of 'reasonable expenses' including 'medical costs, costs for insurance, legal consultation, loss of time and income, suffering or any other reasonable expenses'. Such a broad approach to the content of 'reasonable expenses' raises concerns about the pure altruistic character of the arrangement that seems to more closely resemble a commercial arrangement. Nevertheless, any payments must be scrutinised and approved. Payments to intermediaries are, however, legal: the amount to be paid is left to the discretion of the commissioning couple and the surrogacy broker.

The most important similarity between the Israeli and the Greek model is that pre-approved surrogacy arrangements are legal and enforceable. The surrogate has an express statutory right to have an abortion (Ch 4 S.18), if she wishes to, but, if she decides to continue with the pregnancy and childbirth, she must then relinquish the newborn to the commissioning parents. This takes place in the presence of a social worker, who must be notified of the event of the delivery within twenty-four hours. From then onwards, the child will be in the custody of the commissioning couple, who must apply within seven days after the delivery to the court for a parentage order so they may be acknowledged as the child's legal parents. Until the granting of the order by the court, legal guardianship belongs to the social worker, and the parties retain their right to change their minds and withdraw from the agreement (Ch 3 SS.13–14). They will, however, have to convince the court of a change in circumstances that justifies that, and the welfare officer must agree that this is in the child's interests (Ch 3 S.11(b)). To this end, the surrogate has very limited chances to renege on the agreement and keep the child. After the parentage order has been made, the Act does not permit withdrawal from the surrogacy agreement. The surrogate-born child's birth must, however, be entered into a special register (Ch 3 S.16(b)). As Shalev notes, this creates 'the danger of stigmatisation of the children' born following surrogacy (1998: 90).

In conclusion, the Israeli surrogacy law is unique, not only because it provides such a complete response to surrogacy; its provisions are also in line with the particular cultural and *halakhic* traditions of Israel. It has facilitated freedom to enter surrogacy arrangements, albeit within state-defined limits and controls in every step of the process. These are thought to effectively protect the interests of both the parties to the arrangement and the child, and also 'promote the state's religious and pronatalistic agendas' (Stoll, 2013). However, Israeli law does not make surrogacy available to same-sex couples, or single parents. This is now, though, under consideration by the Israeli Parliament, and it is to be hoped that important changes are forthcoming (see Cassidy, 2014; Oryszczuk, 2014).[30]

Conclusion

Prohibiting payments for surrogacy in the UK in the way the Brazier Committee recommended was always likely to be counter-productive in the sense that it

30 Patricia Cassidy, 'Israel's Cabinet approves surrogacy for same-sex couples and single people', BioNews 757, 09/06/2014 (accessed 20/07/2014): <http://www.bionews.org.uk/page_427299.asp>; Stephen Oryszczuk, 'Israel surrogacy for gay couples one step closer', Jewish News Online, 28/10/2014 (accessed 3/11/2014).

would drive more people to 'underground' and completely unregulated surrogacy services (Freeman, 1999). These days, any restrictions on surrogacy, whether on access, payments or even to the acquisition of legal parenthood is likely to drive those who want to use surrogacy to find ways around their particular problem. People will turn increasingly to the internet to find surrogates in this country via 'introduction sites' or social media, resulting in them making arrangements that are potentially illicit and almost certainly unwise (see Jackson, this volume).[31] Beyond that, people seeking 'easy' access to surrogates are likely to continue to go overseas, to those destinations where it is known surrogacy can be bought for a price, via agencies or businesses that facilitate arrangements on a commercial basis and where the surrogate herself will be incentivised by the prospect of payment. If we are genuinely concerned about the harms that internationalised surrogacy may bring, such as exploitation of potentially vulnerable or underprivileged women who act as surrogates in countries where they have little or no protection, or the problems that conflicting laws on legal parenthood and nationality have been shown to bring about for the children born from such arrangements,[32] then perhaps making surrogacy more attractive in the UK is the answer.

Further, it would appear that at least in some instances, there is evidence that not only those commissioning surrogates but also some agents acting on their behalf in the UK simply do not know enough about the law as it stands.[33] To have your dreams of parenthood shattered when you have done things right but someone else who you seek advice from or you place your trust in has not must be incredibly difficult. However, the hardships encountered in such cases would arguably be removed if we were to move to a more facilitative regulatory model, perhaps containing some aspects found in the Greek and/or Israeli models, but which certainly must at least consider the idea that parenthood might presumptively rest with the commissioning parents, that payments (perhaps within a regulatory framework) be recognised for what they are and that dedicated agencies and advisors ought to be able to receive payment for professionalised advice. When judges retrospectively authorise payments beyond reasonable expenses on a routine basis, because not to do so would contravene the principle that the child's best interests are paramount, and even go so far as to extend the period of time in which a Parental Order can be applied for from that outlined in statute, this is surely an indication that our laws on surrogacy are deeply flawed, or not adequate to meet

31 Note also that 'partial' surrogacy arrangements, where the surrogate uses her own egg and is inseminated outside of a clinical setting, are totally unregulated by UK law, indicating another potential danger of too-restrictive regulation.

32 Notably, France has recently been held to have been in violation of Article 8 of the European Convention on Human Rights in its failure to grant citizenship and/or recognition of legal parenthood to children born to surrogates in the US: *Mennesson v France* (application no. 65192/11) and *Labassee v France* (no. 65941/11). French law is set to change accordingly, though the actual practice of surrogacy will remain illegal.

33 See e.g. MacFarlane J's comments in *Re G* (Surrogacy: Foreign Domicile) [2007] EWHC 2814 (fam), at [29] and the recent case *JP v LP & Others* (Rev 1) [2014] EWHC 595 (Fam).

the demands posed by twenty-first century surrogacy. Momentum for change is picking up, with increasing academic criticism mirrored by those experiencing surrogacy in day-to-day practice (Gamble, 2014; Ghevaert, 2014; Prosser, 2013), and with surrogacy taken up as an issue in Parliament in October of 2014,[34] with indications from the Minister for Public Health (Jane Ellison MP) that government will consider whether UK surrogacy law should be reviewed, after hearing opinions from other MPs. The European Parliament has already commissioned its own study on surrogacy laws and practice across Europe (McCandless et al, 2013; also see Hague Conference on Private International Law, 2014), further indicating that surrogacy law in this country is ripe for review.[35] The leader of one of the main political parties, in the run up to the 2015 General Election, also indicated that reform of surrogacy laws should be undertaken (Swinford, 2015).

There will never be universal agreement about surrogacy. Our nearest neighbours on the European continent think it abhorrent and even protest about it on the streets. But all recent signs indicate that the law regulating surrogacy in the UK is not 'fit for purpose' and that a big opportunity for informed debate leading to reform was missed when the 1990 Act was updated. Reform is necessary in order to offer commissioning parents from the UK the safest and fairest route to parenthood through surrogacy as well as to protect the welfare of children and it may be that in considering future directions, we should consider all options, as well as look to learn from the facilitative legislative models of Greece and Israel.

References

Aggouridi, V., (2014) 'NAMAR has been "resurrected"' (16 October 2014, Virus.com).

Ahmad, A. and Brooks, J., (2015) 'Thai surrogates battle for babies birthed for Japanese millionaire' *BioNews* 786 (19 January 2015, Progress Educational Trust).

Benshushan, A., and Schenker, J.G., (1997) 'Legitimizing Surrogacy in Israel' 12(8) *Human Reproduction* 1832.

Birenbaum-Carmeli, D., (2007) 'The Politics of "The Natural Family" in Israel: State policy and kinship ideologies' 69 *Social Science & Medicine* 1018.

Brazier Committee Report, (1998) *Surrogacy: Review for Health Ministers of Current Arrangements for Payments and Regulation, Report of the Review Team* (London: HMSO) Cm 4068.

Brilliant Beginnings, (2014) 'UK Parliament debates surrogacy reform' (15 October 2014) <http://www.brilliantbeginnings.co.uk/blog/uk-parliament-debates-surrogacy-reform>

British Medical Association, (1996) *Changing Conceptions of Motherhood: The Practice of Surrogacy in Britain* (London: British Medical Association).

Callaghan, S. and Newson, A., (2014) 'Surrogacy, motherhood and Baby Gammy' *BioNews* 766 (11 August 2014, Progress Educational Trust).

34 Hansard, 14 October 2014, Column 1WH.

35 Additionally, The Hague Conference on Private International Law has been conducting a long-term investigation into the possibility of creating a new *global* convention on international surrogacy, taking into account information gleaned from those working with surrogacy about issues arising from international surrogacy arrangements. It recently published its report on the 'desirability and feasibility' of taking the project forward (Hague Conference on Private International Law, 2014).

Cassidy, P., (2014) 'Israel's Cabinet approves surrogacy for same-sex couples and single people' *BioNews* 757 (9 June 2014, Progress Educational Trust).

Crawshaw, M., Blyth, E. and van den Akker, O., (2012) 'The changing profile of surrogacy in the UK – Implications for national and international policy and practice' 34(2) *Journal of Social Welfare and Family Law* 267.

Department of Health (2005) *Review of the Human Fertilisation and Embryology Act: A public consultation* (London: Department of Health).

Dorner, D., (2000) 'Jurisprudence in the age of biotechnology: An Israeli case analysis' 913(1) *Annals of the New York Academy of Sciences* 188.

Fox, M., (2009) 'The Human Fertilisation and Embryology Act 2008: Tinkering at the Margins' 17(3) *Feminist Legal Studies* 333.

Freeman, M., (1999) 'Does surrogacy have a future after Brazier?' 7 *Medical Law Review* 1.

Frenkel, D.A., (2001) 'Legal regulation of surrogate motherhood in Israel' 20(4) *Medicine & Law* 605.

Gènéthique, (2014) 'Greece. The New Eldorado for infertile couples' (11/08/2014) [Online] <http://www.genethique.org/en/greece-new-eldorado-infertile-couples-61946.html>

Ghevaert, L., (2014) 'UK surrogacy gone wrong' *BioNews* 746 (17 March 2014, Progress Educational Trust).

Golombok, S., MacCallum, F., Murray, C., Lycett, E. and Jadva, V., (2005) 'Surrogacy families: parental functioning, parent-child relationships and children's psychological development at age 2' 47(2) *Journal of Child Psychology and Psychiatry* 213.

Golombok, S., Casey, P., Readings, J., Blake, L., Marks, A. and Jadva, V., (2011) 'Families created through surrogacy: Mother-child relationships and children's psychological adjustment at age 7' 47(6) *Developmental Psychology* 1579.

Hague Conference on Private International Law, (2014) 'The Desirability and Feasibility of Further Work on the Parentage/Surrogacy Project' *Preliminary Document No 3 B of April 2014*.

Harkov, L., (2014) 'Ministers approve surrogacy for singles, same-sex couples' *The Jerusalem Post* (6 January 2014).

Hatzis, A., (2009) 'From soft to hard paternalism and back: the regulation of surrogate motherhood in Greece' 49(3) *Portuguese Economic Journal* 217.

Hatzis, A., (2010) 'The Regulation of Surrogate Motherhood in Greece' [Online] <http://users.uoa.gr/~ahatzis/Surrogacy.pdf>

Horsey, K., (2010) 'Challenging presumptions: Legal parenthood and surrogacy arrangements' 4(22) *Child and Family Law Quarterly* 449.

Horsey, K. and Sheldon, S., (2012) 'Still hazy after all these years: The law regulating surrogacy' 20(1) *Medical Law Review* 67.

House of Commons Science and Technology Committee, (2005) *Human Reproductive Technologies and the Law* (Fifth Report of Session 2004–2005, HC 7–1).

House of Lords, House of Commons Joint Committee on the Human Tissue and Embryos (Draft) Bill, (2007) Vol. 1: Report, Session 2006–2007, HL 169–1, HC 630–1 (July 2007).

Jackson, E., (2001) *Regulating Reproduction: Law, Technology and Reproductive Autonomy* (Oxford: Hart Publishing).

Jadva, V., Casey, P., Blake, L. and Golombok, S., (2012) 'Surrogacy families ten years on: Relationship with the surrogate, decisions over disclosure and children's understanding of their surrogacy origins' 27 *Human Reproduction* 3008.

Kahn, S.M., (2000) *Reproducing Jews: A Cultural Account of Assisted Conception in Israel* (Durham: Duke University Press).

Kaiafa-Gbandi, M., Kounougeri-Manoledaki, E. and Symeonidou-Kastanidou, E. (eds.), (2012) *Assisted Reproduction in Human Reproduction: 10 Years after the Implementation of La 3089/2002* (in Greek) (Athens-Thessaloniki, Greece: Sakkoulas Publications).

Karlatira, P., (2014) 'Without license the 67 fertility clinics in Greece' (in Greek), *Newspaper Proto Thema* (15 October 2014) <http://www.protothema.gr/ugeia/article/418527/horis-adeia-oi-67-monades-upovoithoumenis-anaparagogis-sti-hora-mas/>

Kounougeri-Manoledaki, E., (2010) *Medically Assisted Reproduction: The Right of an Unmarried and Single Man to Have a Child through Surrogacy* (in Greek) (Athens-Thessaloniki, Greece: Sakkoulas Publications).

Kounougeri-Manoledaki, E., (2005) *Assisted Reproduction and Family Law. The Greek regime: Laws 3089/2002 and 3305/2005* (in Greek) (Athens-Thessaloniki, Greece: Sakkoulas Publications).

Kovacs, S., 'La Grece, L' Eldorado de la GPA', *Le Figaro* (3 October 2014) (in French) <http://www.lefigaro.fr/mon-figaro/2014/10/03/10001-20141003ARTFIG00288-en-grece-l-eldorado-de-la-gpa.php>

McCandless, J. et al, (2013) *A Comparative Study on the Regime of Surrogacy in EU Member States*), European Parliament. Full text available at: <http://www.europarl.europa.eu/RegData/etudes/etudes/join/2013/474403/IPOL-JURI_ET(2013)474403_EN.pdf>

McCandless, J. and Sheldon, S., (2010) 'The Human Fertilisation and Embryology Act (2008) and the tenacity of the sexual family model' 73(2) *Modern Law Review* 175.

Millbank, J., (2014) 'Rethinking 'commercial' surrogacy in Australia' *Journal of Bioethical Inquiry* (July 2014).

Natalie Gamble Associates, (2014) 'Court unlocks "nonsensical" law for surrogacy parents who miss six month deadline to secure parental status' (NGA Blog) <http://www.nataliegambleassociates.co.uk/blog/2014/10/03/court-unlocks-nonsensical-law-for-surrogacy-parents-who-miss-six-month-deadline-to-secure-parental-status/>

Oryszczuk, S., 2014 'Israel surrogacy for gay couples one step closer' *Jewish News Online* (28 October 2014).

Prosser, H., (2013) 'Surrogacy overseas – legal and ethical issues', Speech delivered to British Infertility Counsellors Association (BICA) at the annual conference of the European Society for Human Reproduction and Embryology (6 July 2013).

Ravdas, P., (2010) 'Surrogate Motherhood in Greece: Statistical Data Derived from Court Decisions', working paper.

Rivas Llanos, M. V., (2013) 'Israeli health minister moves to lift surrogacy restrictions for singles and gay couples' *BioNews* 735 (Progress Educational Trust, 16 December 2013).

Rozenberg, J., (2014) 'High Court put justice before statutory requirements in surrogacy case' *The Guardian* 9 October 2014.

Schenker, J.G., (2003) 'Legal aspects of ART practice in Israel' 20(7) *Journal of Assisted Reproduction and Genetics* 250.

Shalev, C., (1998) 'Halakha and patriarchal motherhood – An anatomy of the new Israeli surrogacy law' 5 *Social Security, Journal of Welfare and Social Security Studies,* Special English edition 74.

Sharpe, J., (2014) 'Thai parliament votes to outlaw commercial surrogacy' *BioNews* 782 (1 December 2014, Progress Educational Trust).

Sperling, D., (2010) 'Commanding the "Be Fruitful and Multiply" Directive: Reproductive Ethics, Law and Policy in Israel' 19 *Cambridge Quarterly Healthcare Ethics* 363.

Stoll, J., (2013) *Surrogacy Arrangements and Legal Parenthood. Swedish Law in a Comparative Context,*

Uppsala Universitet. Full text available at: <http://www.diva-portal.org/smash/get/diva2:649875/FULLTEXT01.pdf>
Swinford, S., (2015) 'Nick Clegg: Consider letting gay couples pay surrogates' *The Telegraph* (10th April 2015).
Teman, E., (2003a) '"Knowing" the Surrogate Body in Israel' in Cook, R., Sclater, S. and Kaganas, F., (eds), *Surrogate Motherhood: International Perspectives* (Oxford: Hart Publishing).
Teman, E., (2003b) 'The medicalization of "nature" in the "artificial body": Surrogate motherhood in Israel' 17(1) *Medical Anthropology Quarterly* 78.
Trokanas, T., (2011) *Human Reproduction – Personal Autonomy and its Limits* (in Greek) (Athens-Thessaloniki, Greece: Sakkoulas Publications).
Van Zyl, L. and Walker, R., (2013) 'Beyond altruistic and commercial contract motherhood: The professional model' 27(7) *Bioethics* 373.
Vyas, K., 'Indian law forbids same-sex surrogate parents' Al Jazeera America (16 June 2014).
Warnock Committee Report, (1984) *Committee of Inquiry into Human Fertilisation and Embryology, Report* (London: HMSO) Cmnd 9314.
Warnock, M., (2002) *Making Babies: Is There a Right to Have Children?* (Oxford: Oxford University Press).

9 Access to genetic and biographical history in donor conception: An analysis of recent trends and future possibilities

*Eric Blyth and Lucy Frith**

Introduction

According to French sociologist Simone Bateman Novaes (1998), 'instrumental insemination' undertaken by medical practitioners to facilitate conception in a woman has been practised in Europe since at least early in the nineteenth century. In a celebrated case reported to have taken place in 1884, Professor William Pancoast inseminated the wife of a man rendered sterile after contracting gonorrhoea, using sperm provided by his 'best looking' medical student. The woman had been anaesthetised and it appears that she never knew about the procedure, although her husband was told – but advised never to disclose what had transpired – as were Pancoast's medical students who witnessed the procedure (no other instances of insemination taking place in the presence of witnesses have ever been reported). Twenty-five years later, one of these former students, Dr Adison Hard, reported Pancoast's ministrations in a letter to a medical journal, claiming to have met the (by now) young man who had been conceived as a result (Hard, 1909).

For many years, the approach espoused by Pancoast, comprising both anonymity and secrecy, uniformly characterised donor insemination (Hurley, 2004) and also came to characterise the donation of oocytes and embryos once the feasibility of these procedures became established. During the past 30 years, however, coinciding with the rapid development of IVF and associated assisted reproductive technologies (ART) and their diverse applications, a variety of cultural, legal, ethical and religious traditions have accounted for the varied ways in which gamete and embryo donation are treated in different countries. This ranges from complete prohibition of all donor procedures in Italy (reflecting the influence of Roman Catholic opposition) – although the law supporting this ban has been challenged – and in certain Islamic nations (e.g. Egypt, Libya, Saudi Arabia, Senegal and Tunisia – although Iran, dubbed 'the Egg Donation Capital of the Muslim World', has developed innovative oocyte donation programmes (Hazrat-e Maryam Fertility Center, undated)), to relatively permissive arrangements that allow all forms of donor conception – often on an overtly commercial basis (e.g. India, Israel and the United States) (International Federation of Fertility Societies, 2013).

While in most jurisdictions in which donor conception is practised anonymity remains a key principle, a small number of jurisdictions have formalised systems requiring donors of gametes or embryos to agree to the release of their identity to any offspring who requests this (usually when reaching the age of majority). In recognition of the changing legal landscape and the accessibility of information via the internet, the Ethics Committee of the American Society for Reproductive Medicine (ASRM) has advised that donor programmes: 'should make it clear to donors that they cannot give guarantees regarding immunity from future contact by offspring' (Ethics Committee of the ASRM, 2014: 676). Opinion regarding the advisability of parents of donor-conceived children telling their children about their conception has also changed. For example, in 1993, the ASRM encouraged anonymous sperm donation (ASRM, 1993); by 2002 it indicated an acceptance of directed, known gamete donation if all parties agree (ASRM, 1998, 2002), and in 2013 it 'strongly encouraged ... [parental] ... disclosure to donor-conceived persons of the use of donor gametes or embryos in their conception' (Ethics Committee of the ASRM, 2013). In the UK, the statutory regulator of clinical assisted conception services, the Human Fertilisation and Embryology Authority (HFEA), initially adopted a neutral stance regarding parental disclosure, requiring centres to take account of 'a child's potential need to know about their origins and whether or not the prospective parents are prepared for the questions which may arise while the child is growing up' (HFEA, 2001: 3.14a). However, in 2005, it changed tack, advising clinics to 'encourage and prepare patients to be open with their children from an early age about the circumstances of their conception' (HFEA, 2005a, 2005b). When the Human Fertilisation and Embryology (HFE) Act was revised in 2008, legislators took the opportunity to give this specific guidance statutory reinforcement, emphasising:

(a) the importance of informing any resulting child at an early age that the child results from the gametes of a person who is not a parent of the child, and
(b) suitable methods of informing such a child of that fact (Human Fertilisation and Embryology Act 2008 s14(3)(6C)).

This chapter examines the regulatory regimes that actively facilitate a donor-conceived individual's ability to learn the identity of his or her donor: Austria, Finland, the Netherlands, New Zealand, Norway, Sweden, Switzerland, the UK and the Australian states of New South Wales, Victoria and Western Australia. Details of relevant legislation in these jurisdictions, including the implementation dates, are summarised in Table 9.1. Space precludes a detailed discussion of the factors contributing to these shifts in greater openness and availability of information about the donor or the arguments for them here (see Blyth, this volume). Rather, the chapter charts the regulatory provisions of those countries and states that require 'non-anonymous' gamete and embryo donation, and identifies the similarities and differences between these different regulatory models, considering the following areas:

1. The organisations that maintain, and manage access to, donor conception records;

2. The length of time that records need to be kept;
3. The age at which a donor-conceived person can obtain the identity of his or her donor;
4. Provisions for earlier access to the donor's identity for a 'special reason' (e.g. health, disability);
5. Ability of a parent/guardian to request the identity of a donor on behalf of a child who is a legal minor;
6. Provisions for access to information prior to the introduction of legislation mandating disclosure of donor identity;
7. Grounds for withholding identifying information when requested;
8. Limits on the number of children who may be born using the gametes of a single donor;
9. Provisions for counselling regarding disclosure of donor information to parents, donors and donor-conceived individuals;
10. Rights of donors to know about offspring born following their donation; and
11. Linking donor conception to birth registration.

In addition we discuss proposals in South Australia and Kenya (where consultations are taking place at the time of writing to establish a formalised registration system) and more limited provisions in Germany and Washington State (US) requiring donors to be identifiable to their offspring, as well as recent developments in the Republic of Ireland. The chapter concludes by outlining further provisions that may be introduced to facilitate access to genetic and biographical information following donor conception.

Organisations that hold information about gamete and embryo donation

In most jurisdictions, a central register is maintained by a government department or agency. In Finland, New South Wales and Norway, this is the government health department or ministry. In the UK and Western Australia, the responsible authority is the regulatory body for ART: the HFEA and the Western Australian Reproductive Technology Council, respectively. In Switzerland, the responsible agency is the federal authority for civil affairs and in the Netherlands, it is the responsibility of a foundation created and financed by central government (Stichting donorgegevens kunstmatige bevruchting). In New Zealand and Victoria, the register is held by the Registry for Births, Deaths and Marriages (BDM). Only Austria and Sweden have no central register; there, doctors and clinics providing donor services are required to maintain relevant records.

Length of time that information on donor registers needs to be kept

Several jurisdictions stipulate specific lengths of time that information must be kept – this is 30 years in Austria and Finland (although names of donors held

Table 9.1 Jurisdictions requiring a gamete or embryo donor to agree to the disclosure of his or her identity to any offspring

Jurisdiction	*Legislation*	*Date of implementation*	*Permitted donor procedures*
Austria	Fortpflanzungsmedizingesetz. 275 Bundesgesetz; FMedG 1992[1]	1 July 1992	Sperm donation
Finland	Act on Assisted Fertility Treatments (1237/2006)	1 September 2007	Embryo, oocyte, sperm donation
The Netherlands	Wet donorgegevens kunstmatige bevruchting 2002[2]	1 June 2004	Embryo, oocyte, sperm donation
New South Wales	Assisted Reproductive Technology Act 2007	1 January 2010	Embryo, oocyte, sperm donation
New Zealand	Human Assisted Reproductive Technology (HART) Act 2004	22 August 2005	Embryo, oocyte, sperm donation
Norway	Act on Biotechnology 2003	1 January 2005	Sperm donation
Sweden	Lag om insemination 1984[3] (replaced by Genetic Integrity Act 2006)	18 March 1985	Oocyte, sperm donation
Switzerland	Federal Act on Medically Assisted Procreation of 18 December 1998 – FF 1996 III, 197 (LPMA)	1 January 2001	Sperm donation
United Kingdom	Human Fertilisation and Embryology Authority (Disclosure of Donor Information) Regulations 2004;	1 April 2005	Embryo, oocyte, sperm donation
	Human Fertilisation and Embryology Act 2008	1 October 2009	
Victoria	Infertility Treatment Act 1995 (amended by the Assisted Reproductive Treatment Act 2008)	1 January 1998; 1 January 2010	Embryo, oocyte, sperm donation
	Assisted Reproductive (Further Amendment) Bill 2013	July 2015	
Western Australia	Human Reproductive Technology Amendment Act 2004	1 December 2004	Embryo, oocyte, sperm donation

1 English translation: Reproductive Medicine Act
2 English translation: The Artificial Insemination (Donor Information) Act
3 English translation: Law on Insemination

on the National Supervisory Authority for Welfare and Health [Valvira] donor register are kept indefinitely); 70 years in Sweden; 80 years in the Netherlands and Switzerland. In New Zealand, information must be kept indefinitely by BDM and for 50 years by service providers, although in practice, most clinics will also keep it indefinitely. In Victoria and Western Australia, destruction of these records at any time is prohibited. Since no time limit is specified in legislation in New South Wales or the UK, it may be assumed that in both jurisdictions no records will be destroyed. Similarly in Norway, no time limit is specified; the information is kept 'as long as it is needed' (according to communication from the Norwegian Directorate of Health), that is, as long as a donor-conceived person can claim their right to their donor's identity including, therefore, for a period beyond the death of the donor.

The age at which a donor-conceived person can obtain the identity of his or her donor

Several jurisdictions specify the age at which a donor-conceived person may learn their donor's identity: 16 years in Austria, the Netherlands and Western Australia; and 18 in Finland, New South Wales, New Zealand, Norway, Switzerland and the UK. In Sweden, although no age is specified, in practice this is assumed to be around 18 years (i.e. at maturity). In Victoria, while 18 is the 'default' age for accessing a donor's identity, a younger donor conceived person who is aged under 18 years can learn her/his donor's identity with the consent of her/his parent/guardian, or with a written opinion from a counsellor that (s)he is sufficiently mature to understand the consequences of receiving the information.

Provisions for earlier access to the donor's identity for a 'special reason' (e.g. health, disability)

In specific circumstances, some jurisdictions allow access to the donor's identity at an earlier age. In Austria, this is for medical reasons only. Similarly in the UK, the identity of a donor could be disclosed by order of a court, either in the 'interests of justice' (s34 of the 1990 Act, as amended) or where a clinic is subject to civil proceedings following the birth of a child with a congenital disability. In deciding whether to make such an order, the court must consider the welfare of any children who might be affected by the disclosure. In New Zealand, in 'exceptional circumstances' (that are not defined and have not been tested) a donor-conceived person aged 16 or 17 years can apply to the Family Court to be treated as though he or she is aged 18.[1] A judge will need to be satisfied that it is in the best interests of the individual to have access to the information requested. In Switzerland, before reaching the age of 18, a donor-conceived person can request the donor's identity if (s)he can demonstrate a 'legitimate interest'.[2] Before providing this information, the authority must, if possible, inform the donor of the request and ascertain his intentions regarding any personal contact.

Ability of a parent/guardian to request the identity of a donor on behalf of a child who is a legal minor

Four jurisdictions only (New South Wales, New Zealand, Victoria and Western Australia) allow the parent or guardian of a donor-conceived child who is a legal minor to access the donor's identity, and only where certain conditions are met.

1 Information received from Joi Ellis – NZ Fertility counsellor at Fertility Associates.

2 English translation of Art 27(2) Federal Act on Medically Assisted Procreation of 18 December 1998.

In New South Wales, a parent or guardian can only request identifying information in order to save a child's life or prevent serious damage to a child's physical or psychological health. As regards the latter, a medical practitioner or psychologist must certify that psychological damage is likely to occur. In New Zealand, a parent or guardian of a donor conceived person who is under 18 years may request, and be provided with, information about the donor from either a service provider or BDM. The parent or guardian must be advised 'of the desirability of counselling' and the donor must be advised that the information has been requested. In Victoria, a parent or guardian can apply to the Central Register and must undergo counselling before any request may be granted. The donor's identity may only be disclosed with their consent. This provision is reported to have proven very popular with parents who wish to thank the donor personally and/or parents who wish to start information exchange/contact with the donor sooner rather than later Victorian Assisted Reproductive Technology Authority (VARTA) (VARTA, personal communication, 16 March 2014).

In Western Australia, the parents or guardians of a donor-conceived child aged under 16 years may consent on their own behalf and on behalf of their child to sharing of identifying information. All parties must give their consent to the release of information and agree not to disclose the identity of anyone who has not given consent. Counselling must be undertaken before this information may be released.

Provisions for access to information prior to the introduction of legislation mandating disclosure of donor identity

Seven jurisdictions (Finland, New South Wales, New Zealand, the Netherlands, the United Kingdom, Victoria and Western Australia) have provisions to facilitate information exchange and contact between a donor-conceived individual and their donor – where mutually agreed – where a donor procedure took place prior to the introduction of legislation mandating disclosure of donor identity. In the Netherlands, New South Wales, New Zealand, the UK, Victoria and Western Australia, arrangements have also been introduced to facilitate information exchange and contact if desired between donor half-siblings, subject to mutual agreement.

In Finland, a donor-conceived person aged 18 years or older may ask the treating clinic to contact the donor and request her/his agreement to register her/his identity on the donor register, although the clinic has no obligation to do so. Regardless of the donor's agreement to identity disclosure, any non-identifying information that (s)he has given to the clinic can be provided to her/his offspring.

In New South Wales, the Health Central Register enables a donor-conceived individual conceived before 1 January 2010 and who has attained 18 years of age and a gamete donor who donated before 1 January 2010 voluntarily to register information about themselves and seek non-identifying and identifying information about others to whom they are related as a result of donation. A parent of a donor-conceived child who was born before 1 January 2010 can apply to the Central Register for non-identifying information, including medical history and other personal information, about their child's donor. On receipt of a request for information, the Ministry of Health will initially contact the treating hospital or clinic to ascertain whether a match can be made with the donor and/or other donor-conceived offspring. Privacy regulations preclude any active approach by the Ministry of Health to seek consent to disclose information that has not already been released. No information may be divulged by the Ministry of Health to a third party unless express permission has been given both as regards the information itself and the potential recipient.

New Zealand's Human Assisted Reproductive Technology (HART) Register also functions as a Voluntary Contact Register for people involved in a donor procedure undertaken prior to 21 August 2005. Most New Zealand clinics began recording information about donors in the 1990s, about the same time that they started restricting recruitment to donors who were willing to be identified (New Zealand Law Commission, 2005). Individuals conceived as the result of a donor procedure during this period may be able to access information from clinics, although there is no legal obligation either on clinics to release the information or on donors to agree to being identified. Generally, individuals conceived before 1990 will be entirely reliant on the voluntary register for any information that they do not already possess. The HART Register also enables donor-conceived siblings and the parent or guardian of a donor-conceived person younger than 18 years of age to share identifying information by mutual consent.

In 2010, Fiom, a national social work agency in the Netherlands with experience in counselling adopted persons and birth mothers, opened a voluntary DNA database in cooperation with the Canisius Wilhelmina Hospital in Nijmegen, for donor conceived people born before 1 June 2004, their donors and donor half-siblings.

UK Donorlink (UKDL), a voluntary contact register, was established in the UK in April 2004 to facilitate information exchange and contact by mutual consent between an individual conceived as a result of a donor procedure undertaken in the UK before 1 August 1991, their donor and any half-siblings. UKDL used DNA profiling to establish a genetic link and provided dedicated counselling services to those using its services (Crawshaw and Marshall, 2008; Crawshaw et al., 2013). On 1 April 2013, UKDL was replaced by the Donor Conceived Register.[3] In addition, in April 2010, the HFEA launched the Donor Sibling Link, which helps donor-conceived people conceived after 1 August 1991 and who are aged over 18 years to find out if anyone else shares the same donor and if so, to share contact information by mutual consent.

Victoria's Infertility Treatment Act 1995 established a Voluntary Register to enable donors, donor-conceived people, their parents, descendants and relatives to voluntarily record identifying details or additional information not included on the Central Register (e.g. photographs and messages). Information on the voluntary register may only be released in accordance with the wishes of the person who registered the information. A 2001 amendment

3 <http://www.donorconceivedregister.org.uk/>

to the Act extended the scope of the Voluntary Register to donor procedures taking place prior to 1 July 1988. In August 2014, the Victorian Parliament approved the Assisted Reproductive (Further Amendment) Bill 2013 which will take effect in July 2015 to extend to individuals conceived with gametes donated before 1988 the ability to obtain non-identifying information about their donor from the Central Register, and identifying information if their donor consents, that is, the rights to information held on the Central Register currently enjoyed by individuals conceived with gametes donated between 1988 and 1997.

In Western Australia, the Reproductive Technology Registers assist information exchange for donors, donor-conceived adults (i.e. those aged at least 18 years of age) and parents of a donor-conceived child who is younger than 18 years, where the donor procedure took place before 2004. The Voluntary Register rules require the written consent of the individual to whom the information relates to be given for the release of any identifying information. In addition, an applicant for identifying information must also receive counselling.

Grounds for withholding the identifying information when requested

Two jurisdictions, New Zealand and Victoria, permit some discretion as to the release of identifying information when requested to do so. In New Zealand, the clinic or BDM may refuse to disclose the information, if satisfied on reasonable grounds that the disclosure is likely to endanger any person. In Victoria, a more general concern regarding a potentially adverse effect on the welfare and interests or the health and safety of a relevant party could result in the information being withheld.

Limits on the number of children who may be born using the gametes of a single donor

With the exception of New Zealand, all jurisdictions impose an upper limit on either the number of children or the number of families that include children who may be born using the gametes of a single donor. Jurisdictions that apply a maximum limit on the number of children are Norway and Switzerland (eight) and the Netherlands (25). Jurisdictions that apply a limit on the number of families are: Austria (three); Finland and Western Australia (five); New South Wales (five women, including the donor's own partner/wife. A lesbian couple count as two women); Sweden (six); the United Kingdom (10); and Victoria (10, which includes the donor's own family). In New Zealand, clinics set their own limits, following guidelines issued by the Fertility of Australia Reproductive Technology Accreditation Committee (2010) and New Zealand standards 8181. On the basis of these, Fertility Associates, New Zealand's largest provider of ART services, imposes a maximum of 10 children in five families (Fertility Associates, personal communication, 17 December 2013).

Provisions for counselling regarding disclosure of donor information to parents, donors and donor-conceived individuals

With the exception of Austria, Norway and Sweden, all jurisdictions have established arrangements for the availability of counselling for donor-conceived individuals in conjunction with their request to discover the identity of their donor.

Rights of donors to know about offspring born following their donations

Donors have a right to know about children born following their donations as follows: in Sweden they can ascertain the number of offspring; in New South Wales and Victoria, the year of birth and gender; in New Zealand, the United Kingdom and Western Australia, the number, gender and year of birth. Conversely, donors in Austria, Finland, the Netherlands, Norway, Sweden and Switzerland have no automatic rights to information about any children born as a result of their donation.

Linking donor conception to birth registration

Self-evidently, provisions enabling a donor-conceived person to ascertain information about genetic relatives they may have as a result of gamete or embryo donation are meaningless if they do not know about their conception in the first place. Clearly, the experiences of ignorance about donor conception can never be examined. However, various studies have indicated relatively low levels of parental disclosure, although some evidence of increasing levels of disclosure has been reported (see Blyth, this volume) and studies of donor-conceived individuals' experiences have highlighted adverse consequences associated with late, accidental or inadvertent disclosure (see, for example, Turner and Coyle, 2000; Kirkman, 2003; Paul and Berger, 2007; Berger and Paul, 2008; Jadva et al., 2009; Blake et al., 2010; Cushing, 2010; Beeson et al., 2011).

Annotation of birth certificates has been referred to as a possible means of encouraging parental disclosure (House of Lords and House of Commons, 2007; International Donor Offspring Alliance, 2007; Blyth et al., 2009; see also Blyth, this volume). To date, only Victoria has introduced provisions, under the Assisted Reproductive Treatment Act 2008, requiring BDM to mark the child's birth entry to note that (s)he is donor-conceived. When a birth certificate is issued to a donor-conceived person (but not to a third party, such as a parent), the certificate must include an addendum stating that further information is available from BDM about the entry.

In New South Wales, following a court ruling in which the name of a sperm donor was removed from a child's birth certificate and replaced with that of the birth mother's former partner,[4] the Committee on Law and Safety of the Legislative

4 *AA v Registrar of Births Deaths and Marriages and BB* [2011] NSWDC 100.

Assembly of New South Wales (2012) advocated adoption of the model in force in Victoria. Although these recommendations were accepted by the New South Wales government (2014), to date no further legislative action has been taken.

Provisions in South Australia, Germany, Washington, Kenya and the Republic of Ireland

In South Australia, the Assisted Reproductive Technology Treatment Regulations 2010 came into force in September 2010, providing for the establishment of a register of donor procedures, the Donor Conception Register, that will enable a donor-conceived individual aged at least 16 years to learn the identity of her/his donor and for the establishment of a voluntary contact register relating to a donor procedure undertaken before the introduction of the Donor Conception Register. In February 2014, the government of South Australia launched a consultation to help determine the contents of the Donor Conception Register and arrangements for access to information contained in it. The consultation period ended on 31 March 2014; at the time of writing the outcome of this is awaited.

In July 2011, Washington became the first of the US states to legislate for a donor-conceived person to learn the identity of her/his donor. A new section of the Revised Code of Washington (the state's legal code) requires any person donating gametes to a fertility clinic in Washington state that are used for family-building, to disclose their identity to the clinic, and the clinic to disclose the donor's identity to any donor-conceived offspring aged at least 18 years who requests it (RCW 26.26). It is unclear what prompted the introduction of this legislation. Its potential impact is significantly constrained since it includes an opt-out clause for donors who do not wish their identity to be disclosed, by means of an affidavit of nondisclosure, so it is comparable more to the hybrid 'double-track' system advocated by Pennings (1997) than to any of the other jurisdictions described in this chapter. As far as it has been possible to ascertain, there have as yet been no efforts to establish any kind of registry or to take other steps to implement the legislation.

Save for prohibitions on both oocyte and embryo donation, Germany has not developed comprehensive regulation of gamete donation. However, various court judgments since 1988 have promoted the rights of donor-conceived individuals to access information about his or her biological origins.[5] (Deutsche Welle, 2013; Thorn, 2013). In January 2015, Germany's highest civil court, the Federal Court of Justice, delivered a landmark ruling[6] following an application by two teenage sisters who wished to learn the identity of their donor and which had been heard by lower courts in previous years. The key decisions made by the court are that, at any age, donor-conceived children have the right to obtain the name of the donor;

5 Bundesverfassungsgericht [BVerfG], 18.1.1988 - 1 Beschluss vom Rundschreiben [BvR] 1589/87, Zeitschrift für das gesamte Familienrecht [FamRZ] 1989, 147.

6 BGH Judgment of 28th January 2015 XII ZR 201/13

parents of a donor-conceived child may demand the donor's identity for the purposes of informing the child. (Deutsche Welle, 2015) However, unlike other jurisdictions whose policies have been analysed in this chapter, Germany still lacks the infrastructure considered necessary for the effective implementation of rights to information, such as a central register of donations and births resulting from gamete donation, protection of donors from legal liability for offspring, provision of counselling and intermediary services to facilitate and support information provision – and if sought – contact.

Developments in both Washington state and Germany represent piecemeal arrangements that, whilst auguring the first steps in promoting the interests of donor-conceived people to learn about their biographical and genetic history, fall well short of the more comprehensive arrangements evident in other jurisdictions cited in this chapter.

Similarly in July 2014, it was reported that Kenyan MP Millie Odhiambo has sponsored an In Vitro Fertilisation Bill in the National Assembly, modelled on UK legislation, which would – among other provisions – establish a donor register, from which a donor-conceived person reaching the age of 18 could obtain information about their donor. Contemporary reports indicate that the Bill enjoys widespread community support, although further information about the Bill's provisions for donor-conceived individuals' access to information about their biographical and genetic history remains sparse (Standard Digital, 2014).

More recently, on 25 September 2014, the government of the Irish Republic approved proposals in the General Scheme of the Children and Family Relationships Bill 2014 which will require clinics and hospitals to provide details of donors and children to a national donor-conceived person register. According to Justice Minister Frances Fitzgerald, the new provisions, expected to become law in 2015, will enable a donor-conceived person to 'know his or her identity' (O'Loughlin, 2014).

Is the Human Fertilisation and Embryology Act fit for purpose in the twenty-first century? Further provisions to facilitate access to genetic and biographical information following donor conception

As long-standing advocates of the rights of donor-conceived people to access information about their biographical and genetic history, where donor conception is permitted, we believe that the use of donors who do not agree to the release of their identity to offspring at some future date should be prohibited. We, therefore, very much welcome the efforts of the UK government and regulatory body to ensure that the UK has for a number of years been at the forefront of the '[shift] away from exclusively anonymous donation to one with considerably more flexibility and openness' (International Federation of Fertility Societies, 2013: 75), especially given the comparative international context, and the still-contested nature of donor-conceived people's rights to information. To our knowledge, the UK was the first – and to date only – jurisdiction to enshrine in law the promotion of advice to parents of donor-conceived children to disclose the nature of their conception to their children while still young. Nevertheless, with increasing understanding of the intra- and inter-personal dynamics of gamete and embryo donation and the interests of a wide range of parties personally affected by donor conception, we have identified further measures that can be taken to promote information acquisition and exchange.

Since many individuals or clinics provide donor services on a commercial basis, the security of records must be able to withstand the consequences of any individual practitioner or clinic going out of business and ceasing to provide a service. The historical review of donor records in Victoria provided by the Law Reform Committee of the Victorian Parliament highlights the perils of insufficient regard to data storage, security and access, noting that records of donor procedure undertaken by defunct service providers have ended up in the Public Records Office to which, ironically, public access is denied (Parliament of Victoria, 2012: 7.1.2.4). Our review indicates that various models appear generally capable of performing the task adequately, including bodies that regulate assisted conception services, government health departments/ministries or registries of births, deaths and marriages, or independent bodies funded by government. A necessary criterion is that the organisation responsible for maintaining and managing access to information has the necessary resources and disposition to carry out the task. In Victoria, responsibility for all donor registries transferred from the (then) Infertility Treatment Authority to the Registry for BDM in January 2010, a move that was widely considered a retrograde one because of BDM's failure to deal adequately with requests for information. This led the Law Reform Committee of the Victorian Parliament to recommend returning stewardship of the registers to the (now-renamed) Victorian Assisted Reproductive Treatment Authority (Parliament of Victoria, 2012: 6.3.2). While this recommendation was not accepted by the Victorian government, proposals to respond to these criticisms have been put forward to ensure that the service provided by BDM is better fit for purpose (Government of Victoria, 2013).

In order to ensure that records are as accurate as possible, donors should be requested to update information on a periodic basis (say every five years) and to provide any relevant health-related information as and when this becomes available, as recommended by the Ethics Committee of the American Society for Reproductive Medicine (2014). This could be achieved through confidential communications from clinics requesting any updated information. Similarly, recipients of donor gametes or embryos should be requested to provide periodic updates and information about health issues in their children that may have a genetic element, that might have implications not only for the health of the donor but also for the health of a donor's future children (Ethics Committee of the ASRM, 2014).

Arrangements should be in place to ensure that service providers and/or register custodians pass on relevant information to donors, recipients of donated gametes and donor-conceived individuals. While in the jurisdictions reviewed in this chapter, the rights of *some* donor-conceived people to learn the identity of their donor has been recognised, no jurisdiction has extended this right to donor-conceived individuals where the donor did not explicitly consent to disclosure of their identity. Where donor registers were established in advance of legislation mandating disclosure of a donor's identity (currently in New South Wales, the UK, Victoria and Western Australia), this has meant that official records exist that provide information linking a donor-conceived individual to his or her donor, but to which the donor-conceived individual has no right of access. Satisfactory resolution of this problem has foundered on the competing rights of donors to privacy and of donor-conceived individuals to personal information. To date, the most extensive investigation of this dilemma has been undertaken by the Law Reform Committee of the Victorian Parliament (Parliament of Victoria, 2012) which investigated the situation of donor-conceived individuals in Victoria who were not entitled to information about their donor under the Infertility Treatment Act 1995 or the amending legislation of 2008. In the course of evidence gathering, the Committee discovered that past clinic practices assumed anonymity and that 'donors were not given a choice as to whether they wished to be anonymous' (Parliament of Victoria, 2012: 2.3.1.1).[7] Acknowledging, therefore, that objections to retrospective disclosure of donor identity that rested on claims relating to donor consent were flawed, the Committee afforded greater weight to the rights of donor-conceived individuals and recommended the retrospective disclosure of donor identity regardless of explicit consent, but that both donors and donor-conceived individuals should be able to place a veto on *contact* from each other. In the event, the government of Victoria rejected the Committee's proposals and introduced the Assisted Reproductive (Further Amendment) Bill 2013 to extend the remit of the existing voluntary contact register. Regardless of the merits of retrospective disclosure and inequities faced by donor-conceived individuals based on the date of their conception, it seems unlikely that any government will implement retrospective disclosure of donor identity in the foreseeable future and as a necessity, donor-conceived individuals who were conceived before the implementation of legislation mandating disclosure of donor identity will have to rely on the mechanisms provided by voluntary contact registers, social media, genealogy websites (Motluk, 2005) or registries independent of government, such as the Donor Sibling Registry.[8] In this regard we consider that governments and service providers need to run relevant educational programmes to facilitate participation in such registers by both donor-conceived people and former donors.

It is important to remember that information available for a donor-conceived person on any form of donor register is meaningful only to the extent that the individual knows about the potential relevance of this information to her/him and, even if they know they are donor-conceived, that they have an interest in obtaining it. Knowledge of being donor-conceived is, therefore, central. Available

7 To our knowledge this is the only attempt that has been made to elicit evidence regarding donor consent to anonymity under regimes that predate donor identity disclosure. We have no reason to suppose that these practices are unique to Victoria.

8 The Donor Sibling Registry was founded by Wendy and Ryan Kramer in 2000. As of 6 September 2014, the DSR had 44,202 registrants and had facilitated connections between 11,569 donor half-siblings and/or donors.

evidence indicates that, historically, recipients of donor gametes have tended to heed the advice of service providers not to disclose to their donor-conceived children information about their conception, although in keeping with the relatively recent changes in policy and professional practice noted earlier in this chapter, parental practices also appear to be changing in favour of increased transparency. As an aid, both to parental disclosure and to donor-conceived individuals' ability to learn about their genetic and biographical history, consideration to annotating birth registration documentation, as has already occurred in Victoria and proposed in New South Wales, could be given by other jurisdictions, including the UK (see Blyth, this volume). Any such arrangements must, of course, pay due regard to individuals' rights to privacy and confidentiality, as we have discussed further elsewhere (Blyth et al., 2009).

Recognition also needs to be given to the potential interests in information and possible contact of a range of individuals who are personally affected by donation – as acknowledged at least in part and in different ways under New Zealand, UK and Victorian legislation. In addition to donor-conceived people themselves, we would like to see the interests of parents, grand-parents, siblings, children and other descendants of donor-conceived individuals; donor half-siblings; donors and their partners, children and parents afforded greater recognition. However, it is beyond the scope of the present chapter to identify the precise mechanisms by which different parties' access to information about others could be best secured whilst paying due regard to individuals' legitimate rights to privacy and non-interference.

Conclusion

This chapter aimed to give an overview of the provisions of those jurisdictions that have allowed donor-conceived people to access identifying information about their gamete donor and/or donor siblings. In the last 30 years or so there has been a trend towards the opening up of gamete donation: allowing legal options for those to find out information and encouraging those using gamete or embryo donation for family-building to tell their children that they were conceived using donor gametes or embryos. In this way it can be argued that the dominant view over how to approach gamete donation has changed – at least in the Western world – and the legislative landscape in the UK reflects this. Since publishing our first overview of legislation in this area over five years ago (Blyth and Frith, 2009), no substantive new legislation affording donor-conceived individuals the rights to learn the identity of their donor has been enacted. In this highly contentious area, the question of whether the UK's legislation is still 'fit for purpose' cannot be measured by any objective criteria but must take account of social attitudes, cultural practices, developing technologies, history and emerging evidence. However, various measures have been introduced, proposed or discussed in various jurisdictions to facilitate increased access to information about genetic and biographical history. Meanwhile, the developments in South Australia, Washington, Germany, Kenya and the Republic of Ireland highlight a perceptible, albeit gradual trend towards increased transparency and recognition of the rights to information by an increasing range of parties, particularly those conceived by donor gametes or embryos (International Federation of Fertility Societies, 2013).

Acknowledgement

It would not have been possible to write this chapter without the help of many individuals who kindly provided information regarding specific jurisdictions. Our thanks go to: Sonia Allen, Kate Bourne, Karlheinz Brandt, Naomi Cahn, Joelle Darwich, Joi Ellis, Marysa Emery, Anne Forus, Elizabeth Hurrell, Wendy Kramer, Claudia Lampic, Miranda Montrone, Iolanda Rodino, Viveca Söderström-Anttila, Tuula Stark, Gunilla Sydsjö, Petra Thorn, Hans van Hooff and Daniel Wirthner.

References

American Society for Reproductive Medicine, (1993) Guidelines for Gamete Donation, *Fertility and Sterility* 59: S1–9.

American Society for Reproductive Medicine, (1998) Guidelines for Gamete and Embryo Donation, *Fertility and Sterility* 70: S1–6.

American Society for Reproductive Medicine, (2002) Guidelines for Gamete and Embryo Donation: A Practice Committee Report, *Fertility and Sterility* 90: S30–44.

Beeson, D., Jennings, P. and Kramer, W., (2011) 'Offspring searching for their sperm donors: how family type shapes the process' 26(9) *Human Reproduction* 2415.

Berger, R. and Paul, M., (2008) 'Family secrets and family functioning: the case of donor assistance' 47 *Family Process* 553.

Blake, L., Casey, P., Readings, J., Jadva, V. and Golombok, S., (2010) '"Daddy ran out of tadpoles": how parents tell their children that they are donor conceived, and what their 7 year olds understand' 25(10) *Human Reproduction* 2527.

Blyth, E. and Frith, L., (2009) 'Donor-conceived people's access to genetic and biographical history: An analysis of provisions in different jurisdictions permitting disclosure of donor identity' 23 *International Journal of Law, Policy and the Family* 192.

Blyth, E., Frith, L., Jones, C. and Speirs, J., (2009) 'The role of birth certificates in relation to access to biographical and genetic history in donor conception' 17(2) *International Journal of Children's Rights* 207.

Crawshaw, M., Gunter, C., Tidy, C. and Atherton, F., (2013) 'Working with previously anonymous gamete donors and donor-conceived adults: recent practice experiences of running the DNA-based voluntary information exchange and contact register, UK DonorLink' 16(1) *Human Fertility* 26.

Crawshaw, M. and Marshall, L., (2008) 'Practice experiences of running UK DonorLink, a voluntary information exchange and contact register for adults related through donor conception' 11(4) *Human Fertility* 231.

Cushing, A., (2010) '"I just want more information about who I am": the search experience of sperm-donor offspring, searching for information about their donors and genetic heritage' 15(2) *Information Research* paper 428.

Deutsche Welle (2013) 'Court rules sperm donors' children have right to know' 6 February.

Deutsche Welle (28 January 2015) 'German court removes age limit for sperm donor disclosure'. 28 January http://www.dw.de/german-court-removes-age-limit-for-sperm-donor-disclosure/a-18222071

Ethics Committee of the American Society for Reproductive Medicine, (2013) 'Informing offspring of their conception by gamete or embryo donation: a committee opinion' 100(1) *Fertility and Sterility* 45.

Ethics Committee of the American Society for Reproductive Medicine, (2014) 'Interests, obligations, and rights in gamete donation: a committee opinion' 102 *Fertility and Sterility* 675.

Fertility of Australia Reproductive Technology Accreditation Committee, (2010) *Code of Practice for Assisted Reproductive Technology Units* (http://www.fertilitysociety.com.au/wp-content/uploads/20101120l-final-rtac-cop.pdf).

Government of Victoria, (2013) *Parliament of Victoria Law Reform Committee. Inquiry into Access by Donor-Conceived People to Information about Donors. Victorian Government Response* (http://www.parliament.vic.gov.au/images/stories/committees/lawrefrom/donor-conceived/Response_to_Donor-conceived.pdf).

Hard, A.D., (April 1909) 'Artificial impregnation' *The Medical World* 163 (letter).

House of Lords/House of Commons, (2007) *Joint Committee on the Human Tissue and Embryos (Draft) Bill* Vol 1: Report (London: The Stationery Office).

Human Fertilisation and Embryology Authority, (2001) *Code of Practice* (5th edition). (London: HFEA).

Human Fertilisation and Embryology Authority, (2005a) *Tomorrow's Children: A Consultation on Guidance to Licensed Fertility Clinics on Taking in Account the Welfare of Children to be Born of Assisted Conception Treatment* (London: HFEA).

Human Fertilisation and Embryology Authority, (2005b) *Tomorrow's Children: HFEA Report of the Policy Review of Welfare of the Child Assessments in Licensed Assisted Conception Clinics* (London: HFEA).

Hurley, M. (2004) In House of Commons Science and Technology Select Committee (2005) *Human Reproductive Technologies and the Law. Fifth Report of Session 2004–05* Vol II. Response to Qs344/345 (London: The Stationery Office).

International Donor Offspring Alliance, (2007) *Human Fertilisation and Embryology Bill. Birth Certificates: The Case for Reform. Briefing for Members of the House of Commons.*

International Federation of Fertility Societies, (2013) Surveillance 2013 (http://www.iffs-reproduction.org/?page=SurveillanceHidden).

Jadva, V., Freeman, T., Kramer, W. and Golombok, S., (2009) 'The experiences of adolescents and adults conceived by sperm donation: comparisons by age of disclosure and family type' 24(8) *Human Reproduction* 1909.

Kirkman, M., (2003) 'Parents' contributions to the narrative identity of offspring of donor-assisted conception' 57 *Social Science and Medicine* 2229.

Legislative Assembly of New South Wales Committee on Law and Safety, (2012) *Inclusion of donor details on the register of births* Report 1/55 (Adelaide: Legislative Assembly of New South Wales).

Motluk, A., (2005) 'Anonymous sperm donor traced on internet' *New Scientist* 2524 3 November.

New South Wales Government, (2014) *NSW Government Response to NSW Legislative Assembly Committee on Law and Safety Inquiries into Donor Conception* (Sydney: NSW Government).

New Zealand Law Commission, (2005) *New Issues in Legal Parenthood – NZLC R 88* (Auckland: New Zealand Law Commission).

Novaes, S., (1998) 'The Medical Management of Donor Insemination' in Daniels, K.

and Haimes, E., (eds) *Donor Insemination: International Social Science Perspectives* (Cambridge: Cambridge University Press) 105–130.

O'Loughlin, A., (2014) 'Anonymous sperm donation is to be banned in Ireland' *Irish Examiner* (26 September 2014).

Parliament of Victoria Law Reform Committee (2012) *Inquiry into Access by Donor-Conceived People to Information about Donors* (Melbourne: Parliament of Victoria).

Paul, M.S. and Berger, R., (2007) 'Topic avoidance and family functioning in families conceived with donor insemination' 22 *Human Reproduction* 2566.

Pennings, G., (1997) 'The "double track" policy for donor anonymity' 12(12) *Human Reproduction* 2839.

Standard Digital (2014) 'How proposed law seeks to protect "Test tube" babies' 28 July.

Thorn, P., (2013) 'Court decision in Germany supports rights of the donor conceived to access their donor's identity' *BioNews* 693 (18 February 2013, Progress Educational Trust).

Turner, A.J. and Coyle, A., (2000) 'What does it mean to be a donor offspring? The identity experiences of adults conceived by donor insemination and the implications for counselling and therapy' 15(9) *Human Reproduction* 2041.

10 Compensating reproductive harms in the regulation of twenty-first century assisted conception

Antony Blackburn-Starza

Introduction

Social and technological developments in assisted conception services have resulted in significant changes to family and kinship arrangements and understandings of genetics and parenthood, rendering the law's interaction with fertility services in need of frequent reform. But while limited changes have occurred to the law on parenthood, the implicit principle of familial autonomy that has underpinned some key aspects of reform has not fully permeated the conceptual underpinnings of fertility regulation and the common law. This can be seen in the lack of attention given to mechanisms to provide redress for errors in assisted conception, of which there are an alarming number.[1]

Mistakes in the provision of assisted conception services have been reported in the UK and elsewhere, including instances of alleged sperm or embryo mix-ups and the accidental destruction of gametes or embryos.[2] Although in some instances the child is born with an unintended defect (Chohan, 2014), in many cases the harms experienced may be less tangible and difficult to conceptualise as legally recognisable damage. For example, sperm mix-ups can lead to the fracture of biological parenthood;[3] or, where the gamete donor used was not the original intended donor, the situation can have an adverse effect on familial relationships and identity.[4] In other cases, the negligent destruction of gametes can represent a loss of patients' chance to have genetically related children.[5] While not strictly

1 See footnotes 14, 15, 16 and 17. See also the Human Fertilisation and Embryology Authority's report, 'Adverse incidents in fertility clinics: lessons to learn (2010–2012)', published 8 July 2014.

2 See (in the UK) *A & B by C (Their Mother & Next Friend) v A– Health & Social Services Trust* [2011] NICA 28 (sperm mix up); *Jonathan Yearworth & Ors v North Bristol NHS Trust* [2009] EWCA Civ 37 (destruction of sperm); *Holdich v Lothian Health Board* [2013] ScotCS CSOH 197; *Leeds Teaching Hospitals NHS Trust v A and Others* [2003] EWHC 259.

3 *Leeds Teaching Hospitals NHS Trust v A & Ors* [2003].

4 In *A & B by C (Their Mother & Next Friend) v A– Health & Social Services Trust* [2011], despite a request for a 'Caucasian' sperm donor, a donor was used from the 'Cape coloured' community in South Africa.

5 For an example, see *Yearworth & Ors v North Bristol NHS Trust* [2009] where sperm deposited by a number of men prior to receiving chemotherapy treatment that can leave the patient infertile was negligently destroyed.

speaking causing actual *losses*, such errors may nonetheless result in manifest *harms* for those affected.

However, the requirement to prove actionable damage in claims for compensation represents a significant obstacle to the pursuit of redress. For example, while the tort of negligence for the most part requires claimants to prove physical damage in the form of personal injury or property damage, harms in the reproductive context are dissimilar from broken bones and are not straightforwardly physical or deleterious (Priaulx, 2010: 82; Witting, 2002). They therefore evade doctrinal or conventional categorisation of actionable damage (Priaulx, 2010: 82; 2015). The result is that many fertility patients are denied access to justice, which not only prevents the recovery of compensation, but (more pertinently for the focus of this discussion) fails to respect the *loss* of reproductive autonomy that may occur. This problem is also indicative of a general failure in the law to explore and articulate the harm resulting from errors in assisted conception.

There has been little discussion of reproductive harms and actionable damage beyond the wrongful life context, with some notable exceptions (Nolan, 2007, 2013; Priaulx, 2007, 2010). Despite a stated commitment to personal autonomy from some members of the judiciary,[6] arguments for the recognition of autonomy in claims for compensation have so far failed to build on this commitment outside 'failure to warn' claims in negligence. Further still, again with significant exceptions (Chico, 2011; Nelson, 2013; Priaulx, 2008), little focus has been given to precisely what version of autonomy is offered in discussions of regulation and civil liability, nor precisely how this links in with the social realities of reproductive decision-making.

The relative lack of attention in academic and legal literature to a legal construction of reproductive harms appears at odds with contemporary debates in bioethics and medical law that seek to situate a normative discussion of different versions of autonomy within moral, social and political agendas. It also contrasts with protections featured in the Human Fertilisation and Embryology Acts 1990 and 2008 (hereafter 'the 1990 Act' and 'the 2008 Act') that can be seen to promote reproductive autonomy and the recognition of alternative family models.

Moreover, the failure to provide redress appears out of step with social practices around assisted conception. The task of the law in keeping up to date with continued technological developments in assisted conception, and the changing social attitudes that accompany them, is made all the more important by an ever greater uptake of assisted reproductive technologies (ART) in the UK. Meanwhile, the regulatory challenge has, arguably, shifted beyond the ethical facilitation and progression of technology, to an increasing demand to give recognition to the interests and expectations of patients and the creation of families. While such trends necessitated law reform that culminated in the 2008 Act, that legislation

6 See for example Lord Steyn in *Chester v Afshar* [2004] UKHL 41, at [24]; *Rees v Darlington Memorial Hospital NHS Trust* [2003] UKHL 52. *Rees* illustrates a version of autonomy relating to reproduction that differs from the respect of medical decision-making in *Chester*.

has now also fallen out of date. It also failed to address the importance of redress in the overarching regulatory goals in the first place.

Mechanisms for redress should, therefore, be an integral part of this overall regulatory project. This is partly due to the technical nature of the reproductive technologies which may increase the likelihood of unintended, adverse incidents occurring. For example, mitochondrial replacement techniques (if developed into treatments (see Riley, this volume)) will alter the germline of embryos, resulting in possible genetic changes for future generations, potentially raising important questions of liability.[7] But it is also because the imposition of liability (and the availability of compensation that comes with it) serves to attribute responsibility to fertility clinics in a way that recognises the obligations generated by delivering a professional service built around patient expectations and interests. The provision of redress also vindicates a person's rights or interests when they have been infringed.

This chapter attempts to flesh out a version of autonomy that may be more amenable to a discussion of civil liability in the context of reproductive harms, and that can serve to form the basis of common law or legislative reform. It explores arguments in favour of the recognition of autonomy as a basis for recognising actionable harm. It also asks to what extent a substantive notion of autonomy can be imbued by the acknowledgement of family building practices and kinship arrangements. For certain families a mistake may infringe upon meaningful kinship expectations that may have real manifest impacts on family relationships, as well as emotional distress for the parent and child (Sheldon, 2011). Building on kinship studies that trace the ways reproductive technologies have transformed processes of family building and kinship arrangements (Franklin, 2013; Franklin and MacKinnon, 2002; Freeman et al, 2014; Nordqvist and Smart, 2014), this chapter draws on such observations made to critique the law's readiness to provide remedy in this context.

The first section identifies implicit principles that may explain certain provisions in the existing legislation (and also the common law) that contrast with a lack of attention to reproductive harms, along with outlining the need for further reform upon clear conceptual lines. The discussion then proceeds to identify the features of what can be termed reproductive harms, highlighting the relational process of family building and importance of resemblance, before developing a framework through which such characterisations may be given normative weight in the legal context. It offers a modified version of autonomy substantiated by reference to the meanings attached to assisted conception processes in family building and the kinship arrangements that they create. This approach presents new frameworks and language for characterising harm that are not contingent on traditional categories of physical deleteriousness. The chapter concludes by identifying possible avenues for law reform, raising questions for further examination.

7 For a discussion of the law on 'toxic torts' applied to developments in genetics in the USA see Grodsky (2007), 59 *Standard Law Review* 1671.

The case for critical attention to legally recognisable harm in the reproductive context

Claims for compensation following mistakes in the provision of ART services may be brought under the law of contract or tort, with claims having been brought in negligence, and damages granted in bailment.[8] In 2002, an error at the UK's Leeds General Infirmary led to a woman's eggs being fertilised with the wrong donor's sperm during IVF, resulting in a mixed-race child being born to a white couple.[9] The proceedings dealt with the children's legal parenthood (BioNews, 2004a).[10] In 2009, a claim for psychiatric damage was brought by five men whose sperm, stored prior to receiving chemotherapy, was negligently destroyed.[11] In 2010, a claim in negligence was brought (unsuccessfully) against a Northern Ireland NHS Trust by children conceived following an alleged failure in the ART provision received by their parents; this resulted in them having a different skin tone from their parents, from each other, and from that which was intended (Sheldon, 2011).[12] In 2013, a claim in negligence and for breach of contract arising from the destruction of sperm following a failure in storage was permitted to proceed to trial by Scotland's Court of Session.[13] Other allegations of errors in the UK have been reported in the media, but appear not to have resulted in litigation,[14] although similar legal proceedings have been brought in the USA,[15] Canada[16] and Singapore.[17]

8 E.g. *Yearworth & Ors v North Bristol NHS Trust* [2009].

9 *Leeds Teaching Hospitals NHS Trust v A & Ors* [2003].

10 Also see the Toft report, which was published in 2004 following a number of incidents at Leeds Teaching Hospitals NHS Trust.

11 *Yearworth & Ors v North Bristol NHS Trust* [2009].

12 *A & B by C (Their Mother & Next Friend) v A– Health & Social Services Trust* [2011].

13 *Holdich v Lothian Health Board* [2013].

14 In 2012, *The Sunday Times* (Frodsham, 2012) reported allegations that the wrong donor had been used at London Women's Clinic after children born looked visibly different; at Guy's and St Thomas' Hospital, London, in 2009, three couples had their embryos destroyed after the wrong sperm donor was used (Shaikh, 2009); at the Diana Princess of Wales clinic at St George's Hospital, women were implanted with the wrong embryos, following a labelling error (BioNews, 2002).

15 In 2004, a Black American couple obtained settlement for an undisclosed sum from a New York clinic after their embryo was mistakenly implanted into another woman (BioNews, 2004b). In *Andrews v Keltz* (2007) NY Slip Op 27139, sperm from an anonymous donor was used instead of the husband's during treatment received in 2004. The owner of the clinic was liable as owner, but not personally. A claim against a doctor who advised the couple and performed implantation was dismissed but another against the embryologist was upheld. The judge sympathised with the complaint's argument that the mistake had particular impact because it resulted in a child who is 'not even the same race, nationality, colour...as they are'. In *Buchweitz* (2004), a US woman who was informed over one year later that the wrong embryo was used was awarded $1m compensation (BioNews, 2004c). In 2014 Jennifer Cramblett brought a claim against Ohio sperm bank for using the wrong sperm donor (see Blackburn-Starza, 2014)

16 In 2010, two claims were brought against Dr Barwin at the Barwin Fertility Clinic in Ottawa by Ms Slinn and Mr Guest, in each case for using the wrong sperm (Jones, 2010).

17 In 2010, Thomson Fertility Centre in Singapore was investigated following an alleged sperm mix-up (Satkunarajah, 2010). A claim by the mother for the costs of the child's upbringing was later rejected.

Bringing such a claim in contract or tort is, however, fraught with difficulty at the outset for both doctrinal and policy reasons. In negligence, a claimant must not only establish that a duty of care was owed to them (particularly problematic for resultant children and other non-patients) and that the negligence caused their 'loss' (made problematic by natural genetic variations and implantation failures),[18] but defining a category of actionable damage is also deeply problematic. The 'gist' of negligence is physical damage, either personal injury or property damage (Stapleton, 1988), and claimants must establish a minimum amount of actionable damage to bring a compensation claim.

Claims for reproductive loss could arguably fare better under contract, which is more comfortable with less tangible losses, such as mental distress (restrictively), pure economic loss or loss of opportunity, all of which are resisted in the tort of negligence. However, short of being compensated for some form of anguish or lost chance, the precise measure of loss remains elusive and is affected by the same lack of language or perspective to achieve recognition as in tort. Furthermore, breach of contract claims may not be available following rules of privity to resulting children, non-patients and also for patients receiving treatment under the NHS.[19]

Such dilemmas are by no means irresolvable, but have to date received little political or judicial attention. This relative lack of attention to the harms experienced by patients resulting from ART errors contrasts with implicit trends underpinning the HFE Acts, dominant themes in contemporary bioethics and other areas of the common law in the medical context that seek to promote patient autonomy and/or bring the law in line with alternative modes of family building.

Upon one view, some of the provisions in the 2008 Act articulated already mobilised normative principles directing law reform initiated within the 1990 Act and further promoted a logic that, on the face of it, pays lip-service to principles of reproductive autonomy and, more substantively, the recognition of non-traditional family models. For example, the removal of the phrase 'need… for a father' from section 13(5), known as the welfare principle, represented a move towards recognising women's reproductive autonomy by allowing single women and lesbians access to treatment (Fenton et al, 2010: 278, and see Blyth, this volume). Also notable are the consent requirements enshrined in the 1990 Act that confer certain rights of control over the use of one's own gametes, which arguably signify the underpinning importance of reproductive autonomy by prioritising consent within the law.

The 2008 Act also gives some recognition to new forms of family building through provisions enabling men and women to acquire legal parenthood in situations where they would not otherwise under the common law (Sheldon and McCandless, 2014: 62–64). The ability of same-sex parents to register as the child's second parent, for example, illustrates an important step towards recognising alternative family models.

18 Discussion of genetic variance between generations is seen in *A & B by C (Their Mother & Next Friend) v A– Health & Social Services Trust* [2011] at [9].

19 For a discussion of the contractual position and NHS services, see *Holdich* [2013].

The lack of attention given to the varying conceptions of harm that occur when family building using assisted conception goes wrong, therefore, falls out of pace with moves to respect the reproductive autonomy of fertility patients and the recognition of the family relationships that ART facilitates. It is also inconsistent with a general characterisation of the fertility industry and its governance in the UK, which largely embraces a system predicated on the profitability of hope, opportunity and, to a certain extent, reproductive choice.

However, the law itself remains significantly inconsistent and qualified in both its form and conceptual foundations. This has contributed to reform, to date, being piecemeal and arguably incomplete, with the 2008 Act representing more of a pragmatic response to a number of issues, rather than overarching principled law reform built around a discernable philosophical framework (Eijkholt, 2011; Fenton et al, 2010: 285). There were a number of missed opportunities in the 2008 Act, including provisions to reform abortion law (Sheldon, 2009), the law on surrogacy (Horsey, 2013), legislating for the creation of artificial gametes and womb transplants (Alghrani, 2009) and, perhaps of central relevance to a debate on reproductive harms, is its failure to overhaul the ethical underpinnings of fertility treatment and embryo research (Fox, 2009).

This lack of conceptual clarity under the HFE Acts presents a case for revitalising key philosophical principles and invites a close examination of reproductive autonomy and how the law is seen to respect the creation of families by ART. The inconsistencies and under-developed concepts within the legislation betray a lack of normative unity. For example, the notion of autonomy that operates around consent serves more as a negative right against the imposition of rights and obligations connected to child rearing without consent,[20] rather than promoting a positive view of autonomous decision-making. This was visible in *Evans v UK* (decided under consent provisions contained in the 1990 Act), where the European Court of Human Rights denied Natallie Evans her request to use her embryos created with her former partner who had withdrawn his consent, thus denying her reproductive autonomy while upholding her former partner's. It held that a right to private life encompasses the right to personal autonomy, which covers 'the right to respect for both the decisions to become and not become a parent'.[21] This is indicative of the general framing of fertility legislation in the UK and, in particular, adopted in the 2008 Act, which although seen to promote versions of reproductive autonomy, in other ways fails to grant recognition to the principle, for example in the areas of cloning, sex selection, 'designer babies', selecting for disability and 'saviour siblings' (Eijkholt, 2012).

20 Conversely, in *Re R (IVF: Paternity of Child)* [2005] UKHL 33, a man's claim for paternity was rejected by the court after his ex-partner conceived through IVF with embryos created using donor sperm when receiving treatment together. The woman had concealed their separation from the clinic in order to continue with IVF treatment. It can be said that the autonomous interests of the man did not fall in line with the operation of consent in this case.

21 *Evans v UK* 46 EHRR 34.

The recognition of alternative families also remains philosophically incoherent. It has been argued that the parenthood provisions in the 2008 Act maintain versions of genetic relatedness that appear to favour certain family models over others (Sheldon and McCandless, 2014: 67). Sheldon and McCandless describe how the law's fixation with genetic relatedness focuses on the male in a way that renders the notion of genetic connections as gendered (2014: 67–71). It has also been suggested that the extension of parenthood rights available to same-sex couples was a logic grounded in equality, following on from civil partnerships (and now also marriage), and thus maintaining the welfare of the child by promoting traditional family stability (Gurnham and Miola, 2012: 44).

It is important to note here that the promotion of autonomy in fertility governance remains elusive and sits, rightly so, in tension with other contending principles that challenge an overly individualistic approach or that emphasise societal morality or welfare considerations for the child. The law also operates within significant technical and financial constraints. The argument here is therefore not for autonomy to take the sole or even a dominant position, but rather its presence as a governing principle invites further conceptual development both through a self-examination of its philosophical underpinnings and relevance to the reproductive context, and for regulation to achieve consistency and completeness.

While the legislation remains in need of conceptual justification, common law judges have been more explicit in their references to upholding patient autonomy. This can be seen in the medical non-disclosure context,[22] and also regarding reproduction.[23] In the common law of negligence, the courts are seemingly prepared to characterise damage in such a way to enable or negate compensation where they feel justice dictates it. The instances of recognition of autonomy seen in *Chester* and *Rees* might be said to illustrate this approach, but the justification for these outcomes and the precise formulation of autonomy remain unclear. There is little judicial consensus or explicit reference to an overriding ethical framework (which is lacking) for the regulation of ART, with *Rees* and *Chester* arguably representing ad hoc decisions outside the mainstream development in this area around parenthood.

There remains a real need for a full and proper principled and conceptual approach to the regulation of ART. A deeper understanding of the harms resulting from errors in assisted conception and the subsequent consideration of a normative framework through which such harms can be given legal effect may allow for sustainable reform. While the undesirability of law reform adopting singular normative narratives around autonomy in the context of a morally pluralistic and culturally diverse society must be acknowledged, the current law reveals a failure to fully engage by exploring various versions of reproductive autonomy and the experiences of patients and their understandings of rights and interests. This appears at odds with an industry orchestrated to promote processes of family building and its legislative facilitation. A bioethical framework of autonomy can

22 *Chester v Afshar* [2004] UKHL 41.

23 *Rees v Darlington Memorial Hospital NHS Trust* [2003] UKHL 52.

be greatly supported by empirical contributions from sociological and anthropological literature that articulate the experiences of patients engaged in ART, and the possible effects when things go wrong. However, empirical contributions seem to be slow to permeate the law, which arguably at present replicates formalist models of family life.

Reproductive harms

An attempt to characterise the harm arising from negligence in ART through conventional categories of physical damage is problematic for a number of reasons. First, reproductive harms can often be intangible or non-physical in nature. Rather than physical damage, the harms incurred after failures in the provision of assisted conception often involve a disruption of genetic parenthood specifically, or parenthood generally, or family associated meanings of resemblance, relatedness and connection. Relatedly, reproductive harms are more subjective, falling within personal decisions over how to build one's family (Priaulx, 2010: 82). Reproductive decision-making is usually seen as quintessentially private and the meanings associated with genetic resemblance and family building are uniquely deployed by each individual family. As Chico explains: 'the essence of the grievance rests on the individual's perception of her circumstances, rather than a universal perception of what is harmful' (2011: 26).

This is particularly problematic for laws of redress – in particular, the tort of negligence. While the law does on occasion compensate for more subjective loss, such as loss of amenity in the provision of general damages for personal injury, such damages are nonetheless contingent on physical or deleterious damage. The law is also prepared to compensate intangible loss in the sense of unquantifiable damage, but this too retains the prerequisite occurrence of manifest physical damage. Rather than constituting a problem about measurability, therefore, it may be that where the entirety of damages is founded upon a subjective loss this could undermine the compensatory principle in negligence that favours actual loss over loss of personal preference.[24] However, while the lack of an objective determinant with which to measure loss is problematic, the recognition of autonomy could form the basis of genomic negligence claims.

Second, reproductive harms are also tied up with new technologies that facilitate reproductive decisions and conception in ways that were previously not imagined. While this is a classic problem for laws that deal with emerging and developing technological phenomenon (Priaulx, 2010), ART presents a unique case: the accompanying social revolution it has caused has changed the way some medical professionals and society more generally understand human biology and reproductive materials (Edwards, 2014; Thompson, 2005).

24 On the other hand, in *Briody v St Helen's & Knowsley Area Health Authority* [2001] EWCA Civ 1010, damages for the costs of surrogacy services were claimed but were not awarded for policy reasons. The costs of fertility treatment necessitated by an earlier negligent act could form an objective basis for the measure of damages under consequential loss.

In respect to the intrinsic worth of stored gametes, the value attached to sperm and eggs is implicated in biotechnological innovation as a whole that adds value to bodily material and transforms an otherwise worthless mass of cells into something rather special according to its reproductive (or research) potential. Gametes can take on value in what they represent and how they are used. The industry built around gamete donation and the fees that donors can command in other jurisdictions evidence the commercial value and, in turn, consumer demand for reproductive materials.

In respect to the use of gamete donors, an increasing awareness of genetics in popular and mainstream thinking may be responsible for the promotion of ideas around genetic determinism that popularise the view that a certain genetic makeup may be responsible for phenotypic traits.[25] In other words, whatever the realities of the assisted conception process, the selection of gamete donors is heavily determined by the desirability of particular traits in the resulting child. These desired traits are used by patients with forward-thinking ideas about family building, fitting in and so on. The selection of a gamete donor is thus implicitly tied to considerations of genetic determinism through the perception of what a child *might* be like (look, act and so on) if a certain gamete donor is used.

The extent to which assisted conception services are provided in a liberal political or ideological framework, involving a retreat from medical paternalism and respect for patient autonomy, might also influence the characterisation of reproductive harms. Although commercial donation is not permitted in the UK,[26] patients may still choose donors from a range available. Clinics can use donor websites that list donor characteristics in easily searchable formats.[27] This introduces the technical option of *choosing* a donor; the implicit goal is to opt for desirable genetic characteristics in the child. The promise of reproductive choice thus also invokes rights and interests around autonomy and procreative liberty, and arguably promotes choice, and encourages patients and their families to believe in the autonomy of their decision. However, the liberal conception does not entirely capture the technical and social realities of family building through ART.

It would be limiting to a discussion of reproductive harms to focus attention on the exercise of autonomy, without broader consideration of the context in which such decisions take place. Although IVF has been practised since the late 1970s (other assisted conception techniques precede it), only in recent years have notions of genetic parenthood and the technological facilitation of reproduction been absorbed into the social rubric around parenting and reproduction. The notion of genetic parenthood is heavily implicated in social constructs around the importance of relatedness prevalent in Western societal thinking. Although this has been criticised for promoting the interests of certain groups

25 Genetic determinism is a contested notion, however, with a number of recent studies affirming the complexity of gene-related conditions and phenotypic traits (see e.g. Photopoulos, 2010). There are very few single gene disorders.

26 See section 12 Human Fertilisation and Embryology Act 1990 (as amended)

27 For examples, see the London Sperm Bank (http://www.londonspermbankdonors.com) and the London Egg Bank (http://www.londoneggbank.com/).

and individual power holders in society (see Roberts, 1996), it may nonetheless have very real effects for families. The loss of chance of genetic parenthood has heavily influenced cases in this area, including *Yearworth*. However, a disruption in genetic parenthood itself does not represent the harms incurred; rather, the infringement involves a disruption of 'relatedness'. This concept can exist – or can be constructed – with or without genetic parentage. This is a particularly important point, because this relational and substantive consideration is not fully supported within a liberal framework of choice. If full effect is to be given to the creation of new families through assisted conception in the regulatory framework, then recognition of families' experiences, as perceivably irrational or unfounded as they may be, needs to preside over discernable truths around genetics and biology.[28]

Nordqvist and Smart observe that family members often use resemblances to construct family relationships in the absence of a genetic connection (2014: 132). Their interviewees claimed to detect resemblances between child and family even in the absence of a genetic connection, allowing then to 'construct links' between the children, parent and wider family. The authors conclude that this 'mapping' of resemblance is an important strategy undertaken by parents to deal with the absence of a genetic connection and to reclaim a sense of genetic connectedness with the child. The loss of ability to have biological children is widely recognised; in contrast, the meanings associated with notions of kinship in family building using donor gametes are less well understood – although kinship bonds can be severely disrupted when the 'wrong' donor is used. It is suggested here that, while the importance of a genetic linkage between parents and children may be a social construct, a disruption of such expectations, even when genetic parenthood is impossible, can have very real manifestations. The loss of genetic parenthood can give rise to significant child welfare and well-being considerations. However, less obviously, it could equally be said that resemblance underpins the notion of relatedness between family members – and that this may form the basis of reproductive harms, rather than genetic relatedness per se. This can be seen in cases where a different sperm or egg donor is used from the one that was intended, where it is more difficult to conceptualise the harm, but where harm might include the psycho-social effects of visual dissimilarity between parent and child on the parent-child relationship (Becker et al, 2005) or the pressure of external perceptions within the family (Marre and Bestard, 2009) and wider community (Culley and Hudson, 2009).

Sheldon (2011) highlights the effect of physical dissimilarity between parent and child using a quotation from a father whose children were conceived with sperm donated by a man from the 'Cape' coloured community in South Africa:[29] 'this

28 A counter-point here could be to explore how family building processes replicate traditional models of family and are resultant of social pressures to conform, orchestrated by power holders in society. Such a critique offers insights into the historical and social processes that surround reproduction (see e.g. Nordqvist, 2012: 658).

29 *A & B by C (Their Mother & Next Friend) v A– Health & Social Services Trust* [2011].

mistake has devastated our family and almost destroyed our marriage. We can't go out together because people openly stare at us. My wife has been asked if she'd had an affair'. Such cases are not therefore about loss of genetic parenthood, but a disruption of resemblance in families that shatters the very notion of relatedness on which a family unit is built and the resulting questions that may arise. An approach is needed to articulate such experiences in the courts, one that is centred upon the actual effect of negligence on families rather than notions of physical loss. Such an approach must also be capable of adopting a more relational understanding of the experience of family building, one that has been acknowledged in the law's treatment of parenthood, which grants recognition to the creation of new families in the absence of a genetic tie.

Conceptualising a framework for the recognition of reproductive harms using autonomy

The construction of a normative framework through which to speak about the harms outlined above is necessary to develop a common language and consistent approach through which the recognition of damage in the assisted conception context may be achieved. One approach is to characterise the harm as an infringement of autonomy, defined broadly as the ability to exercise free decisions about how one lives one's own life, with an interest in autonomy already attracting limited recognition in law, as noted above. Although the concept of autonomy is multi-faceted and has attracted a number of critiques, it is a useful starting point in the fertility context because as a principle it encapsulates reproductive decision-making, as well as the experiences of fertility patients, their expectations and interests in family building using ART.

The promotion of some form of autonomy has been suggested as a possible basis for conceptualising reproductive harms (Chico, 2011; Nelson, 2013; Nolan, 2007; Priaulx, 2010). Although it is true that the harms cited above can all be characterised as infringements of autonomy, precisely what version of autonomy is compatible to conceptualise a recognisable form of actionable damage is unclear. Indeed, the very notion of autonomy is subject to rigorous theoretical challenges and interpretations.

The first notion of autonomy to consider is one that can be thought of as procedurally independent. It is an individualistic or liberal conception that protects people – particularly medical patients – from positive infringements. It is a negative, procedural right, already recognised to an extent by the courts.[30] However, being content-neutral (Chico, 2011), this version of autonomy may lack the normative force to constitute a legally recognisable form of damage in its own right. The development of this form of procedural autonomy can be explained by a backlash to medical paternalism in bioethics. A liberal account of procedural

30 For example, see *Re T* [1992] EWCA Civ 18, per Lord Donaldson, para 3 – a competent adult patient has an 'absolute right' to refuse medical treatment. In the reproductive context, see *Briody* [2001].

autonomy is concerned with protecting autonomous decision-making in healthcare (Nelson, 2013: 19). However, such a procedural account of autonomy merely serves to ensure that the correct conditions are in place in which autonomous decision-making can be made and respected, and does not ensure that decisions are made in accordance with a person's autonomously held beliefs (Nelson, 2013). Protection of procedural autonomy does not ensure that autonomously made decisions are actually fulfilled or are respected, as they fall short of a 'right' and are more about choosing what is on offer.

Given the limitations of procedural autonomy, a more substantive version that focuses on the ultimate needs of a person, not the process by which ends are achieved, may perhaps better capture the harms outlined above. A substantive account of autonomy can be informed by considerations of kinship and family building. It may well be that procedural autonomy is also implicated in family building, but if it is possible to define some welfare considerations for patients, children and families, perhaps around identity and family relationships, then such principles could support a more substantive version of autonomy.

Consequently, autonomy could be developed along relational understandings (Nedelsky, 1989). The overly individualistic and atomistic approach of liberal autonomy fails to take into account the notion that people are socially embedded (Nelson, 2013; Jackson 2001). The liberal model is not suited to acknowledging the constitutive nature of social relations to one's sense of self and self-determination (Nelson, 2013: 23). It is not possible to make decisions that are isolated from the relationships around an individual and a relational view of autonomy is able to take into account a broader set of social relations, not just interpersonal relations. However, Nelson recognises that characterising autonomy through a relational lens alone is limiting (at 27). There is a risk that relational theories of autonomy could be used to justify paternalistic ideas about what is autonomous and generate concerns about 'oppressive socialisation' (29).

Developing a workable conception of autonomy in the ART context is therefore difficult, but although the notion of autonomy may evade clear conceptual boundaries, its constitution as a complex conception of procedural, substantive and relational aspects is not without appeal. The social aspect to autonomy is inescapable, but the importance of individual agency that gives autonomy its normative force cannot equally be overlooked. A greater attention is needed on the context of decision-making, but also which gives effect to the decision-maker (Nelson, 2013: 45). Recognising the status of patients not as beneficiaries of medical technology, but as presumptive parents whose reproductive choices (and associated expectations) are *facilitated* by technology, for example, may better acknowledge their experience of family building. A patient's autonomous choices are in fact those that are offered by a fertility clinic, but a procedural view of what goes on in clinics misses the meaningful processes that take place. A fertility clinic is a place where expectations are built and, it could be argued, at least impliedly promised. The role of fertility clinics is to help patients conceive, thus giving effect to reproductive autonomy. The lack of responsibility or legal recognition when this expectation-generated autonomy is infringed by negligence, for example, is therefore in stark contrast with the very business of the fertility industry. Instead, a notion of 'familial autonomy' could provide a more substantive version with material consequences for the health and wellbeing of parents and children.

It is important to note that while the suitability of autonomy as a philosophical concept *per se*, although providing a normative framework through which to speak about reproductive harms, may be insufficient on its own to facilitate law reform. It does, however, offer a way of ensuring consistency and a conceptual justification through which to approach doctrinal questions around compensating harms in assisted conception, should there be the political and judicial will to do so, as well as identifying situations where an infringement of autonomy can give rise to a prima facie right to redress.

Rethinking the law on reproductive harms

The above discussion offers both a critique of the law's failure to expand the momentum of reform and the implicit principles behind it to a discussion over the recognition of reproductive harms, and a proposed reworking of autonomy that is able to capture the 'harm' in reproductive harms upon which a discussion of actionable or legally recognisable damage can take place. Taking these ideas forward requires a great deal of critical attention to the role of autonomy in the reproductive context and the extent to which it is desirable to formulate law reform on this basis. However, if one is to cautiously proceed, then both legislation and common law options present potential avenues through which compensation for reproductive harms can be delivered.

From a legislative approach, one approach may be to establish a statutory redress scheme to grant compensation for infringements of autonomy – proposed by Clark and Nolan (2014) for non-disclosure claims. Compensation could be provided on a 'conventional basis', as in *Rees*, for example. Indeed, the provision of statutory redress is in keeping with the regulatory aims of the law as enshrined in the statutory-born HFEA, which monitors adverse incidents in fertility clinics.

However, inevitably, the provision of a conventional sum for an infringement of autonomy would once again fail to utilise the law's willingness to measure loss on a case-by-case basis. Alternatively, a workable definition of reproductive autonomy – or a set of overarching principles – could signify Parliament's intention to determine legal cases in such a framing. Such a conceptual approach can be evidenced in the work of the Nuffield Council on Bioethics. Its reports on donor information sharing and the donation of human bodies for research demonstrates a principled and ethically consistent approach to policy making, forwarding compound concepts like 'solidarity' and 'altruism' to rationalise workable conclusions (Blackburn-Starza, 2013).

Fertility clinics, operating in an industry worth over £500 million a year and backed up by insurance, could also operate a compensation fund, thereby reducing the costs and time associated with litigation. Again, however, there remains the need for reproductive harms to be measurable in such a way that is meaningful for those affected.

The provision of compensation through tort or contract does allow for an examination of loss in each individual case, but such a move would necessitate a reassessment of the conception of harm in assisted conception perhaps to a greater extent that a conventional award would. Cases that have grappled with the dilemma of awarding compensation in this area have to date provided a somewhat inadequate response. The Court of Appeal's decision in *Yearworth* to characterise the destruction of sperm as property damage for the purposes of a tortious action has attracted attention for crossing the line against ownership of the human body (Dickens and Cook, 2010: 93).[31] However, the property attribution is limited to claims in tort and it is clear that its application in other cases is restricted. The 'ownership' envisaged by the court did not establish a new property interest in human gametes enforceable against persons generally (Rostill, 2013: 17). Indeed, another criticism of the decision is that the property model is a legal fiction that distorts legal conceptions of actionable damage. While the deposit of sperm may generate property-like rights, sperm itself is widely recognised as not property as such. Furthermore, it is clear that it was not the attachment the men had to the sperm itself, rather the potential of fatherhood the sperm represented that motivated the *Yearworth* claimants.[32] This interpretation, however, emphasises a possession and use of gametes that conforms to a procedural account of reproductive autonomy. A property-contract or damage to property in tort does not capture the loss that is perhaps experienced in the loss of genetic parenthood that is more akin to loss of fertility (a personal injury that is not caused by the negligence in such cases). Instead, a language to articulate the material effects of the loss of ability to become a genetic parent is needed to give proper recognition to such harm and a substantive version of parental autonomy outlined above might serve such a purpose.

The Northern Ireland situation (discussed above) shows that, where the property model is inapplicable, the law defaults to a no-compensation result.[33] Notwithstanding the array of policy considerations and the difficulties of establishing duty of care and causation, the Northern Ireland Court of Appeal failed to even engage in an articulation of harms involved in the case, declining to open up a debate of actionable damage.

While acknowledging that the outcome would not have been any different, Sheldon highlights how the court failed to engage in proper consideration of the issues by refusing to engage with the harms experienced by the parties, with no mention of human rights or use of empirical evidence on demography and racism (2011: 667). Perhaps a discussion of family building and the norms that operate

31 The Ontario Superior Court of Justice has recently held that human tissue removed from the body is capable of being personal property in a case concerning genetic testing: *Piljak Estate v Abraham* 2014 ONSC 2893. See also *Lam v University of British Columbia* 2013 BCSC 2094.

32 See comments of Lord Stewart in *Holdich* [2013] ScotCS CSOH 197.

33 *A & B by C (Their Mother & Next Friend) v A– Health & Social Services Trust* [2011].

around kinship in the fertility context could have shed a different light on the claimant's case in a way that is ethically justified.[34]

Conclusion

The discussion has sought to outline a perceived failure to characterise the harms resulting from errors in the provision of assisted conception services that appears in tension with an underpinning respect for reproductive autonomy and the recognition of family building implied in the 2008 Act, but that also falls out of step with continuing trends in bioethics and calls for further law reform. This undermines the ability of the law to provide redress, which is an important part of the overall regulatory regime. It also proposed a version of autonomy that captures the processes involved in family building and meanings of kinship arrangements generated by assisted conception that may support substantive notions of reproductive autonomy.

References

Alghrani, A., (2009) 'The Human Fertilisation and Embryology Act 2008: a missed opportunity?' 35 (12) *Journal of Medical Ethics* 718.

Becker, G., Butler, A. and Nachtigall, R., (2005) 'Resemblance talk: A challenge for parents whose children were conceived with donor gametes in the US' 61 *Social Science & Medicine* 1300.

BioNews, (2002) 'IVF mistake was "labelling error"' *BioNews* 182 (4 November 2002, Progress Educational Trust).

BioNews, (2004a) 'Report of IVF "blunders" inquiry is published' *BioNews* 264 (24 June 2004, Progress Educational Trust).

BioNews, (2004b) 'US couple are compensated for IVF mix-up' *BioNews* 276 (20 September 2004, Progress Educational Trust).

BioNews, (2004c) 'US woman receives $1m compensation for IVF error' *BioNews* 270 (9 August 2004, Progress Educational Trust).

Blackburn-Starza, A., (2013) 'Report review: Donor information sharing – preservation of personal liberty or the indirect control over people's private lives?' *BioNews* 702 (29 April 2013, Progress Educational Trust).

Blackburn-Starza, A. (2014) 'The Ohio sperm-mix up: What's the harm in giving birth to a healthy, beautiful baby girl? *BioNews 783* (8 December 2014, Progress Educational Trust).

Chico, V., (2011) *Genomic Negligence: An Interest in Autonomy as the Basis for Novel Negligence Claims Generated by Genetic Technology* (Abingdon: Routledge).

Chohan, N., (2014) 'Out-of-court settlement for girl conceived with abnormal donor sperm' *BioNews* 740 (3 February 2014, Progress Educational Trust).

Clark, T. and Nolan, D., (2014) 'A critique of *Chester v Afshar*' 34(3) *Oxford Journal of Legal Studies* 1.

34 See, for example, comments on the Jennifer Cramblett case in McKnight, 2014 in *The New Yorker*, 'The Ohio Sperm-Bank Controversy: A New Case for Reparations?' <http://www.newyorker.com/news/news-desk/ohio-sperm-bank-controversy-new-case-reparations>.

Culley, L. and Hudson, N., (2009) 'Commonalities, difference and possibilities: Culture and infertility in British South Asian communities' in Culley, L., Hudson, N. and van Rooij, F., (eds) *Marginalised Reproduction: Ethnicity, Infertility and Reproductive Technologies* (Abingdon: Routledge).

Dickens, B. and Cook, R., (2010) 'The legal status of in vitro embryos' 111 *International Journal of Gynecology and Obstetrics* 91.

Edwards, J., (2014) 'Undoing kinship' in Freeman, T., Graham, S., Ebtehaj, F. and Richards, M., (eds) *Relatedness in Assisted Reproduction: Families, Origins and Identities* (Cambridge: Cambridge University Press).

Eijkholt, M., (2011) 'Procreative autonomy and the Human Fertilisation and Embryology Act 2008: Does a coherent conception underpin UK law?' 11(2) *Medical Law International* 93.

Fenton, R., Heenan, S. and Rees, J., (2010) 'Finally fit for purpose? The Human Fertilisation and Embryology Act 2008' 32(3) *Journal of Social Welfare & Family Law* 275.

Fox, M., (2009) 'The Human Fertilisation and Embryology Act 2008: Tinkering at the Margins' 17(3) *Feminist Legal Studies* 333.

Franklin, S., (2013) *Biological Relatives: IVF, Stem Cells and the Future of Kinship* (Durham, NC and London: Duke University Press).

Franklin, S. and McKinnon, S., (2002) *Relative Values: Reconfiguring Kinship Studies* (Durham, NC and London: Duke University Press).

Freeman, T., Graham, S., Ebtehaj, F. and Richards, M., (eds) (2014) *Relatedness in Assisted Reproduction: Families, Origins and Identities* (Cambridge: Cambridge University Press).

Frodsham, G., (2012) 'Couple has children from different racial backgrounds following alleged IVF mix-up' *BioNews* 655 (8 May 2012, Progress Educational Trust).

Grodsky, J., (2007) 'Genomics and Toxic Torts: Dismantling the risk-injury divide' 59 *Standard Law Review* 1671.

Gurnham, D. and Miola, J., (2012) 'Reproduction, rights, and the welfare interests of children: The times they aren't a-changin' 23 *King's Law Journal* 29.

Horsey, K., (2013) 'Swept under the Carpet: Why surrogacy law needs urgent review' in Priaulx, N. and Wrigley, A., (eds) *Ethics, Law and Society: Volume 5* (Farnham: Ashgate Publishing).

Jackson, E., (2001) *Regulating Reproduction: Law, Technology and Autonomy* (Oxford: Hart Publishing).

Jones, B., (2010) 'Canadian fertility doctor sued over sperm mix-up claims' *BioNews* 576 (20 September 2010, Progress Educational Trust).

Marre, D. and Bestard, J., (2009) 'The family body: Persons, bodies and resemblance' in Edwards, J. and Salazar, C., (eds) *European Kinship in the Age of Biotechnology* (Oxford: Berghahn Books).

McKnight, M., (2014) 'The Ohio sperm-bank controversy: A new case for reparations?' *The New Yorker* 14 October 2014.

Nelson, E., (2013) *Law, Policy and Reproductive Autonomy* (Oxford: Hart Publishing).

Nolan, D., (2007) 'New forms of damage in negligence' 70 *Modern Law Review* 59.

Nolan, D., (2013) 'Damage in the English law of negligence' 4(3) *Journal of European Tort Law* 247.

Nordqvist, P. and Smart, C., (2014) *Relative Strangers: Family Life, Genes and Donor Conception* (Basingstoke: Palgrave Macmillan).

Photopoulos, J., (2010) 'A tall story: genetic factors in height determination' *BioNews* 578 (4 October 2010).

Priaulx, N., (2007) *The Harm Paradox: Tort Law and the Unwanted Child in an Era of Choice* (Abingdon: Routledge-Cavendish).

Priaulx, N., (2008) 'Rethinking progenitive conflict: Why reproductive autonomy matters' 16(2) *Medical Law Review* 169.

Priaulx, N., (2010) 'Managing novel reproductive injuries in the Law of Tort: The curious case of destroyed sperm' 17 *European Journal of Health Law* 81.

Priaulx, N., (2015, unpublished) 'Injuries that matter: Manufacturing Damage in Negligence' *Express O* <http://works.bepress.com/nicolette_priaulx/2>.

Roberts, D., (1996) 'Race and the new reproduction' 47 *Hastings Law Journal* 935.

Rostill, L.D., (2013) 'The ownership that wasn't meant to be: *Yearworth* and property rights in human tissue' 40(1) *Journal of Medical Ethics* 14.

Satkunarajah, N., (2010) 'Singapore fertility clinic faces sperm mix-up probe' *BioNews* 583 (8 November 2010, Progress Educational Trust).

Shaikh, N., (2009) 'Fertility watchdog investigates serious IVF mix-ups at London hospital' *BioNews* 506 (3 May 2009, Progress Educational Trust).

Sheldon, S., (2009) 'A missed opportunity to reform an outdated law' 4 *Clinical Ethics* 3.

Sheldon, S., (2011) 'Only skin deep? The harm of being born a different colour to one's parents *A (a minor) and B (a minor) by C (their mother and next friend) v A Health and Social Services Trust* [2010] NIQB 108; [2011] NICA 28' 19(3) *Medical Law Review* 657.

Sheldon, S. and McCandless, J., (2014) 'Genetically challenged: The determination of legal parenthood in assisted reproduction' in Freeman, T., Graham, S., Ebtehaj, F. and Richards, M., (eds) *Relatedness in Assisted Reproduction: Families, Origins and Identities* (Cambridge: Cambridge University Press).

Stapleton, J., (1988) 'The gist of negligence: Part 1. Minimal actionable damage' 104 *Law Quarterly Review* 213.

The Telegraph,. (2014) 'You're big business now baby' <http://www.telegraph.co.uk/women/womens-health/11171311/youre-big-business-now-baby.html>

Thompson, C., (2005) 'Making parents: The ontological choreography of reproductive technologies' (MIT Press, Inside Technology Series).

Witting, C., (2002) 'Physical damage in negligence' 61(1) *Cambridge Law Journal* 189.

11 'A less than perfect law': The unfulfilled promise of Canada's Assisted Human Reproduction Act

Pamela White

Introduction

'Is there something truly unique about assisted human reproduction that requires specific and overarching regulations and strict penalties?' (Lemmens, 2011). In the UK, the response has been emphatically in the affirmative (Burns, 2012). By way of contrast, in the US, a public policy silence has delegated assisted reproductive technology (ART) governance to state-level family law, consumer-driven clinics, the American Society for Reproductive Medicine (ASRM) and professional medical societies and associations (Briggs, 2010; Thompson, 2005). Canada, in seeking to avoid the negative lessons of commercialisation that typified the stance of its southern neighbour, turned to the UK example of centralised legislation and regulation (Jones and Slater, 2010).

Modelled on Britain's Human Fertilisation and Embryology Act 1990 (the 1990 Act), and its centralised approach to ART regulation, Canada's comprehensive 2004 Assisted Human Reproduction Act (AHRA) also offered ethical conceptual depth that the UK legislation has been criticised as lacking (Brazier, 1999). Canada's AHRA (s2) – like New Zealand's Assisted Reproductive Technology Act 2004 (s3, s4) and the Australian State of Victoria's 2008 Assisted Reproductive Technology Act (s5) – establishes from the outset the ethical and moral parameters of the regulation of ART. Explicit ethical principles are not found in the UK legislation though the 'twin pillars of consent and best interests of the child' underscore its administration.

However, the promise of Canada's restrictive 2004 pan-Canadian legislation setting to regulate IVF clinics and the practice of ART in manner not dissimilar to the UK remained unfulfilled. Once passed, the AHRA became the subject of a constitutional division of powers debate with Quebec challenging the federal government's authority to regulate in areas designated as provincial constitutional responsibilities. Canada's Supreme Court (SCC) was bitterly split (4:4:1) on the 'evil posed by assisted human reproduction' that warranted the use of Criminal Code powers. Six years after the AHRA was passed, the 2010 SCC decision in *Reference Assisted Human Reproduction Act* 2010 SCC 61 (*AHRA Reference*) rendered much of the AHRA *ultra vires* on the basis that the provinces and not the federal government have the constitutional authority to regulate the practice of medicine and research.

At the time the AHRA was passed, Canadian legislators were advised to consider the implications of striving to attain perfection to the exclusion of 'attaining the good'. While the legislative goal of 'attaining the good' may have been well intended, both the AHRA and its implementation were flawed. This chapter reviews the unfulfilled promise of Canada's misguided legislation. It examines the federal AHRA and its remit post *AHRA Reference*, alongside recent provincial legislative efforts and emerging private sector governance. The chapter concludes with a discussion of possible future directions for Canadian ART regulation.

Canada's 2004 AHRA: Comprehensive pan-Canadian regulation reinforced by criminal code penalties

Canada's first IVF baby was born in 1983, some five years after the birth in the UK of Louise Brown (cbc.ca archives). For Canadians, the ability of embryonic ART to overcome the medical obstacles of infertility offered considerable hope to childless couples and individuals and the LGBT community. Yet the widespread application of ART introduced social, ethical and legal concerns, including the threat of eugenics and a redefinition of the 'family'. ART created the opportunity for the commercialisation of human procreation, with surrogacy being viewed as especially troubling (Miall, 1993). While offering hope to the infertile, the regulation of ART enabled an unprecedented opportunity for state intervention in family life and scientific endeavour (Alghrani and Harris, 2006).

In response to mounting social and political pressure, Canada created a commission of inquiry and held extensive public consultations. Britain's Warnock Committee provided a model for Canada's Royal Commission on New Reproductive Technologies, appointed in 1989 and chaired by Dr Patricia Baird. The Baird Commission was given a broad mandate, similar in scope to the one accorded to Warnock (Baird, 1993: 2).

The 1993 Baird Report, *Proceed with Care*, was comprehensive, extensive and voluminous.[1] Central to Baird's recommendations was the view that federal regulation based on the peace, order and good government clause of the Constitution Act 1987 was justified given the potential of ART to endanger the health and safety of Canadians, especially women and children. In summary, the Commissioners reached three overarching conclusions about the delivery of new reproductive technologies: i) an urgent need existed for well-defined boundaries around the use of ART; ii) accountable regulation should protect the interests of those involved as well as society as a whole; and iii) given the increasing pace of knowledge and development, a flexible and continuing response to evolving technologies that involves wide input from Canadians was essential to their responsible delivery. Baird also recommended the creation of a New Reproductive Technologies

1 *Proceed with Care: Final Report of the Royal Commission on New Reproductive Technologies* consists of two volumes (1,200 pages) accompanied by 15 volumes of research. It made 293 recommendations. However, the Commission was stalked by controversy and its activities hotly debated (Eichler, 1993; Weir and Habib, 1997).

Commission similar in scope to the UK's Human Fertilisation and Embryology Authority (HFEA).

Canada's Parliament, as had been the case in the UK following Warnock, did not respond immediately to implement the Commission's recommendations. Two years after Baird reported, the government placed a voluntary moratorium on reproductive technologies deemed contrary to Canadian values and ethics, notably cloning. A year later, in 1996, it took steps to address a most pressing health need: the transmission of disease from use of untested donor sperm. Some 11 years after *Proceed with Care*, following a series of legislative attempts,[2] further consultation,[3] a final round of House of Commons debates and Senate Committee Hearings culminated in the passing of Canada's AHRA (2004). The AHR Agency was established in 2006.

Though the AHRA passed without amendment, it was recognised as being imperfect legislation. Failure to address federal/provincial constitutional division of powers even though questions about the constitutionality of the AHRA had been present since its conception (Von Tigerstrom, 2011), together with delays in legislative implementation, mismanagement by the AHR Agency, and federal regulatory paralysis characterise Canada's federal ART legislative and regulatory record (Baylis and Downie, 2013).

In 2004, Quebec initiated a series of court proceedings alleging that the federal government had strayed into and interfered with matters under provincial constitutional jurisdiction: the practice of medicine and research (Décret, 1177–2004; Décret, 73–2006). The Attorney General of Canada's appeal to the SCC of the 2008 Quebec Federal Court decision on the matter was heard on 17 April 2009. After many months, the Court rendered its decision on 22 December 2010 (*AHRA Reference*).

The characterisation of ART as both a moral evil and a beneficial medical technique that needed to be controlled bitterly divided the SCC (Gaudreault-DesBiens and Karazvian, 2012). Chief Justice McLachlin asked whether the Act should be characterised as legislation which curtails 'the negative impacts associated with AHR or rather as legislation that promotes positive medical practices?' (*AHRA Reference*, p.6). The McLachlin faction argued that the pith and substance of the entire Act was to uphold morality and prohibit a public health evil and, as such, it held a valid criminal law purpose. Justices Le Bel and Deschamps set apart the challenged sections as being rules to govern the practice of medicine

2 The 1996 Bill C-47, Human Reproductive and Genetic Technologies Act, was dropped from the *Order Paper* when Parliament was prorogued, spring 1997. In 2002, Bill C-56 (An Act Respecting Assisted Human Reproduction) included provisions for the establishment of an AHR Agency; renamed C-13, the Act was reintroduced following adjournment of Parliament in 2003 and again in January 2004 introduced as C-6 (An Act Respecting Assisted Human reproduction and Related Research). The AHRA was given Royal Assent on 29 March 2004.

3 The Advisory Committee on the Interim Moratorium on Reproductive and Genetic Technologies chaired by S. Martin established December 1996; Standing Committee on Health, Bonnie Brown. December 2001; *Assisted Human Reproduction: Building Families*; House of Commons consultations on a draft AHR Act C-6.

and research which do not fall within the remit of federal criminal code powers. The tie-breaking opinion of Justice Cromwell disagreed with the Chief Justice's analysis, sided largely with LeBel and Deschamps JJ, and found a compromise by including within the federal constitutional remit the sections of the AHRA dealing with consent (s8) and donation by youth for the purposes of fertility preservation (s9) (Mitchell, 2011; Whyte, 2011).

The Baird Commission's vision of comprehensive federal legislation and regulation, similar in scope to the UK's, was shattered by the *AHRA Reference* decision rendering *ultra vires* the sections of the Act that sought to licence and regulate the practice of ART and research.[4] The SCC ruled that these sections exceeded the legislative authority of the Parliament of Canada under the Constitution Act 1867 as they sought to regulate and promote the benefits of medical practice and research which are provincial constitutional responsibilities. The absolute prohibitions in the Act which had not been contested were upheld as criminal law.

Ogbogu (2013) observes that *AHRA Reference* serves to remind Canadian legislators that in the context of health matters the valid use of criminal law for public purpose is restricted to the suppression of a legitimate public health evil. From an ART policy standpoint Hogg (2014) considers the decision to be unfortunate. Cameron and Gruben (2014) argue that from a feminist perspective the SCC in striking down the licencing regime (s10), the AHR Agency and the health reporting information registry (s17) failed to recognise the Act's beneficial impact on women's reproductive health. From a governance perspective, Canada's post-*AHRA Reference* legislative landscape, rather than having one uniform and standard approach as had been established in the UK, must evolve separately in each provincial jurisdiction, likely in a patchwork fashion (Mitchell, 2011).

Quebec moved quickly to regulate ART medical treatment and research (CQLR.C-A-5.01; CQLR.C-A-5.01, r.1). Funding of ART began in late 2009, consultation and assessment of the program occurred in 2013 with a report published in 2014 (White, 2013, 2014). Quebec remains Canada's sole province to fund IVF through the provincial healthcare program, though the recently elected majority liberal government in Ontario announced funding for one cycle of IVF (Government of Ontario 2014 Budget, 31).

In the common-law provinces, oversight for the medical and clinical practice of ART has been left to the self-regulating medical and clinical bodies such as the Colleges of Physicians and Surgeons, professional associations and the private sector. Still, as Guichon et al. (2013) observe, only the Alberta and Saskatchewan Colleges of Physicians and Surgeons have adopted ART practice guidelines. Accountability, standard setting and certification have been entrusted increasingly to Accreditation Canada (AC), the Canadian Standards Association (CSA) and to professional associations such as the Canadian Fertility and Andrology Society

4 *Assisted Human Reproduction Act*, 2010 SCC 61, [2010] 3 SCR 457 at 5. Sections rendered *ultra vires*: ss10, 11, 13, 14–18, 40(2), (3), (3.1), (4) and (5) and 44(2) and (3). The SCC decision also stated that ss 40(1), (6) and (7), 41–43, 44(1) and 44(4), 45–53, 61 and 68 are constitutional to the extent that they relate to constitutionally valid provisions.

(CFAS). Provincial courts, family law and public institutions are responding to ART matters on a case-by-case basis,[5] with strong consumer demand shaping IVF clinic policies.[6] The prospect of federal punitive legal action until recently has had little deterrent impact on the providers of services to surrogates and egg donors (Motluk, 2010).[7]

In 2012, two years after *AHRA Reference*, the federal government amended the AHRA. During the days following the announced legislative changes found buried in an omnibus tax budget Bill,[8] it was the elimination of the federal AHR Agency, resulting in an expected savings of $10 million, that caught the media's attention. However, as the story developed the discussion shifted to the actual amount of the savings that were likely to be achieved: a sum of barely $5 million, as Assisted Human Reproduction Canada (AHRC) had never spent its annual budgetary allowance (Blackwell, 2012). The realisation of a lower financial saving was soon accompanied by stinging commentaries focusing on AHRC's lack of effectiveness (Kingston, 2012), the unsightly public disagreements between AHRC's President and the board members, the failure to enforce prohibitions on gamete selling and commercial surrogacy, as well as on Health Canada's utter incapability to bring forward regulations (CBC *The Current*, 2012). Critical commentary together with a review of the previous 25 years of public debate served to cast a dismal pall of failure on Canada's ART project with several prominent bioethicists, lawyers and political scientists expressing a considerable degree of displeasure and disappointment over Canada's misdirected foray into the realm of ART regulation (Baylis and Downie, 2013).

Canada's amended AHRA 2012: Protection of morality, health and safety

The 2012 amendments to the AHRA have been labelled as being no more or less a re-run of the earlier failed legislative project (Cattapan and Cohen, 2013). Certainly there is much truth to the view that little has changed. While the legislative remit is narrower, the Act continues to rely on Criminal Code powers to prohibit selected ART activities, unless permitted by regulation (Norris and Tiedemann, 2012). The regulatory apparatus of Health Canada (HC), the department now responsible for administrating the AHRA, remains paralysed and moribund as no regulatory activity has been undertaken.

In response to Canada's failed AHRA three differing but complementary policy analyses have occurred. Baylis and Downie (2013) invite the federal government to respect its fiduciary duty to Canadians by showing leadership and initiating the regulatory process. Several legal scholars (Cameron and Gruben, 2014; Hogg,

5 *Pratten v British Columbia (Attorney General)* 2011 BCSC 656.

6 See, e.g. comments on Canadian IVF clinic websites about failure of government to respond to patients' requests for mitochondrial DNA donation to be legalised in Canada www.genesis.ca.

7 *R v Leia Picard and Canadian Fertility Consulting Ltd* 2013.

8 C-38: *Jobs, Growth and Long-term Prosperity.*

2014; Mitchell, 2011; Snow and Knoff, 2012) have examined other regulatory models including Australia and Quebec. Medical legal ethicists have explored the ethical guidance offered by s2 of the AHRA as suggestive of a way forward (Couture et al, 2014; Guichon et al, 2013).

To understand the current tensions in ART policy debate it is important to examine Canada's amended AHRA. I argue that the Act rests on three pillars set out in legislation: i) establishment of a bright line between a select number of activities which due to their irrefutable moral implications warrant prohibition and those ART activities which can be permitted if they adhere to ethical principles of non-discrimination, non-commoditisation, consent and altruism; ii) the protection of the morality, health and safety of Canadians, narrowly conceived as a regulated reimbursement of expenses scheme for surrogates and gamete donors and a national health and safety testing regime for donated sperm and ova; and iii) strong Criminal Code powers enabling inspection, compliance enforcement and prosecution.

Pillar 1: Ethical values define the bright line separating prohibited and sanctioned ART activities

Canada's amended AHRA begins with a set of 'principles not customarily advanced by the criminal law' (Mitchell, 2011: 637). All principles are of equal importance, an ethical stance similar to the one adopted by New Zealand (s3, s4). This schema contrasts with the Australian State of Victoria's 2008 Act (s5) which lists five underpinning ethical principles in descending order of importance (Atkin, 2004). By way of contrast, neither the UK's 1990 nor amended 2008 Human Fertilisation and Embryology (HFE) Act lay out an explicit set of underlying ethical principles.

Section 2 AHRA reflects Parliament's desire to establish the ethical guidelines intended to shape Canada's ART governance response. As the guidelines are enshrined in a 'statutory declaration', the principles have greater legal force than had they been set out in a preamble (Hébert et al, 2003; Interpretation Act, s13). Section 2 provides regulatory guidance to the organisations mandated to fulfil the requirements of the Act (Rivard and Hunter, 2005). The ethical principles are national in scope and given that *AHRA Reference* left this section of the legislation untouched, I argue that they serve as guidance to provincial legislators and the private sector governance groups as well as HC. Thus all parties involved in ART governance have an obligation to consider and respect the scope and intent of the overarching ethical principles set out in s2 AHRA.

Rivard and Hunter (2005: 36) argue that the 'the principles recognise the impacts of these technologies both on the larger society and on the individuals involved with their use and who are created by them, as well as their families'. Similar ethical concerns are evidenced in Chapter I (1.1 and 1.2) of the Quebec Act (Respecting Clinical and Research Activities Related to Assisted Procreation) which identify the necessity to protect the health of persons, especially women and the children born of ART activities, with the Civil Code enabling the filiation of such children (Chapter I.1.1). The objective of Quebec's regulation of clinical and research activities is to ensure high-quality, safe and ethical practices and to encourage ongoing improvement of services (Chapter I.1.2).

The ethical principles set out in s2 AHRA are drawn from a disparate set of sources. In part, their genesis can be found in the deliberations of the Baird Commission (1993, Chapter 3). Jones and Slater (2010) note that the National Action Committee on the Status of Women and the Women's Legal Education and Action Fund led the lobbying to have non-discrimination included in the Act. The 2001 Standing Committee of Health Report (Assisted Human Reproduction: Building Families) emphasised the requirement for informed consent.

The protection of the health and well-being of women and children is singled out as a priority consideration (s2(a)) with recognition being given to the particular consequences of ART for women as compared with men (s2(c)). As noted above, this concern is mirrored in the Quebec legislation (Chapter I.1.1). The benefits of ART for families and individuals are to be secured by taking appropriate measures for the protection and promotion of human health, safety, dignity and rights in the use of these techniques and in research (s2(b)). Stated affirmatively, free and informed consent is viewed as being a foundational value to be reflected in law (s2(d)). Discrimination in the conduct of assisted production is not acceptable (s2(e)). Commercialisation and trade in the reproductive capabilities of men and women, and the exploitation of children raise health and ethical concerns sufficient to justify their prohibition (s2(f)). The final declaratory principle recognises the ability of ART to do harm to human individuality and diversity, and to the very notion of what it means to be human (s2(g)). The paradigmatic examples of human cloning and the mixture of human and non-human genomic materials (chimera) were singled out for attention as having the potential to confront human dignity, thus mandating their prohibition.

The UK's HFE Act 2008 permits admixed embryo research and allows for regulations to be passed allowing that human embryos can be altered as a result of mitochondrial DNA donation (Section 3ZA(5) and see Riley, this volume).[9] In contrast, the strong ethical position taken by Canada regarding experimental cloning and DNA transfers has not gone without comment. Some view Canada's position as potentially detrimental to future scientific research (Caulfield, 2001); others have expressed doubt about the scientific justification for chimera and admixed embryo research (Baylis and Robert, 2007), and about the ethics of mitochondrial DNA transfers (Baylis, 2013).

The ethical principles of autonomy (free and informed consent), justice (avoidance of discrimination), beneficence (promotion of the wellbeing of women and children) and non-malfeasance (avoidance of commercialisation) are privileged. The final principle speaks to the ability of ART to harm human individuality, diversity and the very notion of what it means to be human.

Present in New Zealand's legislation but missing from Canada's list of ethical principles is recognition that access to information about ART complements consent and promotes the well-being of those undergoing or conceived as a result

9 In the UK, mitochondrial DNA donation will likely be permitted by Regulations in 2016.

of ART techniques (Atkin, 2004). This omission proves problematic in light of the *AHRA Reference* decision as s17, which legislated for the Health Information Registry, was ruled *ultra vires*. The Quebec legislation restores the population health aspects of such a registry, though as Couture (2014) argues, compliance with s2 requires greater beneficent treatment of the duties owed to the children conceived using donated third-party gametes than exists in Quebec, which favours anonymous donor gametes.

The declaratory power of these principles establishes an ethical bright line supporting prohibition of specific behaviours defined as being detrimental to human dignity and Canadian society, and of others rendered permissible in certain circumstances as specified in regulation. Human cloning and creation of admixed embryos (s5) are prohibited. Altruistic surrogacy (s6) and gamete donation (s7) is mandated. Free and informed consent is required for the creation, use and donation of embryos (s8). Underage participation in ART is prohibited except in cases of fertility preservation (s9). Failure to comply with these prohibitions carries the prospect of stiff Criminal Code sanctions.

The UK's HFE Act 2008 privileges embryo research (including on admixed human embryos) subject to close regulation by the HFEA. The HFE Act 1990 mandated altruistic gamete and embryo donation, and pursuant to the 2008 amendment the creation and storage of embryos by persons under age 18 (Consent, Schedule 3, 2008 HFE Act) is also permitted. The 2008 Act has also clarified embryo use upon death of a partner and in the event of disagreements about use. As recent jurisprudence attests, failure to obtain 'informed' consent prior to the commencement of treatment can have serious implications for the attribution of legal parenthood.[10]

Pillar 2: Protection of the morality, health and safety of Canadians

The second pillar of the AHRA rests on the federal fiduciary remit: protection of public morality, health and safety. Narrowly conceived, the focus concerns the testing and screening of donated gametes, the reimbursement of expenses incurred by gamete donors and surrogates and the regulation of consent. Here, I will discuss briefly the s10 and s12 amendments concerning the testing and screening of sperm and ovum donors, and the reimbursement of expenses incurred by gamete donors and surrogates. Consent to donate gametes and embryos to a third party and to research, creation and use of embryos for reproductive purposes, and use of embryos following death were enshrined in AHRA (s8: Consent) Regulations. This is the only AHRA regulation currently in force.

Testing of sperm and ovum (s10), and the reimbursement of expenses incurred by surrogates and gamete donors (s12)

As amended, the AHRA states that the changes made to s10 were undertaken to reduce risks to human health and safety arising from the reproductive use of

10 *Re E and F (Assisted Reproduction: Parent)* [2013] EWHC 1418 (Fam).

human sperm and ova (disease transmission). In this amendment, the federal government draws on the ethical principle 2(b) requiring the taking of appropriate measures to ensure safety and promotion of health. The amended Act at section 10(2), 10(3) and 10(4) brings the testing of both sperm and ova under the Criminal Code powers of the AHRA.

It has been acknowledged since 2005, that the 1996 Processing and Distribution of Semen for Assisted Conception Regulations did not also address health and safety issues pertaining to ova (Rivard and Hunter, 2005). Health Canada (HC) never took the legislative steps necessary to regulate screening and testing of ova under the Food and Drug Act as it had done with sperm. At least one IVF clinic director indicated reluctance to use third-party donated ova due to the lack of Canadian testing standards (*CBC News*, 2012). Yet evidence exists that Canadian IVF clinics are importing frozen human eggs and that the freezing of third-party ova occurs (Downie and Baylis, 2013a; Lui and Greenblatt, 2012).

Since the 2012 amendments, no s10 regulations have been tabled in the House of Commons or the Senate and no discussion has occurred at the Health Committee. HC might be tempted to argue that the s10 regulatory void has been partially filled by the CSA who, in association with IVF clinic directors and embryologists, developed an ova and sperm testing and screening standard which was adopted for use by the CFAS in December 2012, though compliance is voluntary (CAN/CSA-Z900.2.1-12). This soft governance private sector regulatory approach to the protection of the health and safety of Canadians, I argue, does not meet the 'pith and substance' of the Act. HC has not indicated when it intends to regulate the testing and screening of ovum.

Reimbursement of expenses incurred by surrogates and gamete donors (s12)

The amended AHRA 2012 replaces s12(1) with the following:

> No person shall, except in accordance with the regulations, reimburse for expenses incurred in the donation of sperm or ovum, transport or maintenance of an in vitro embryo, or reimburse a surrogate mother for expenditures.

To date, no regulations have been passed. One can only conclude that the federal government appears unable to determine how to regulate the reimbursement of gamete donation and surrogacy without being seen to promote the commercialisation of these activities. Thus absent of a legal ruling, the HC statement indicating that the selling of gametes is illegal but their purchase is not, reflects the government's policy position (Downie and Baylis, 2013b; Mainland and De Rose, 2014).

The government's lack of regulatory action in association with its failure to prosecute those persons involved in what has been labelled a 'human egg trade' has been severely criticised (Downie and Baylis, 2013a; Gruben, 2013). Recommendations for HC action have included the issuing of clarifying statements as regards the remit of the AHRA prohibitions, drafting of regulations, enforcement of the Act, preparation of guidance documents for provincial and territorial officials, and initiation of federal/provincial forums on infertility and donation of excess frozen eggs (Downie and Baylis, 2013a). No HC response has as yet been forthcoming.

Pillar 3: Strong Criminal Code penalties – tough sanctions, no regulations and little guidance

The AHRA's strong criminal law powers equip HC to take the regulatory and enforcement actions required to meet its responsibilities. Yet the government has demonstrated prolonged reluctance to prosecute those suspected of being involved in egg selling and commercial surrogacy (Motluk, 2010). The first prosecution under the AHRA initiated in response to evidence obtained by American law enforcement agencies resulted in the conviction for fraud of a private IVF clinic owner who advertised and supplied surrogacy services.[11]

Critics argue that the Act's prohibitions are misplaced and counter-productive, achieving the reverse outcome than that intended by potentially endangering women to a greater extent than would have occurred had a more open approach to the donation of eggs and surrogacy been in place (Cattapan, 2013). Certainly the federal reluctance to regulate reveals a profound failure to put into force the ethical principle 2(b) which speaks to the 'benefits of ART and related research being effectively secured by taking appropriate measures for the protection and promotion of human health, safety, dignity and rights in the use of these technologies and in related research' (also see Horsey and Neofytou, this volume, who comment similarly on the UK's position). Protection has been viewed solely through a lens of policing further complicated by regulatory paralysis.

The scope of federal health protection permitted by the amended AHRA speaks to a narrow interpretation of health which does not align well with the World Health Organisation (1946) declaration that 'Health is a state of complete physical, mental and social well-being and not merely the absence of disease or infirmity'. Section 2(a) AHRA acknowledges Parliament's recognition that the well-being of the child born through the application of ART must be given priority, and in s2(c) that the well-being of women must be protected in the application of these technologies. The responsibility to ensure the well-being of women and of children conceived using ART and the examination of health issues related to infertility by such means as health surveillance and health promotion is a public health policy area seemingly vacated by the federal government even though HC and its sister department, the Public Health Agency of Canada, possess health promotion and surveillance mandates.

Compliance with ethical principles of beneficence and justice described in s2(a) and s2(c) now fall to provincial legislatures and private sector self-appointed actors through a case-by-case application of provincial family law, specific provincial regulations and development of codes, practices and ethical protocols adopted by private sector governance bodies. These approaches do not imply that there will

11 *R v Leia Picard and Canadian Fertility Consulting Ltd* 2013; Blackwell, 2013.

necessarily be less regulation, only that there could be less transparency with considerable potential for uneven law and governance as a patchwork of regulation is developed across the country.

Canada's misguided and imperfect legislation cannot be attributed solely to a misjudgement of constitutional responsibilities (Snow and Knoff, 2012). Regulatory paralysis combined with failure to enforce existing AHRA prohibitions characterises the federal response to its fiduciary duties in this area. The neoliberal privileging of self-regulation reveals a desire to enable private sector regulators to occupy an ever larger place in the ART arena as evidenced by HC's seemingly tacit acceptance of the voluntary CSA screening and testing of reproductive tissues (sperm and ovum) standard.

The federal government could demonstrate leadership by facilitating federal/provincial/private sector dialogue with a view to encouraging the development of provincial standards for the training and certification of embryologists. It could foster the development of uniform law where currently there exists confusion and conflicting legal approaches in areas such as surrogacy and parenthood, birth registration and medical standards. The precedents for such pan-Canadian agreements within the spirit of federal/provincial cooperation are well established and often cited (e.g. Securities). Regrettably, HC shows little appetite for such an approach though under previous federal administrations provincial/territorial/private sector collaborations were common and frequently productive as is evidenced by cooperative legislative and policy setting in the areas such as information privacy and population health (e.g. Personal Information Protection and Electronic Documents Act; the Canadian Institute for Health Information).

Canada's ART governance is at the crucial stage marked by federal regulatory inaction, widespread provincial legislative disinterest and the unknown ability of private sector soft governance mechanisms (standards, certification and policies) to crystallise (Casey and Scott, 2011). In Quebec, a 2014 report commissioned by the *Commissaire à la santé et au bien-être,* entitled '*Avis dètaillé sur les activités de procreation assistée au Quebec*', contained several recommendations that draw from the UK experience; notably the screening of IVF patients for parental suitability, limiting of access based on age and voluntary sterilization, and uniform clinic practices sparked discussion about regulatory change (White, 2014). Fiscal restraint measures adopted by the recently elected Liberal government (2014) have resulted in a proposed scaling back of the province's IVF program and a tightening of the admissibility criteria. In Ontario, the funding of one cycle of IVF may also provide the impetus needed for the province to regulate IVF activities.

In the UK, by way of contrast, the 1990 HFE Act was revised in 2008 and the 8th edition of the HFEA's Code of Practice is in place. Since 1991, the HFEA has licensed clinics, authorised research, mandated open-identity gamete donation, regulated egg sharing, updated its consent regime and established a registry to collect treatment data and to retain information on the identity of gamete donors. It has tackled difficult ethical issues including best interests of the child and non-discrimination (McCandless, 2013), 'savour siblings' (Smith, 2013), sex selection for 'family balancing' (Wilkinson, 2008), prenatal genetic diagnosis

(Porter and Smith, 2013), same-sex parenting and the need for a father (Lee et al, 2014; McCandless and Sheldon, 2008) and disagreements among embryo donors (HFEA, 2008).

Such legislative and policy changes have not been without controversy, as the chapters in this volume attest. During the 2010 Conservative government's 'Bonfire of the Quangos' the HFEA came close to being merged with the Human Tissue Authority. However, the groundswell of support for the HFEA and recognition of its important coordinating and consultative role and regulatory expertise resulted in its retention, though operational efficiencies are expected to be achieved.

In the context of a national legislative framework, a strong argument can be made for the establishment of a central regulatory authority. In the aftermath of *AHRC Reference* Canada's amended AHRA retains no centralised governance capacity or regulatory agency. The future of Canada's regulatory project must involve all of the players, notably patients, federal and provincial governments, private sector clinics, professional associations and accreditation bodies. I argue that the ethical principles set out in s2 AHRA provide guidance. However, the crucial next step must be the serious engagement with ART governance by all parties: federal, provincial and private sector with the federal government making the first move by bringing forward legislation to regulate ovum testing and screening (s10) and reimbursement of gamete donors and surrogates (s12). Better yet would be a reconsideration of the punitive regime imposed by the Act: does gamete donation, screening and testing, and surrogacy truly warrant criminal code penalties?

References

Alghrani, A. and Harris. J., (2006) 'Reproductive Liberty: Should the Foundation of Families be Regulated?' 18(2) *Child and Family Law Quarterly* 175.

Atkin, B., (2004) 'Regulation of Assisted Human Reproduction: The Recent New Zealand Model in Comparison with Other Systems', RJP/NZACL Yearbook, vol.11, 81–100.

Baird, P., (1993) *Proceed with Care: Final Report of the Royal Commission on New Reproductive Technologies* (Ottawa: Minister of Government Services Canada).

Baylis, F., (2013) 'The Ethics of Creating Children with Three Genetic Parents' *Reproductive Biomedicine Online* 531.

Baylis, F. and Downie, J., (2013) 'A Tale of Assisted Human Reproduction Canada: A Tragedy in Five Acts' 25(2) *Canadian Journal of Women and the Law* 183.

Baylis, F. and Robert, S.J., (2007) 'Part-Human Chimeras: Worrying the Facts, Probing the Ethics' 7(5) *The American Journal of Bioethics* 41.

Blackwell, T., (2012) 'Government Shutters Agency that Oversees Canada's Fertility and Assisted Reproduction Industry' *National Post* (30 March 2012).

Blackwell, T., (2013) 'Illegal Purchase of Sperm, Eggs and Surrogacy Services Leads to 27 Charges against Canadian Fertility Company and CEO' *National Post* (15 February 2013).

Brazier, M., (1999) 'Regulating the Reproduction Business?' 7 *Medical Law Review* 166.

Briggs, L., (2010) 'Reproductive Technology: Of Labour and Markets' 36(2) *Feminist Studies* 359.

Brown, B., (2001) *Standing Committee on Health. Assisted Human Reproduction: Building Families* December 2001 (Ottawa: House of Commons).

Burns, S., (2012) *The Law of Assisted Reproduction* (Hayward's Heath: Bloomsbury Professional Ltd).

Cameron, A. and Gruben, V., (2014) 'Quebec's Constitutional Challenge to the *Assisted Human Reproduction Act*: Overlooking Women's Reproductive Autonomy?' in Patterson, S., Scala, F. and Sokolen, M. K., (eds) *Fertile Ground: Exploring Reproduction in Canada* (Montreal: McGill-Queen's University Press).

Casey, D. and Scott, C., (2011) 'The Crystallization of Regulatory Norms' 39(1) *Journal of Law and Society* 76.

Cattapan, A., (2013) 'Rhetoric and Reality: Protecting Women in Canadian Public Policy on Assisted Human Reproduction' 25(2) *Canadian Journal of Women and the Law* 202.

Cattapan, A. and Cohen, S., (2013) 'The Devil We Know: The Implications of Bill C-38 for Assisted Human Reproduction in Canada' 35(7) *Journal of Obstetrics and Gynaecology Canada* 654.

Caulfield, T., (2001) 'Clones, Controversy and Criminal Law: A Comment on the Proposal for Legislation Governing Assisted Human Reproduction' 39 *Alberta Law Review* 335.

CBC News (2012) 'Test Imported Human Eggs, Doctors Urge: Ova should Meet Same Safety Standards as Human Sperm' 27 April.

CBC Radio 1, The Current (2012) 'The Future of Assisted Human Reproduction' 11 April.

Couture, V. et al, (2014) 'Strengths and Pitfalls of Canadian Gamete and Embryo Donor Registries: Searching for Beneficent Solutions' 28 *Reproductive BioMedicine Online* 369.

Downie, J. and Baylis, F., (2013a) 'Transnational Trade in Human Eggs: Law, Policy and (In)action in Canada' *Journal of Law, Medicine and Ethics* (Spring) 224.

Downie, J. and Baylis, F., (2013b) *Letter to Ms. Lynn Mainland* (16 December 2013) www.noveltechethics.ca.

Eichler, M., (1993) 'Frankenstein meets Kafka: The Royal Commission on New Reproductive Technologies' in Basen, B., Eichler, M. and Lippman, A. (eds) *Misconceptions: The Social Construction of Choice and the New Reproductive Technologies* (Ottawa: Voyegeur Press), 196–222.

Gaudreault-DesBiens, J.-F. and Karazvian, N., (2012) 'Canada's New Reproductive Technologies: A Moral Evil, or Signs of Beneficial Medical Progress?' *Public Law* (January) 147.

Gouvernement du Québec (2014) *Commissaire à la santé et au bien-être, Avis dètaillé sur les activités de procreation assistée au Quebec* www.csbe.gouv.qc.ca.

Government of Ontario (2014) *Building Opportunity, Securing our Future, 2014 Ontario Budget Papers* (Toronto: Queen's Printer for Ontario).

Gruben, V., (2013) 'Women as Patients, Not Spare parts: Examining the Relationship between the Physicians and the Women Egg Providers' 25(2) *Canadian Journal of Women and the Law* 249.

Guichon, J., Mitchell, I. and Doig, D., (2013) 'Assisted Human Reproduction in Common Law Canada after the Supreme Court of Canada Reference: Moving beyond Regulation by Colleges of Physicians and Surgeons' 25(2) *Canadian Journal of Women and Law* 315.

Hébert, N., Chenier, M. and Norris, S., (2003), *Legislative Summary Bill c-13: Assisted Human Reproduction Act*, Parliamentary Research Branch, Library of Parliament. LS-434 E.

Hogg, P., (2014) *Constitutional Law of Canada*, vol. 1 (Toronto: Thomson Carswell).

Jones, M. and Slater, B., (2010) 'Proceeding Carefully: Assisted Human Reproduction Policy in Canada' 19(4) *Public Understanding Science* 420.

Kingston, A., (2012) 'Assisted Human Reproduction Canada: The Budget Cut Everyone Missed' *McLean's Magazine* (2 April 2012).

Knight, C. and Smith M.K., (2013) 'The Human Fertilisation and Embryology Act 2008' 32(2) *New Genetics and Society* 107.

Lee, E., Macvarish, J. and Sheldon, S., (2014) 'Assessing Child Welfare under the Human Fertilisation and Embryology Act 2008: A Case Study in Medicalisation?' 36(4) *Sociology of Health and Illness* 500.

Lemmens, T., (2011) 'The Assisted Human Reproduction Act and the Supreme Court of Canada' www.tvo.org (4 November 2011).

Liu, K.E. and Greenblatt, E.M., (2012) 'Oocyte Cryopreservation in Canada: A Survey of Canadian ART Clinics' 34(3) *Journal of Obstetrics and Gynecology Canada* 250.

Mainland, L. and De Rose, C., (2014) 'Response to Downie and Baylis Open Letter' www.noveltechethics.ca (6 February 2014).

McCandless, J., (2013) 'Cinderella and her Cruel Sisters: Parenthood, Welfare and Gender in the *Human Fertilisation and Embryology Act* 2008' 32(2) *New Genetics and Society* 135.

McCandless, J. and Sheldon, S., (2008) 'No Father Required? The Welfare Assessment in the Human Fertilisation and Embryology Act 2008' 18(3) *Feminist Legal Studies* 201.

Miall C.E., (1993) 'The Regulation of Reproduction: The Relevance of Public Opinion for Legislative Policy Formation' 7 *International Journal of Law and the Family* 18.

Mitchell, G.G., (2011) 'Not a General Regulatory Power — A Comment on *Reference re Assisted Human Reproduction Act*' 54 *Supreme Court Law Review* 633.

Motluk, A., (2010) 'The Human Egg trade: How Canada's Fertility Laws are Fooling Donors, Doctors and Parents' *The Walrus* 1–8.

Norris, N. and Tiedemann, M., (2012) *Legal Status at the Federal level of Assisted Human Reproduction in Canada*. Library of Parliament: Publication No. 2011–82-E (July 2012).

Ogbugu, U., (2013) 'The Assisted Human Reproduction Act Reference and the Thin Line Between Health and Crime' 22(1) *Constitutional Forum* 93.

Porter, G. and Smith, M., (2013) 'Preventing the Selection of "Deaf Embryos" under the Human Fertilisation and Embryology Act 2008: Problematising Disability' 32(2) *New Genetics and Society* 171.

Rivard, G. and Hunter, J., (2005) *The Law of Assisted Human Reproduction* (Markham: LexisNexis Canada).

Smith, M., (2013) 'The Human Fertilisation and Embryology Act 2008: Restrictions on the Creation of "Saviour Siblings" and the Relevance of the Harm Principle' 32(2) *New Genetics and Society* 154.

Snow, D. and Knopff, R., (2012) 'Assisted Reproduction Policy in Federal States: What Canada Should Learn from Australia' 5(12) *School of Public Policy Research Papers* 1.

Thompson, C., (2005) *Making Parents: The Ontological Choreography of Reproductive Technologies* (Cambridge, Mass: MIT Press).

Von Tigerstrom, B., (2011) 'Federal Health Legislation and the *Assisted Human Reproduction Act Reference*' 74 *Saskatchewan Law Review* 33.

Weir, L. and Habib, J., (1997) 'A Critical Feminist Analysis of the Final Report of the Royal Commission on New Reproductive Technologies' 52 *Studies in Political Economy* 137.

White, P.M., (2013) 'Quebec Government Orders a Review of IVF Funding' *BioNews* 706 (28 May 2013, Progress Educational Trust).

White, P.M., (2014) 'Quebec's Assisted Human Reproduction Program' http://impactethics.ca/2014/07/15/quebecs-assisted-human-reproduction-program/ (15 July 2014).

Wilkinson, S., (2008) 'Sexism, Sex Selection and 'Family Balancing'' 16(3) *Medical Law Review* 369.

World Health Organisation (1946) 'Preamble to the Constitution of the World Health Organisation as adopted by the International Health Conference (New York, 19–22 June 1946).

Whyte, J.D., (2011) 'Federalism and Moral Regulation: A Comment on the *Reference re Assisted Human Reproduction Act*' 74 *Saskatchewan Law Review* 45.

12 The regulation of PGD for medical sex selection and the gendering of disability in the UK and Australia

Isabel Karpin

Introduction

In Australia and the UK, as in a number of other jurisdictions,[1] diagnostic testing of an embryo prior to implantation (preimplantation genetic diagnosis (PGD)) is permitted primarily to avoid the birth of a child with a 'serious' disability or illness.[2] The use of a regulatory threshold of 'seriousness' for PGD has prompted debate regarding what constitutes a serious disability (Karpin and Savell, 2012; Scott, 2007). While there is no normative consensus and very little in the way of legislative guidance, in both the UK and Australia ethical practice guidelines and licensing conditions have created a space for clinics to take account of some contextual factors. For example, the 8th *Code of Practice* of the UK's Human Fertilisation and Embryology Authority (HFEA) requires clinics, when deciding whether to provide PGD to a patient, to consider not only medical factors but also the patient's familial and social circumstances, and the patient's views about the condition.[3] At the same time, the use of PGD to test for so-called 'social' characteristics or what might be described as undesired 'normal' physical variations, has been repeatedly rejected (see Snelling and Gavaghan, this volume). Indeed, this distinction is relied on to draw a sharp line between permissible and impermissible PGD for sex selection in both the UK and Australia. Both the Australian National Health and Medical Research Council's ART guidelines (NHMRC, 2007)[4] and

1 Australia: National Health and Medical Research Council *Ethical Guidelines on the Use of Assisted Reproductive Technology in Clinical Practice and Research 2007* (NHMRC ART Guidelines) para 12.2; UK: Human Fertilisation and Embryology Act 1990 (HFE Act) Sched 2 para 1ZA(1) and (2); see further Karpin, I. and Savell, K., (2012), chapter 4.

2 A notable exception is the USA where, in most states, access to PGD is not limited by law. In Australia and the UK, PGD is also permitted to increase the chance of a live birth using assisted reproductive technology (ART) by checking for chromosomal abnormalities (otherwise known as preimplantation genetic screening (PGS)) and to identify a tissue match for an existing ill child who will benefit from cord blood when the tissue-matched child is born.

3 Paras 10.5–10.7. A similar approach is taken in Western Australia where the Reproductive Technology Council (RTC) recommends consideration of the significance of the risk *for* the person seeking the testing at para 8 of the Policy on the Approval of Diagnostic Procedures Involving Embryos (March 2008).

4 Paras 11 and 12.2.

the UK Human Fertilisation and Embryology Act 1990 (HFE Act)[5] prohibit the use of PGD for non-medical sex selection – that is sex selection that is not being used to facilitate the prevention of a disease or disability.

While the ethical and regulatory debate has typically been concerned with whether, and in what circumstances, non-medical sex selection should be a permissible use of PGD, in this chapter I focus on the currently permissible *medical* sex selection or sex selection to avoid the birth of a child with a sex or gender-related disorder.[6] The legal facilitation of this form of sex selection raises important and under-examined questions regarding the significance of the gendering of disability.

The gendering of disability

In both the UK and Australia, regulations limiting access to PGD require the presence of an 'abnormality' or a 'defect'. Thus it seems clear that PGD would not be permitted to select against 'normal' traits that are merely undesirable physical variations. There is evidence, however, that suggests that what constitutes a 'normal' physical variation can possess a gendered dimension. Normative gender stereotypes can, and do, inform how disability is constructed. What is viewed as a disability in one sex can be viewed as a trivial variation, or even a positive trait in the other sex. Catherine Mills (2011) describes this phenomenon in a case involving a couple whose foetus was identified as having no left hand at the 19-week morphology ultrasound scan. The couple, who decided to terminate, were, according to Mills, 'strongly influenced by the knowledge that the foetus was female' (Mills, 2011: 1). She notes the significance 'social norms' play in decisions regarding termination and 'the role such norms play in establishing the conditions of what appear as reasonable decisions in the first place' (Mills, 2011: 3). Although there is no information provided about why gender influenced the couple's decision-making, Mills speculates the decision was based on concerns about female attractiveness.

In the context of PGD, a gendered understanding of disability may be present where sex selection of embryos is used as a risk reduction strategy because it is not possible to identify a single gene or set of genes for the relevant disorder. Non-Mendelian conditions or conditions that are polygenic are not usually the subject of PGD testing unless it can be shown that there is a higher incidence of the condition in one sex than the other. In those cases it has been argued that sex selection is an effective risk reduction strategy because it identifies embryos that are less vulnerable by virtue of their sex. These embryos are then transferred in preference to embryos of the other sex. However, the causes and diagnosis of non-Mendelian conditions that may have a polygenic, epigenetic and environmental component are often highly contested. Where there is a purported sex prevalence that assessment may also be impacted by gender stereotypes. There is significant

5 Sched 2 para 1ZB(1).

6 Sched 2 para 1ZA(1)(c) and 1ZB(3).

scholarly discussion of precisely this situation with autism. A number of highly regarded researchers contest the oft-repeated orthodoxy that autism is four times more likely to affect boys than girls (as will be shown later in this chapter) and suggest instead that there may be significant gender bias both in diagnosis of the condition and construction of the statistics (Gillis-Buck and Richardson, 2014; Goldman, 2013).

Thus, regulations that specifically allow PGD for sex selection based on biomedical claims while prohibiting sex selection based on social or psychological desires may be insisting on a false dichotomy. What, then, is the existing regulatory landscape for PGD and sex selection in the UK and Australia?

The regulatory landscape in the UK and Australia

The UK has regulated to permit access to and use of PGD in some manner since 1990, although direct reference to PGD in the HFE Act first occurred with the 2008 amendments (see Snelling and Gavaghan, this volume). It is thus not surprising that the HFE Act has been a model for other jurisdictions, such as Australia where PGD coupled with IVF is a thriving industry. As in the UK, there has been regulation of PGD in Australia since the early 1990s in the jurisdictions of Victoria, South Australia and Western Australia. However, only Western Australia has retained a system of detailed oversight similar to the current approach taken by the HFEA (Karpin and Savell, 2012).[7] Furthermore, compliance with the national NHMRC ART Guidelines is a condition of accreditation for all Australian ART clinics mandated under the Commonwealth *Research Involving Human Embryos Act 2002*. Below I will draw out some of the more salient elements of the regulatory oversight of PGD in the UK and Australia with respect to medical sex selection.

The regulation of medical sex selection and PGD in the UK

As a consequence of the 2008 amendments to the HFE Act, a licence for treatment can include an authorisation for embryo testing where there is a risk of a genetic, chromosomal or mitochondrion abnormality that will lead to the development of a serious physical or mental disability in the person to be born.[8] Schedule 2 para 1ZA(1)(c) states that embryo testing can be carried out to establish the sex of an embryo 'in a case where there is a particular risk that any resulting child will have or develop (i) a gender-related serious physical or mental disability, (ii) a gender-related serious illness, or (iii) any other gender-related serious medical condition'. Schedule 2 para 1ZA(3) states further, that 'for the purposes of subparagraph (1)(c), a physical or mental disability, illness or other medical condition

7 Human Reproductive Technology Act 1991 (WA).

8 Sched 2 para 1ZA(1)(b) and 1ZA(2). Note under para 1ZA(1)(a) PGD can also be used for 'establishing whether the embryo has a gene, chromosome or mitochondrion abnormality that may affect its capacity to result in a live birth'. This is sometimes described as PGS and is aimed at improving the success rate of ART rather than avoiding the birth of a disabled child, although it will also result in the avoidance of the transfer of embryos with chromosomal abnormalities.

is gender-related if the Authority is satisfied that (a) it affects only one sex, or (b) it affects one sex significantly more than the other'.

In the latter part of this chapter I will focus specifically on the circumstances of sub-paragraph (3) (b) namely where the condition (in this case autism) is alleged to 'affect one sex significantly more than the other' because it is in these circumstances where diagnostic gender bias may significantly inform statistical claims which provide a 'biomedical platform' (Gillis-Buck and Richardson, 2014) for the legal selection of sexed embryos. It is notable in this regard that the language of the HFE Act 1990 as amended in 2008 refers to gender-related conditions rather than sex-related conditions. There is no explanation for this in the legislation itself, the Explanatory notes or the 8th edition of the HFEA *Code of Practice*. Further, this language does not appear in earlier iterations of the *Code*, or in the 2002 HFEA Consultation document on sex selection (HFEA, 2002) or the 2003 report on that consultation (HFEA, 2003) except with respect to the potential for non-medical sex selection to endorse gender stereotyping. The use of this language is not insignificant since 'sex' is generally used to indicate a biological or genetic identity whereas 'gender' tends to describe a psycho-social construct (Goldman, 2013). It is possible that the use of 'gender' in paragraph 1ZA is inadvertent and further research will be necessary to ascertain a definitive answer to that question. However, whatever the basis for its inclusion, its presence is highly productive, reminding us that though an embryo possesses only a biological sex, the person to be born with the relevant condition will possess both a biological sex and a socially constructed gender. In this way, the legislation signals (whether it means to or not) that there may be a social dimension to the determination of sex-based disablement. Further, the language makes it a clear requirement that the relevant condition must be capable of being described as a *serious* mental or physical disability, without defining what that might include. The seriousness of a condition, already very much dependent on contextual factors such as the availability of economic and social resources, may also be contingent on gendered understandings of social norms of acceptable and challenging behaviour.

The HFEA's PGD Licensing Committee has the final say in determining whether a particular condition satisfies the legislative criteria. It does this by taking into account a number of factors including age of onset of the condition, symptoms and their variability, the treatability of the condition and the effect on quality of life, amongst other things (HFEA, 2010). When applying to test for a new disorder, the HFEA requires clinics to provide the *On Line Mendelian Inheritance in Man* (OMIM) system number and that number is used in all the deliberations of the Licensing Committee.[9] The OMIM number focuses on the phenotypic expression of an identified genetic condition or disorder. Phenotypic information is more useful for determining seriousness since it describes all the observable characteristics that a condition might manifest.

On 30 January 2014, the HFEA Licensing Committee made a determination refusing a request to allow sex selection using PGD for Autism Spectrum Disorder

9 HFEA website 'PGD conditions licensed by the HFEA' http://guide.hfea.gov.uk/pgd/ <last accessed 14 October 2014>.

(ASD) (OMIM #209850).[10] An # symbol before an entry indicates that it is a descriptive entry, usually of a phenotype and does not represent a unique locus. The centre making the request wanted to establish the sex of embryos in families with at least two severely affected males, in order to avoid the inheritance of ASD as they viewed the condition to be a gender-related serious medical condition. While the assignment of a #OMIM suggests a level of consensus that there is a hereditary component to the condition, the licensing committee nevertheless preferred to follow the advice of two peer reviewers who they state:

> expressed concern about the use of PGD for Autism Spectrum Disorder (Classic) … and the request to apply sex selection. The peer reviewers noted that even where a family has two affected male children this does not guarantee that female children will be free of the disorder, or indeed that in any particular family affected in this way that a female is at any less risk than a male (para 11).

The committee therefore found that it 'could not see a way of authorising sex selection for the purpose of *possibly* reducing the risk of this family having another affected child' (para 19). The fact that it could not be described in terms other than as a mere 'possibility' in relation to the specific family was determinative. The committee did not address the question directly of whether the legislative threshold that it 'affects one sex significantly more than the other' had been reached; however, it did note in para 7 that ASD is 'diagnosed in approximately four times as many males'.

The regulation of medical sex selection and PGD in Australia

While Australia lacks a national oversight body equivalent to the HFEA, the NHMRC's ART Guidelines have taken on a quasi-regulatory effect via accreditation rules requiring clinical compliance.[11] The Guidelines, last amended in 2007, are currently undergoing a comprehensive review and provide that PGD should be available only to test for serious disease or illness. They state that '[p]ending further community discussion, PGD must not be used for:

- prevention of conditions that do not *seriously harm* the person to be born
- selection of the *sex* of an embryo *except to* reduce the risk of transmission of a serious genetic condition; or
- selection in favour of a genetic defect or disability in the person to be born' (my emphasis).[12]

10 HFEA Statutory Approvals Committee, 30 January 2014 Centre 044 (The Centre for Reproductive and Genetic Health (CRGH) – PGD application for Autism Spectrum Disorder OMIM #209850.

11 Research Involving Human Embryos Act (Cth) 2002 s11.

12 At [12.2]. The 'Explanation of Key Terms' in the NHMRC ART Guidelines does not attempt to define 'serious'.

Non-medical sex selection is also prohibited under s 11.1 of the Guidelines.

Furthermore in two states, Western Australia and Victoria, the use of PGD and sex selection to reduce the risk of autism has been approved. In Western Australia, the RTC will not grant approval for any diagnostic procedure on an embryo unless 'there is a significant risk of a serious genetic abnormality or disease being present in the embryo'.[13] The RTC Policy also includes a specific statement regarding the use of PGD for sex selection that indicates it would be available where it satisfied the requirements for testing for a specific condition as described above.[14] Unlike its UK counterpart, the Western Australian RTC has approved the use of PGD to identify the sex of embryos in families with children with autistic boys to avoid the transfer of male embryos.[15]

Up until 2010 when the 2008 amendments to the Victorian reproductive technology legislation came into force, Victoria too had a reproductive technology authority that played a significant role in regulating access to PGD. The Infertility Treatment Authority (ITA) imposed conditions or restrictions on ART licences that it granted.[16] In 2003, it developed a policy limiting access to PGD using three lists (Victoria ITA, 2003). Conditions that required no prior approval were in lists A and B. List A included conditions that lead to pregnancy failure and chromosomal abnormalities, while List B included sex-related disorders such as Fragile X, and single gene disorders such as Huntington Disease, and familial adenomatous polyposis. A third category (List C) contained conditions to be approved on a case-by-case basis. As early as 2009 the ITA approved the use of PGD for sex selection in the case of autism. The ITA's 2009 annual report shows that approval was given to include on list C several conditions where there was a higher instance in one sex, but inconclusive genetic evidence about the transmission of that condition including BRCA, and Haemophilia A as well as autism (Victoria ITA, 2009: 8). Although the ITA was the governing authority, it was guided by clinical and scientific evidence, and advice from both clinical geneticists and other IVF and health practitioners (Karpin and Savell, 2012: 201). In a study of PGD I conducted with Dr Kristin Savell, one interviewee discussing the role of the ITA in approving the use of PGD for sex selection for autism stated:

> For a while the authority required an individual application in relation to genetic testing using sex selection to implant embryos that were female rather than male to reduce the risk of autism… As time went on, the use of PGD to eliminate, or to minimise the risk of autism became more common… And so

13 Human Reproductive Technology Act 1991 (WA) s14(2b)(a)(ii).

14 See note 3.

15 WA RTC Annual Report 1 July 2012 to 30 June 2013. http://www.rtc.org.au/reports/docs/AR2013.pdf <last accessed 30 Mary 2014>. See page 13 Table 2 for a list of conditions for which approval for PGD was given in the year of the report. Autism Spectrum Disorder is the first listed in the table titled Genetic Conditions. Given as stated earlier that there is as yet no identified genetic locus or marker for ASD this might be viewed as a premature conclusion.

16 Infertility Treatment Act (1995) (Vic) s8(3)(b) and s106(1).

it was really in situations where genetic inheritance wasn't as clear or it was a novel use that the application was required.

(Karpin and Savell, 2012)

The ITA was abolished at the end of 2009 and was replaced by the Victorian Assisted Reproductive Technology Authority (VARTA) in 2010. Though no longer operational, these earlier regimes – which shared some important similarities with the UK regulatory system – have had the effect of creating a list for which PGD is now routinely available in those jurisdictions. For example, the list of conditions for which PGD was used in Victoria between 2010 and 2012 can be found on the website of the new authority (VARTA) which, although it no longer has a role in approving licences, gathers data, monitors clinic practices and offers information and educational services. The list, entitled 'Single Gene Disorders', is followed by a paragraph referring to the use of sex selection for autism.[17]

The importance of social context in laws regulating PGD

From 1993 through to 2008 there was a series of attempts by the HFEA to refine the understanding of what constituted a sufficiently serious condition to warrant PGD. In the 1993 HFEA consultation on sex selection, PGD was viewed as ethically acceptable when there was a 'high risk of a life threatening disease' (HFEA, 1993: [28]). An example of a 'sex-linked' condition that the review did not consider to be very serious was 'colour blindness' (HFEA, 1993: [14]), whereas both Duchenne's muscular dystrophy and haemophilia were described as sufficiently serious.

The Advisory Committee on Genetic Testing (ACGT),[18] as it then was, used similar language when it conducted its consultation on PGD six years later in 1999. There it was stated that PGD should be available 'for certain severe or life-threatening disorders' (ACGT, 1999: [10]). Disorders that were discussed as obvious candidates for PGD and thus appear to have been uncontroversial were single gene disorders. There was, however, discussion of whether late-onset disorders satisfied the criteria and whether screening should be allowed for carrier embryos and for conditions that were genetically complex.[19]

Importantly, the Consultation Report displays a complex approach to disability and the relevance of the question of seriousness. Alongside the seriousness of the condition, the report recommends consideration of the familial and social context and the support and services available. For instance, it is noted that:

17 http://www.varta.org.au/preimplantation-genetic-diagnosis/.

18 The commission has since been incorporated into the Human Genetics Commission.

19 Examples listed included cystic fibrosis, Duchenne muscular dystrophy, haemophilia, Huntington's disease, the thalassaemias, sickle cell disease and a number of uncommon hereditary cancers (at [5]).

> the impact on the quality of life of a child born with a disability, as well as their families will depend on a number of factors. These will include the seriousness of the disability, the circumstances of the family, as well as the emotional and material support available.
>
> (ACGT, 1999: [21])

This idea that what constitutes a serious disability is contextually determined would seem to stand in tension with the impulse for state regulation of access to PGD. In fact the Consultation Report goes on to suggest that:

> [e]ach family should be free to make their own choices in this respect and their view will be *one* of the most important determining factors in assessing the justification for PGD.
>
> (ACGT, 1999: [21])

However, both the HFEA and the ACGT do rely on a shared understanding that distinguishes disability or disease from social and psychological characteristics. While the former are considered candidates for PGD depending on their seriousness, the latter are viewed as entirely inappropriate:

> The HFEA and the ACGT do not think it would be acceptable to test for any social or psychological characteristics, normal physical variations, or any conditions which are not associated with disability or a serious medical condition.
>
> (ACGT, 1999: [22])

The problem with these kinds of statements is that they rely on a normative consensus that simply does not exist. While we might be able to agree that some disabilities have a medical status, many disabilities are characterised by their physical variation from the norm rather than any ongoing need for medical services. For example, one can be blind, deaf or short statured and healthy at the same time, to offer a few obvious examples. Nevertheless, these forms of physical variation would typically be viewed as not falling within the range of 'normal physical variation' and would likely be included in the category of disability. Disability scholars, Adrienne Asch and David Wasserman offer a compelling critique of prenatal testing for disability as a form of synecdoche – a 'characteristic response to a stigmatized trait, in which the part obscures or effaces the whole' (Asch and Wasserman, 2005). In these cases the disabling dimensions of the social and psychological constraints take on more prominence than the impairment itself.

The regulatory constraints on PGD, then, to disallow its use to test for social and psychological characteristics, fail to account for all the ways in which so-called serious medical conditions for which testing is already permitted may be conditions that are understood as seriously disabling only within a particular social context. This context may involve reliance on gender stereotypes as well.

In 2002, the HFEA undertook a major consultation on the question of whether to allow PGD for sex selection (HFEA, 2002) and produced a report in 2003 that concluded that there was substantial public opposition to sex selection for non-medical reasons and it should not be permitted (HFEA, 2003). Sex selection for medical reasons was, however, supported and the Department of Health review of the HFE Act undertaken prior to the 2008 amendments, reiterated the view that sex selection for non-medical reasons should be prohibited while sex selection to prevent transmission of a disorder was accepted as appropriate treatment for a serious disability or disease (Department of Health, 2006).

However, as already noted, what constitutes a 'serious medical condition' has not been defined in the legislation. It was, however, briefly touched on in the parliamentary debates on the 2008 amendments to the HFE Act in the context of the amendments to formalise the use of PGD for human leukocyte antigen (HLA) tissue typing; that is to select an embryo that is a tissue match for an existing sibling. The aim of the latter procedure is to enable the harvesting of cord blood from the birth of the tissue-typed embryo, in order to use the product of that blood to save an existing ill child (the sibling of the putative child).

The discussion does, however, offer interesting insights into what members of the two Houses of the UK Parliament understood by the term 'serious'. Despite a commitment to a flexible definition that would allow a certain degree of clinician discretion, some members of the House went into quite specific details about what they viewed would and would not constitute a serious condition. One example that is particularly interesting given current Australian practices around PGD and sex selection for autism and the HFEA's recent decision to refuse a request for PGD for autism, is the comment by Baroness O'Cathain that '[w]hile I would never wish to minimise the significant difficulties that autism presents, it is not a condition for which the production of a tissue-typed child should be the solution'.[20]

The regulatory constraints on PGD, as I have stated above, thus not only limit the capacity to use the technology to test for conditions that are not viewed as serious physical or mental disabilities, diseases or conditions but also for social characteristics. Conditions that do not fall within the range of normal variation but are viewed as non-serious conditions would not be found to be appropriate candidates for PGD. Yet, there has been significant debate about when to allow the transfer of an embryo known to be affected by a condition or trait. This practice is currently prohibited in the Australian NHMRC ART guidelines with no reference to seriousness. The guidelines state that PGD must not be used for 'selection in favour of a genetic defect or disability in the person to be born'.[21]

In 2008, when the UK amended its legislation, the idea of favouring an embryo with a genetic defect or disability was also considered unacceptable, but it was acknowledged that there may be circumstances where it was reasonable to transfer

20 *Hansard*, HL, vol. 698, col. 14, 21 January 2008 (Baroness O'Cathain).
21 At [12.2].

such an embryo where there were no unaffected alternatives. Rather than prohibiting the choice in favour of an affected embryo altogether, the amended legislation prohibited making a preference for embryos known to have an abnormality that will result in a serious physical or mental disability, illness or condition over those that do not.[22] The amended legislation also introduced the same limit for embryos *known to be of a particular sex* that carried a particular risk, compared with embryos not of that sex.[23] Thus, were sex selection for autism to be approved in the UK, a clinic might feel it was obligated to prefer female embryos where there was evidence of autism in boys in the patient's family. In this hypothetical scenario it would only be in the case where there were no suitable female embryos that the clinic would be allowed to transfer a male embryo.

Sex selection and the welfare of the future child

Before moving on to examine the specific issue of the gendering of disability and the viability of medical sex selection, the idea of what is a serious 'medical' condition must be considered against one further regulatory frame – the requirement in section 13(5) of the HFE Act (as amended) and in para 2.5 of the Australian NHMRC ART Guidelines as well as some specific Australian State legislation that ART treatment only be offered after taking into account the welfare of any child who may be born as a result of the treatment. This welfare or well-being principle frames obligations to prospective children and inevitably has flow on effects to decisions made by clinics about when and if to test an embryo using PGD and what may be done with embryos that test positive for a condition or genetic marker or that are of a sex at a higher risk of having the condition.

It does seem reasonably clear that in both Australia and the UK, the principle of the welfare of the future child could potentially operate as a barrier to treatment for those prospective parents who might pass on a disability or an inheritable disorder including where there is a higher incidence in one sex compared with the other.

There are very few cases where the welfare principle has been relied on to deny access to treatment and fewer still that involve sex selection. However, one case worth mentioning is the Victorian case of *JS and LS* v *Patient Review Panel* (2010) involving the denial of a request by a couple for PGD to sex select under s28(2)(b) of the Victorian Assisted Reproductive Treatment Act (2008) which allows non-medical sex selection at the discretion of the Patient Review Panel. In coming to a decision to deny the couple's request to choose the sex of their child the court relied on the guiding principles in s5(a) of the Victorian Act, which closely follows the NHMRC ART Guidelines. It states:

> the welfare and interests of persons born or to be born as a result of treatment procedures are paramount.

22 HFE Act, s13(9).
23 HFE Act, s13(10).

In this case the couple made a special case for sex selection based on their circumstances: they had three children of the same sex, and had lost a pregnancy at birth – possibly due to medical negligence – of a child of the opposite sex to the existing children. They had been deeply affected by the loss of that child and argued that they suffered from post-traumatic stress disorder. They felt that being allowed to have a child of the same sex as their lost child would go some way to allowing them to move on with their lives. Indeed, they were so committed to the process that, having been denied the right to sex select using PGD, they went ahead and became pregnant a further four times. The first child was not of the desired sex, the second pregnancy resulted in a spontaneous miscarriage, and the third – a twin pregnancy – had to be terminated as there was only one placenta. On the fourth occasion they used IVF to become pregnant with twins but when these were revealed as the non-desired sex, the pregnancy was terminated. At the hearing, the couple indicated that they would continue in this way if they did not obtain approval for PGD for sex selection. In denying that request, the Victorian Civil and Administrative Tribunal stated 'we do not consider it is in the interests and welfare of the child to be born, that permission should be given to permit the use of an embryo which has been sex selected for the purpose of producing or attempting to produce a child of the desired sex' (at [80]). It went on to say 'in our view, arguments based on completion of family, replacement of a child, or family balance do not advance the welfare interests of a child born to fulfil that end' (at [82]).

While this is clearly not a case involving the potential transmission of an inheritable disability or disease, nevertheless, the parental distress and trauma is not simply a social preference. Clearly the psychological well-being of the parents in this case was tied to the outcome of the case. There was evidence presented to the tribunal from psychologists that the birth of a child of the desired sex may not ameliorate the post-traumatic stress disorder that these parents were clearly suffering. However, that does not seem like an adequate argument for denying them the possibility that it might. It is an interesting line to draw when we recall how jurisdictions such as the UK and Western Australia consider the social and familial circumstances of the patients when determining the availability of PGD to avoid the birth of a disabled child.

The gendering of disability and the case of medical sex selection for autism

The use of PGD to deselect male embryos in families where there is a history of autism spectrum disorder has been approved in both Western Australia and Victoria and rejected by the UK HFEA licensing committee as noted above. In the last part of this chapter I want to explore what happens when the disability or disease sought to be prevented by sex-selective procedures is itself embedded in gender stereotypes.

Amor and Cameron (2008) describe autism as an example of a condition which is substantially more common in one sex than another but that is not caused by a single gene and does not follow Mendelian inheritance patterns. They consider it to be a condition that is caused by multiple genetic influences, where the contributing genes are either unknown or poorly understood, where specific gene testing is not available and where environmental influences may be important (Amor and Cameron, 2008: 729). Relying on the claim that four times as many boys are diagnosed with autism, they suggest that for a couple with one autistic child, gender selection in favour of female embryos could reduce their risk of having an affected child from 5% to 2% (Amor and Cameron, 2008: 730). Putting aside for the moment the fact that the clinical range in autism is broad, 'ranging from relatively minor difficulties with communication and socialization to individuals with severe intellectual impairment who are unable to communicate' (Amor and Cameron, 2008, p732), in the case of autism another interesting dimension must be considered and that is the gendered construction of the condition itself and its diagnosis. Indeed Gillis-Buck and Richardson (2014) argue that the two points are not unrelated. They note that there are numerous studies that show that the historical inclusion of high functioning autistics or people with Asperger's is responsible for the 'often-cited dramatic male prevalence'. They state 'male prevalence is significantly less pronounced in autistic individuals with intellectual disability, showing a sex ratio typical of all developmental disorders with mental impairments' (Gillis-Buck and Richardson, 2014: 7). Goldman (2013) too points out that the male prevalence of 4:1 in autism is 'highly modulated by cognitive function' and that 'as IQ decreases the skewness of the sex ratio decreases'.

There is, as yet, no biological test or marker for autism. Currently the standard research based measures used in assessment of autism are tests such as the Autism Diagnostic interview and the Autism Diagnostic Observation schedule.[24] The first is a parent interview and the second measures observed behaviours. While there are some instances where autism is associated with conditions that do have a biological marker such as Fragile X syndrome and tuberous sclerosis, what is interesting about the fact that autism is diagnosed in this way is that recent studies have shown that the testing itself may contain gender bias. Goldman points out that autism is not a disease but a 'developmentally defined syndrome characterized by a set of behavioural symptoms, not validated biomarkers' (Goldman, 2013: 676). She then notes that to 'arrive at a diagnosis of autism, clinicians rely on a series of observations, and scores on descriptive behavioural tests based on magnitudes of departure from expected norms at specific ages'.

It is not surprising then that even with comparably high levels of ASD traits, girls are substantially less likely to be diagnosed than boys unless their conditions are compounded by cognitive and other behavioural deficits (Constantino

24 Other tests include the Childhood Autism Spectrum Test and the Development and Wellbeing Assessment (Falkmer et al, 2013). Other versions of these tests are the Childhood Autism Spectrum Test (CAST) – a behavior and personality test usually answered by a parent and the DAWBA (the Development and Wellbeing Assessment) again an interview-based test with parents, the child and the child's teacher.

and Charman, 2012). According to another study, doctors are more likely to miss autism in girls even when the severity of the symptoms is held constant for both boys and girls (Russell et al, 2011). The general belief that girls do not get autism may be having an influence on diagnosis in these cases. It was also found that it requires a relative increase in the total symptom burden in a female to cross the threshold of a diagnosis of autism compared with a boy. It was thus suggested that this was either 'a significant problem in current diagnostic approaches or indicates that, in the absence of accompanying cognitive or behavioural deficits, girls exhibit better adaptation to the same levels of diagnosis in boys' (Constantino and Charman, 2012). This study and a spate of other recent studies suggest that with available diagnostic tests, higher functioning girls with autism are being diagnosed either later than boys or are altogether missed. The authors therefore suggest developing gender-specific thresholds which may go some way to addressing the problem. Goldman points out that 'the majority of the behavioural instruments used to diagnose autism have been standardized using male cohorts and very few studies have tested their sensitivity for identifying girls with autism biomarkers' (Goldman, 2013: 677). However, it is clear the problem goes somewhat deeper. Simon Baron-Cohen's theory, for example, that autism is a form of extreme male brain is based on his view that autistic people are hypersystematisers. On average, he argues male brains are more systematising while the female brain has a higher capacity for empathising (Baron-Cohen, 2003; Baron-Cohen et al, 2009). Baron-Cohen is well regarded in the field; however, he has come under criticism for this theory and there are a number of feminist responses that challenge both the premise that autistic people are, on the whole, hypersystematisers and that this can be characterised as a masculine brain trait or indeed that there are only two types of brain (e.g. Fine, 2010; Jack, 2014). Gillis-Buck and Richardson refer to a recent study by Oldershaw that suggests that 'females diagnosed with anorexia nervosa, a classically female-biased disorder, exhibit high levels of systemizing behavior that meets the diagnostic criteria for autism' (Gillis-Buck and Richardson, 2014: 8). Without diverging into an entirely different discussion it is worth noting that as yet no one has suggested PGD and sex selection for anorexia despite its sometimes fatal consequences and new claims that it may have a hereditary component (Innes, 2013).

Baron-Cohen associates the systematising brain with engineering, mathematical and science skills which he says are fields dominated by men. He has also argued that when so-called 'geeks' are attracted to each other they tend to produce autistic kids (Baron-Cohen, 2006). Further it is interesting that Baron-Cohen has not identified a pathology associated with the extreme female brain and in fact has suggested that a tendency to hyperempathise would not involve pathology. Nancy Bombaci has argued that the alignment between the very small component of the group that are classified as Aspergers and genius also aligns with a construction of genius that is gendered male (Bombaci, 2012). Thus extreme femaleness or hyperempathy (were there such a thing) may not be valued or noticed to quite the same extent as hypersystematising.

Conclusion

Gillis Buck and Richardson state that:

> the 4:1 sex ratio ubiquitously cited in autism and sex differences research relies on two assumptions: (1) that the pronounced prevalence of males among [High Functioning Autistics], Asperger's and average to high IQ individuals – representing 20 per cent of those on the autism spectrum – carries insight into the general etiology of the condition and (ii) that current diagnosis rates of males and females reflect organic facts about autism and not gender stereotypes in diagnostic practices.
>
> (Gillis Buck and Richardson, 2014: 8)

While it is not the aim of this chapter to settle this debate, this case study provides a concrete example of the limits and ambiguities inherent in the regulatory distinction between medical and non-medical sex selection that appears in both the UK and Australian legislation and guidelines. Autism spectrum disorder is not unique in having a gendered dimension. Goldman notes that 'autism is just one among many developmental disorders such as dyslexia, ADHD or conduct disorders which affect more boys than girls' (2013: 676) and it is notable that dyslexia is something that has already been discussed in the media as a potential candidate for PGD (Corderoy, 2013).

The example of medical sex selection thus shows how important it is to be aware of the cultural framing of disability and gendered notions of harm in the regulation of technologies such as PGD. Neither the recent changes to the UK's HFE Act nor the ongoing review of the NHMRC ART Guidelines in Australia address the possibility that there are gendered assumptions behind how we understand what is 'normal' and 'abnormal' and what is in the welfare interests of a future child and what will harm them. Yet heavy reliance is placed on the workability of these concepts within the regulatory framework. The net result is that access to technologies such as PGD are limited without a clear justification.

References

Advisory Committee on Genetic Testing, (1999) *Consultation Document on Preimplantation Genetic Diagnosis.*

Amor, D.J. and Cameron, C., (2008) 'PGD Gender Selection for non-Mendelian Disorders with Unequal Sex Incidence' 23(4) *Human Reproduction* 729.

Asch, A. and Wasserman, D., (2005) 'Where is the Sin in Synecdoche? Prenatal Testing and the Parent-Child Relationship' in Wasserman, D. and Bickenback, J. (eds), *Quality of Life and Human Difference* (Cambridge: Cambridge University Press).

Baron-Cohen, S., (2003) *The Essential Difference: The Truth about the Male and Female Brain* (New York: Basic).

Baron-Cohen, S., (2006) 'The Hyper-systemizing, Assortative Mating Theory of Autism' 30(5) *Progress in Neuro-Psychopharmocology and Biological Psychiatry* 865.

Baron-Cohen, S., et al, (2009) 'Talen in Autism: Hyper-systemizing, Hyper-attention to Detail and Sensory Hypersensitivity' *Philosophical Transactions of the Royal Society B* 364.

Bombaci, N., (2012) 'Popular Discourses on the Neurotypical Woman: Conformity, Authority and Post-War Feminities' 23(2) *Women: A Cultural Review* 139.

Constantino, J.N. and Charman, T., (2012) 'Gender Bias, Female Resilience and the Sex Ration in Autism' 51(8) *Journal of the American Academy of Child and Adolescent Psychiatry* V.

Corderoy, A., (2013) 'Why IVF Parents are Choosing Girls over Boys' *Sydney Morning Herald* (26 December 2013).

Department of Health, (2006) 'Review of the Human Fertilisation and Embryology Act' (London: HMSO).

Falkmer, T., Anderson, K., Falkmer, M. and Horlin, C., (2013) 'Diagnostic Procedures in Autism Spectrum Disorders: A Systematic Literature Review' 22(6) *European Child Adolescent Psychiatry* 329.

Fine, C., (2010) *Delusions of Gender: The Real Science behind Sex Differences* (London: Icon Books).

Gillis-Buck, E.M. and Richardson, S., (2014) 'Autism as a Biomedical Platform for Sex Differences Research' 9 *BioSocieties* 262.

Goldman, S., (2013) 'Sex, Gender and the Diagnosis of Autism – A Biosocial View of the Male preponderance' 7 *Research in Autism Spectrum Disorders* 675.

HFEA, (2002) *Sex Selection: Choice and Responsibility in Human Reproduction Consultation Document* (London: HFEA).

HFEA, (2003) *Sex Selection: Options for Regulation* (London: HFEA).

HFEA, (2010) 'Pre-implantation Diagnostic Testing ("PGD") Explanatory Note for Licence Committee' <http://www.hfea.gov.uk/docs/2010-10-28_Licence_Committee_PGD_explanatory_note.PDF>.

Innes, E., (2013) 'Does Anorexia have a Genetic Link? New Theory Suggests the Disorder May Not be Purely down to Social Pressures' *Daily Mail* (13 September 2013).

Jack, J., (2014) *Autism and Gender: From Refrigerator Mothers to Computer Geeks* (Urbana: University of Illinois Press).

Karpin, I. and Savell, K., (2012) *Perfecting Pregnancy: Law Disability and the Future of Reproduction* (New York: Cambridge University Press).

Mills, C., (2011) *Futures of Reproduction: Bioethics and Biopolitics* (New York: Springer).

National Health and Medical Research Council, (2007) *Ethical Guidelines on the Use of Assisted Reproductive Technology in Clinical Practice and Research.*

Russell, G., Steer, C. and Golding, J., (2011) 'Social and Demographic Factors that Influence the Diagnosis of Autistic Spectrum Disorders' 46(12) *Social Psychiatry and Psychiatric Epidemiology* 1283.

Scott, R., (2007) *Choosing between Possible Lives: Law and Ethics of Prenatal and Preimplantation Genetic Diagnosis* (Oxford: Hart Publishing).

Victoria Infertility Treatment Authority, (2003) 'Genetic Testing and the Requirements of the Infertility Treatment Act 1995: Policy in Relation to the use of Preimplantation Genetic Diagnosis' (reviewed 2009) [no longer available electronically, on file with author].

Victoria Infertility Treatment Authority, (2009) 'Annual Report 2009' <http://varta.org.au/annualreports/w1/i1003573/>.

13 New wine in old bottles and old wine in new bottles: The judicial response to international commercial surrogacy in the UK and Australia

*Anita Stuhmcke**

Introduction

International commercial surrogacy is entered into for the purpose of family formation, so it ought to be simple and logical for family law to apply to these arrangements. However, in both Australia and the UK the legal rules governing this area suggest otherwise. In place of simplicity and clarity of legal regulation there remains ongoing complexity and confusion. This observation is disappointing given that both jurisdictions have recently targeted legislative reform as a means of future-proofing the law in this area of human reproduction. In the UK, the Human Fertilisation and Embryology Act 2008 (hereafter 'the 2008 Act') was widely billed as an opportunity to ensure the law would remain 'fit for purpose for the 21st century' and in Australian state jurisdictions recent legislative reform has concentrated upon providing alternative legal pathways to parenthood for uncompensated surrogacy arrangements.

In both jurisdictions the law proceeds on the assumption that the most important aspect of commercial surrogacy is the resulting child, yet imposes no universal rule upon these arrangements. Transnational commercial surrogacy exposes gaping holes in the ability of domestic family laws to provide a comfortable resolution to jurisdictional difference. Courts in both Australia and the UK have been faced with novel legal issues including children being born stateless[1] and/or with different jurisdictions recognising different legal parents;[2] the death of a commissioning parent and subsequent allocation of parental responsibility;[3] and who may access legal parentage.[4] The legal process has proven to be both illogical and complex as surrogacy cases may take numerous hearings 'to pick a way through

* Thanks to Jenni Millbank, Kirsty Horsey and the anonymous reviewers for their thoughtful comments. This research was supported by Discovery Project Grant 0986213 from the Australian Research Council and funding from UTS: Law.

1 *X & Y (Foreign Surrogacy)* [2008] EWHC 3030 (Fam).

2 See *Re C (A child)* [2013] EWHC 2413 (Fam); *Re K* (Minors) *(Foreign Surrogacy)* [2010] EWHC 1180 (Fam).

3 *A and A and P and P and B* [2011] EWHC 1738 (Fam).

4 *O'Connor & Kasemsarn* [2010] FamCA 987.

the legal maze'[5] raising global issues of power and vulnerability[6] and exposing tension between public policy and the best interests of the child born from such arrangements.[7] It is troubling that such significant legal issues remain given that international commercial surrogacy arrangements are growing in prominence and number (Crawshaw et al, 2013; Millbank, 2013) and that the practice of commercial surrogacy has a long history (Stuhmcke, 2004).

Australia and the UK offer interesting points of comparison on the inter-relationship between family law, public policy and international commerce in surrogacy. In England and Wales the activity of commercial surrogacy has itself never been a criminal offence yet the Surrogacy Arrangements Act 1985 imposes restrictions with the aim of preventing the development of a commercial surrogacy industry. One such restriction is the incorporation of criminal offences within the legislation. As a rare example of this being applied in practice, most recently the High Court determined that in drawing up a surrogacy agreement for payment, solicitors had committed a criminal offence under section 2 of the Surrogacy Arrangements Act 1985, noting that such agreements can lawfully be drawn up free of charge.[8] In Australia, criminal law is applied to the act of commercial surrogacy itself in all state and territory jurisdictions (with the exception of the Northern Territory). Despite this difference in public policy the judiciaries in both jurisdictions approach the determination of parenthood in transnational surrogacy with almost identical goals and concerns. This chapter identifies and discusses this thematic similarity in the judicial response.

This comparative analysis suggests urgent review of the law pertaining to commercial surrogacy in both jurisdictions. Judicial decisions in both Australia and the UK prioritise the best interests and welfare of children born through such arrangements. Of conflicting, yet secondary, concern for the judiciary is public policy aimed at criminalising or at least not facilitating a commercial surrogacy industry. Without public policy approval of international commercial surrogacy, the historical status quo will remain, ensuring existing regulation remains at best a legal minefield, such as that which exists in the UK (see Horsey and Sheldon, 2012), and at worst a legal fallacy, such as that which operates in Australia.

What is cross-border commercial surrogacy and how is it regulated?

These two questions are intertwined. Commercial surrogacy is not always easy to identify. Often contrasted with the practice of altruistic surrogacy, commercial surrogacy is generally construed as a profit-making exercise. However, it can often be difficult to distinguish between surrogacy which is altruistic, and surrogacy which is commercial. This is particularly the case when the surrogate's

5 *Re G (Surrogacy : Foreign Domicile)* [2007] EWHC 2814 (Fam).
6 *Mason & Mason and Anor* [2013] Fam CA 424.
7 *Re: X and Y (Foreign Surrogacy)* [2008] EWHC 3030 (Fam).
8 *JP v LP and Others* [2014] EWHC 595 (Fam).

'expenses' are able to be paid in an altruistic arrangement. While this distinction is irrelevant in countries where commercial and altruistic surrogacy are both 'legal' such as India and certain states in the United States, it is highly relevant in jurisdictions such as South Africa and Australia where commercial surrogacy is a criminal offence while altruistic surrogacy is allowed. It is also a critical distinction in jurisdictions where the practice is not criminal yet not facilitated such as the UK.

There are difficulties with the conceptualisation of commercial surrogacy. Firstly, surrogacy arrangements can be commercialised to varying degrees. At one end of the spectrum are informal arrangements in which no benefit is provided to the surrogate mother. At the other end are fully commercial contracts brokered by a professional surrogacy agency. There are also intermediate possibilities, such as relatively informal arrangements that nonetheless involve monetary or other benefits being provided to the surrogate mother. These arrangements may include unregulated ways of accessing surrogates such as using international surrogates or family friends. As such, they may involve varying degrees of lawfulness. For example in Australia such informal arrangements have been expedited by the birth mother using the intended mother's Medicare card for the purposes of hospital admission and giving birth under the other woman's name. Secondly, the very creation of categories between the two types of surrogacy is in and of itself questionable. For example, Van Zyl and Walker (2013) reject the categorisation of altruistic surrogacy as gift relationship and contract surrogacy as non-gift noting that contract motherhood should not be organised according to the norms of the gift relationship. Attention has also been drawn to an absence of convincing ethical arguments to distinguish the binary style of surrogacy regulation imposed by altruistic versus commercial surrogacy (Stuhmcke, 1996).

The internationalisation of commercial surrogacy brings additional economic, social and political challenges. The operation of the global commercialised market in low-resource countries such as Thailand (Hibino and Shimazono, 2013; Whittaker, 2011) and India (Pande, 2009; Unnithan, 2013) has created a range of benefits and negative impacts. In low-income countries benefits include the generation of business. Dangers include whether this will create a two-tiered health system for the western elite and the poorly resourced public (Whittaker, 2011). In high-income countries such as the UK a national benefit of cross-border commercial surrogacy is to allow citizens to go off-shore to pursue commercial surrogacy while not allowing the practice on moral grounds in the home jurisdiction (Storrow, 2010) while disadvantages include inaccurate legal advice to those who pursue surrogacy overseas, as well as the inadequacy of domestic law to handle aspects of international commercial surrogacy (Storrow, 2013).[9]

The numbers of individuals and couples pursuing international commercial surrogacy is growing. In the UK, a 2014 roundtable convened by the Project Group on Assisted Reproduction (PROGAR) and funded by the Society for Reproductive

9 See *Re G ((Surrogacy: Foreign Domicile)* [2007] EWHC 2814 (Fam); *Re X and Y (Foreign Surrogacy)* [2008] EWHC 3030 (Fam).

and Infant Psychology (SRIP) was advised that more than 1,000 babies are brought to the UK each year, but it could not be identified with authority that these were all surrogacy babies as there are no special procedures for passport applications following a surrogacy arrangement. While many of this number may well relate to babies following a surrogacy arrangement, there is no way to be sure. In the UK, each year around 100 Parental Orders are sought. It has been suggested that a majority of commissioning parents may not subsequently apply for a Parental Order for transfer of legal parentage (Blyth et al, 2014). The General Register Office of England and Wales notes that in approximately 26 per cent of the 939 Parental Orders made between January and October of 2011 (i.e. 133 births) the births took place overseas, contrasting with 13% in 2010, 4% in 2009, 2% in 2008 and 0% in 1995, the first year of registration (Crawshaw et al, 2013). The increasing numbers of international commercial surrogate births is recognised as a pressing regulatory challenge in the UK (Gamble, 2013; Horsey and Sheldon, 2012).

Similar issues exist in Australia. Complicated by differing federal and state regulation, continued eligibility restrictions to altruistic surrogacy (Smith, 2013), as well as the inability of many prospective parents to engage previously unknown surrogates (as a result of domestic bans on advertising and payment) and egg donors has led to Australians increasingly travelling for international commercial surrogacy to India, Thailand and the US, among other countries (Department of Immigration, 2013). While the exact numbers are unknown, clearly an increasing number of Australians are engaging in cross-border commercial surrogacy. From the period 2007 to 2010, 69 distinct families had been involved in surrogacy. These 69 families included 44 who had travelled to 'evade restrictive local laws or to access donor gametes unavailable in home jurisdictions' (Millbank, 2011). Travel to another Australian state was reported in nine arrangements while international travel occurred in 35 cases. In 2010–11, there were 16 recorded surrogacy births within Australia as a result of regulated assisted reproductive treatment, while 394 babies were born in India to Australian citizens in the same year, the majority of them almost certainly via commercial surrogacy (Millbank, 2014). The International destination point is variable – with India and Thailand recently ceasing to be a viable destination for Australians.

This increased utilisation of international surrogacy is occurring in both jurisdictions despite public policy. Using the lens of legislative regulation, the next part of this chapter examines the current state of public policy with respect to international commercial surrogacy in both jurisdictions. Judicial decision-making with respect to international commercial surrogacy is further addressed in the subsequent section.

Public policy: Legislative disapproval of cross-border commercial surrogacy

In the UK and Australia, public policy in this area was borne from uncertainty. In both jurisdictions the laws concerning surrogacy continue to evolve in a haphazard fashion (Jackson, 2014; Millbank, 2011).

This lack of thoughtful review has been questioned by an original architect of UK surrogacy public policy. Dame Mary Warnock, the Chair of the influential 1984 Warnock Report observed in 2002 that 'I now believe that it would be better if the process were officially regulated, and more openly discussed between doctors, prospective parents, surrogates, and, later, with the resulting children' (Warnock, 2002: 92) and further that:

> the hasty legislation was rushed through in the UK at the end of a Parliamentary session in 1989...on a wave of revulsion against anything so vulgar and exploitative as the American commercial companies who were hovering on the shores of Britain. The general sentiment was 'not in our backyard'. If people wanted to enter into surrogacy contracts, let them go across the Atlantic to do it. I do not remember any very serious discussion of whether or not surrogacy was so intrinsically immoral, or its consequences so socially disastrous, that legislation against it must be enacted…I increasingly believe that one social ill we need to be aware of is that of excessive governmental regulation. If surrogacy were allowed in the UK, on the American model, though some people might be offended, I doubt if we would be harmed…I suspect that the legislation hastened through at the time of the Committee of Inquiry into Human Fertilisation and Embryology was mistaken.
>
> (Warnock, 2002: 92–93)

In Australia, regulation of surrogacy was also heavily influenced by the Warnock Report. The first Commonwealth enquiry into surrogacy resulted in the 1985 Family Law Council recommendation of uniform Australian legislation which would reflect that 'as a matter of public policy, surrogacy arrangements are seen as contrary to the welfare and interests of the child' (Family Law Council, 1985). The report went on to make a distinction between altruistic and commercial surrogacy, recommending the prohibition of commercial surrogacy while being less explicit on the practice of altruistic surrogacy. Unsurprisingly, Victoria, the first Australian state to introduce legislation in 1986 by way of the Infertility (Medical Procedures) Act 1984 which dealt specifically with surrogate motherhood prohibited both commercial and altruistic surrogacy. This legislation was based upon findings by the Victorian Waller Committee which condemned commercial surrogacy arrangements as being 'the buying and selling of a baby' (Victorian Committee, 1984). The legislation criminalised commercial surrogacy, a legal position subsequently adopted by all other Australian jurisdictions. This prohibition has never been questioned by policy makers and, similarly to the UK, has never been opened to public debate (Stuhmcke, 2011).

Australian public policy: Legislative regulation of cross-border commercial surrogacy

In most Australian jurisdictions while altruistic surrogacy is variously allowed but difficult to engage in, commercial surrogacy is a criminal offence. The absence of regulation of commercial surrogacy at a federal level means that surrogacy legislation remains state and territory specific. Commercial surrogacy is formally prohibited – and a criminal act – in all jurisdictions which have legislation.[10]

In contrast to the UK approach outlined by Dame Warnock, where the policy was one of 'not in our backyard' and '[i]f people wanted to enter into surrogacy contracts, let them go across the Atlantic to do it', the offence of commercial surrogacy is extraterritorial in three Australian jurisdictions. In New South Wales (NSW), the Australian Capital Territory (ACT) and Queensland (Qld) it is an offence for residents to enter into overseas commercial surrogacy arrangements, carrying a punishment of a fine or imprisonment ($110, 000 AUD or up to three years' imprisonment). These prohibitions also apply to residents of NSW, the ACT and Qld seeking inter-*state* arrangements. The ACT and Qld introduced the provisions in 1994 and 2010, respectively (although Qld had introduced an earlier provision in 1988), and NSW did so in 2011. It is somewhat extraordinary that three Australian state jurisdictions have this prohibition given that it was only recently, in 2010, that Turkey became the first country to introduce such prohibition at a national level – introducing laws to regulate against its citizens seeking third-party reproductive assistance through donor gametes or surrogacy (Gürtin, 2011).

In all three Australian jurisdictions the extraterritorial criminal provisions which apply to commercial surrogacy have never been enforced. This remains the case despite the existence of high-profile legal and media cases where residents of the ACT, Qld and NSW have used international commercial surrogacy. It is also the case despite courts in Qld and NSW granting parentage and parental responsibility orders for such arrangements. The only prosecutions arising from surrogacy in Australia have been for an act committed within a single jurisdiction. There have been prosecutions of several women and a doctor under the now repealed Surrogate Parenthood Act 1988 (Qld) which criminalised both altruistic and commercial surrogacy; these individuals received lenient treatment from the courts (Emmerson, 1996). The absence of effective prosecutions indicates that the role of criminal law in this area is both unnecessary and pointless.

Despite the legislative criminalisation of the practice, applications come to the Family Court for parenting orders under section 64C of the Family Law Act 1975 (Cth) (FLA). Such orders can be granted in circumstances where the law fails to recognise a person as a legal parent. The basis for making such an order is that the applicant is a 'person concerned with the care, welfare or development of the child' (see s 65C(c) of the FLA). These orders are pursued through the courts by Australian citizens returning to Australia with a foreign born child with whom they usually have a genetic link and a primary caregiving role, but no legally recognised relationship. While the parameters of parenting orders are extensive, they are not as far-reaching as legal parentage as they terminate when the child turns 18 and do not grant legal parenthood status as such. Parenting orders do give the

10 Surrogacy Act 2010 (Qld), s 56; Surrogacy Act 2010 (NSW), s 8; Parentage Act 2004 (ACT), s 41; Assisted Reproductive Treatment Act 2008 (Vic), s 44; Surrogacy Contracts Act 1993 (Tas), s 4(4); Family Relationships Act 1975 (SA), s 10H; Surrogacy Act 2008 (WA), s 8.

intended parents responsibility for making decisions concerning the welfare of the child such as the name a child will be called, the school a child will attend and important medical decisions. These orders also include where and with whom a child will live and with whom a child will spend time (see s 64B of the FLA).

However, parenting orders do not solve the complex legal issues which arise in respect of international commercial surrogacy. Generally, Australian family law will not recognise legal parentage granted in other jurisdictions. This means that in the absence of Australian parentage, children brought back to Australia by their genetic Australian parents and primary caregivers may be both stateless and parentless (such as where the child was born in India). It is true, as Millbank observes, that Australian decision makers have had to be creative to 'try to "find" a parent in order to avoid outcomes such as leaving children stateless orphans abroad' and in doing so have given recognition 'through ad hoc liberalisation of interpretations of "parent" and "child" in particular pieces of legislation, which has left parents in a state of ambiguous, labyrinthine and "limping" legal parentage' (Millbank, 2013: 137).

United Kingdom public policy: Legislative regulation of international commercial surrogacy

As noted previously, surrogacy legislation in the UK originated in the findings of the 1984 Warnock Report. Although divided, the Warnock Committee's view was that the operation of agencies to promote commercial and altruistic surrogacy should be prevented. The legislation which was enacted (and is still in force), the Surrogacy Agreements Act 1985, aims primarily to prohibit commercial surrogacy through criminal penalties (which do not apply to the parties to the agreement).[11]

Today in the UK, to obtain parental responsibility for a child born through international commercial surrogacy, the commissioning parents must apply for a Parental Order under section 54(1) of the 2008 Act. Section 54 prescribes that the court must consider the age and genetic relationship of the commissioning parents to the child, the timing of the application and location of the applicants. Payments (of 'expenses') made to the surrogate mother may be authorised by the courts. However, courts in the UK must, under section 54(8) be satisfied that the surrogacy arrangement was altruistic and if so satisfied have discretion to authorise payments retroactively. Interestingly, UK courts are retroactively allowing and approving the applications of commissioning parents for a Parental Order even where the surrogacy arrangement appears to be commercial. Here then is an apparent divergence between the law and public policy and the practice of decision-makers. However, as is discussed further in the following section, this

11 The Warnock Report provides the following reason for this selective application of the criminal law at [8.19] 'We do not envisage that this legislation would render private persons entering into surrogacy arrangements liable to criminal prosecution, as we are anxious to avoid children being born to mothers subject to the taint of criminality'.

response by the courts is perhaps both to be expected and is illustrative of the misapplication of current law to international commercial surrogacy.

Importantly, the judicial retroactive approval of commercial surrogacy has been aided by the Human Fertilisation and Embryology (Parental Orders) Regulations 2010 which inserted section 1 of the Adoption and Children Act 2002 into section 54 of the 2008 Act, rendering the welfare of the child the paramount consideration of the court when considering an application for a Parental Order. The significance of this amendment is captured by Hedley J in *Re L (A Minor)*[12] (at [10]):

> The effect of that must be to weight the balance between public policy considerations and welfare (as considered in *Re X and Y*) decisively in favour of welfare. It must follow that it will only be in the clearest case of the abuse of public policy that the court will be able to withhold an order if otherwise welfare considerations supports its making.

This approach has been endorsed in numerous subsequent international commercial surrogacy decisions.[13] Throughout, the judiciary has been clear in these decisions that a child born through international commercial surrogacy will be granted a Parental Order. This explains why in all reported cases where section 54(8) of the HFEA has been considered the court has retroactively approved payments beyond reasonable expenses.[14]

The courts and public policy: Thematic similarity in jurisdictional response

New wine in old bottles: Prioritising the welfare of the child and deprioritising public policy

Family courts in both jurisdictions have, rightly and without exception, elevated the interests of the child over public policy. The judicial response to disputes in international commercial surrogacy matters is not to ignore, but rather to deprioritise public policy. This approach embodies conceptualising international commercial surrogacy as being a traditional issue about a child's welfare. The family courts deprioritise public policy by minimising, where possible the impact of criminal law (in Australia) and the commercial nature of the agreement (in the UK). For example, in a 2012 Australian family law decision, Ryan J granted the applicants a certificate under section128 of the Evidence Act 1995 (Cth) to

12 [2010] EWHC 3146 (Fam).

13 See e.g. *Re X and Y (Children)* [2011] EWHC 3147 (Fam); *G v G* [2012] All ER (D) 138; *Re D and L (Children) (Surrogacy Parental Order)* [2012] EWHC 2631 (Fam); *Re A& B (Parental Order Domicile)* [2013] EWHC 426 (Fam); *Re P-M* [2013] EWHC 2328 (Fam); *Re C (A Child)* [2013] EWHC 2413 (Fam); *Re C (A Child)* [2013] EWHC 2408 (Fam); *Re W* [2013] EWHC 3570 (Fam); *J v G* [2013] EWHC 1432 (Fam).

14 Payments of up to $56,750 (US) have been approved. See *J v G* [2013] EWHC 1432 (Fam).

enable the parties in the international commercial surrogacy case[15] to speak freely. This certificate ensured that evidence could not be used in criminal courts. In that case Justice Ryan observed the difficulty that the court faces when balancing public policy with the welfare of the child:

> ...[o]f course imprisonment of the applicants would see two much loved children inexplicably separated from the only people they have known as parents. The potential for long term psychological and emotional harm to the children were such an event to come to pass is obvious.
>
> (At [3])

Prioritisation of the best interests of the child over the enforcement of a criminal penalty in cross-border surrogacy was predicted in Australia some 20 years ago. In the passing of the Surrogate Parenthood Act 1988 (Qld) it was observed that:

> If a Queensland resident went to Victoria or South Australia to legally undergo a [surrogacy] and then returned to Queensland, in principle that person could be thrown into gaol for three years. The legislation is silent about what would happen to the child who was born as a result of that act, an act which was perfectly legal in the place where it was carried out.
>
> (Queensland Parliamentary Debates: Mr Wells, 1988: 683)

The best interest and welfare of the child has long and consistent treatment by the family courts. Hence there is no surprise in the inevitability of family courts completing international commercial surrogacy arrangement through granting parental responsibility to the commissioning parents. This is evidenced in the UK where it has been noted that such orders 'will provide lifelong security for the children's relationship with the applicants, which is what the welfare of each child overwhelmingly demands'.[16] As Mr Justice Hedley in *Re X and Y* [2008] EWHC 3030 (at [24]) states:

> I feel bound to observe that I find this process of authorisation most uncomfortable. What the court is required to do is to balance two competing and potentially irreconcilably conflicting concepts. Parliament is clearly entitled to legislate against commercial surrogacy and is clearly entitled to expect that the courts should implement that policy consideration in its decisions. Yet it is also recognised that as the full rigour of that policy consideration will bear on one wholly unequipped to comprehend it let alone deal with its consequences (i.e. the child concerned) that rigour must be mitigated by the application of a consideration of that child's welfare. That approach is both humane and intellectually coherent. The difficulty is that it is almost impossible to imagine a set of circumstances in which by the time the case comes to court,

15 *Ellison v Karnchanit* [2012] Fam CA 602.
16 *Re W (Rev 1)* [2013] EWHC 3570 (Fam) at [30].

> the welfare of any child (particularly a foreign child) would not be gravely compromised (at the very least) by a refusal to make an order.

As Hedley J observes, the family court process is *fait accompli*. In the absence of such judicial completion of the international surrogacy arrangement the child would, in some circumstances (such as birth in India), be both stateless and parentless; in others the child would have the citizenship of the birth country (USA, Thailand) but no parents there (California, British Columbia); or only a mother there (Thailand) (Keyes, 2011; Storrow, 2012).

That said, there is constant tension in this area between the public policy of disapproval of commercial surrogacy and the parameters of family law. As is evident from Hedley J's statement in *Re X and Y*, the courts explicitly acknowledge the conflict between public policy and family law. This is particularly so in Australia and clearest in two 2011 decisions of the Family Court of Australia. In both decisions Justice Watts referred the international commercial surrogacy cases (where the children had been born to surrogate mothers in Thailand) to the Director of Public Prosecutions (DPP). The court, after making orders that it was in the best interest for the children to live with the commissioning parent applicants, made an additional order that a copy of the judgement be provided to the DPP for consideration of whether a prosecution should be instituted against the applicants under section 3 of the Surrogate Parenthood Act 1988 (Qld).[17] There have been no resulting prosecutions.

Similarly, UK courts recognise this 'supervisory' role of regulatory authorities in surrogacy. For example, in *Re G*[18] McFarlane J authorised a copy of the judgement to be sent to the Minister of State for Children, Young People and families as he thought 'it is questionable whether the role of facilitating surrogacy arrangements should be left to groups of well-meaning amateurs' (at [29]).[19] Also, Mrs Justice Thies DBE, in *J v G*,[20] when dealing with a US surrogacy case referred the British Surrogacy Centre of California ('BSC'), which operates in the UK from an address in Essex, to the Department of Health stating:

> During this period the applicants decided to cease using the BSC. It has not been necessary, in the circumstances of this case, to consider the role played by BSC. However, I have directed the applicant's solicitors to send a copy of this judgment to the Department of Health, which has regulatory responsibility in this area.
>
> (At [6])

17 See *Dudley and Anor v Chedi* [2011] at [32] FamCA 502 and *Findlay and Anor v Punyawong* [2011] FamCA 503 at [32].

18 [2007] EWHC 2814 (Fam).

19 This reference was to COTS (Childlessness Overcome through Surrogacy), a non-commercial surrogacy agency founded in the UK in 1988 with the aim of providing advice, help and support to surrogates and intended parents see <http://www.surrogacy.org.uk/About_COTS.htm>.

20 [2013] EWHC 1432 (Fam).

The role of the courts in this area has not been to police the enforcement of criminal laws; rather it has been one of effectively completing the commercial arrangements. In placing the 'new wine' of international commercial surrogacy into the 'old bottle' of determining disputes with reference to the child's welfare the issue becomes one as to whether the continued application of criminal law to this area of family formation is unnecessary and pointless.

Old wine in new bottles: Deconstructing and reconstructing altruistic commerce

The application of prohibitive public policy to international commercial surrogacy has also resulted in judicial creativity. New constructions or recognitions of the inter-relationship between altruism and commerce have been applied to allow the courts to place children with commissioning parents. One example of this is the development and application of what is here termed 'altruistic commerce'. This concept allows courts to resolve the legislative tension in the UK between profit and morality and in the Australian context it facilitates the family courts locating the issue within the realm of family rather than criminal law.

Most simply, UK courts authorise commercial payments against a background of altruism. For example, in the first Russian surrogacy case before the UK High Court (*Re C (A Child)*),[21] Mrs Justice Theis DBE noted the total sum of 50,000 euros paid to an agency and stated that 'on the figures that are available about half of the global fee went to the agency' (at [17]). She also noted that the amount paid to the surrogate 'equates to about 1–2 years average wage' (at [19]) but added that 'there is no evidence to suggest the will of the First Respondent has been overborne by the offer of payment' (at [20]). Theis J then concluded that 'all the evidence points to the sum being within the range of similar arrangements made in Russia and all the information regarding the First Respondent's actions support the conclusion that she entered into this arrangement of her own free will' (at [21]).

This 'new' framework of altruistic commerce creates two main contradictions, and even contortions, in legal reasoning. The first of these is that in paying reasonable expenses there must be no 'moral taint' upon the commissioning parents.[22] This is a judicial imperative in the UK due to section 54(8) of the 2008 Act. The application of this notion gives rise to a simultaneous narrative of vulnerability and strength in international commercial surrogacy cases. In the UK, many judicial decisions characterise the commissioning parents as undergoing a harrowing journey, described variously as: 'a trek through a thorn forest';[23] 'a long and arduous [journey], both emotionally and financially',[24]and often noting the number and duration of IVF treatments: 'Over the last 16 years they have

21 *Re C (A Child)* [2013] EWHC 2413 (Fam).
22 *Re W* [2013] EWHC 3570 per Mrs Justice Thies DBE at [27].
23 *Re X and Y* [2008] EWHC 3030 (Fam) per Mr Justice Hedley at [2].
24 *J v G* [2013] EWHC 1432 (Fam) per Mrs Justice Thies DBE at [22].

had a long and arduous journey to become parents, involving 15 IVF cycles both here, in Italy and then Russia'.[25] The second point of incongruity is that altruistic surrogacy assists the surrogacy industry – the opposite result of what public policy in this area has stated to be its aim. In the UK the legislative statement in section 54 of the 2008 Act that says expenses paid to a surrogate may contravene public policy if they are 'disproportionate to expenses reasonably incurred' results in disadvantage for the surrogate and profit for the industry – the very thing that the Warnock Report originally disapproved of. For example, in *Re P-M*,[26] the court observed that the surrogate was paid $17,700 as altruistic payments and a payment of $48,000 was made to the agency – with a net profit of $21,500 identified by the court. Thies J held that such payments must be included in the consideration of the court but that the legality of that arrangement in the jurisdiction where the surrogacy takes place (here the US) together with the reality of 'a legal commercial framework which is driven by supply and demand' (at [19]) were relevant, holding that the sum paid to the clinic 'was not so disproportionate to expenses' (at [24]).

The lack of legislative guidance as to what constitutes commercial surrogacy contributes to the courts imputing layers of altruism into the commerciality of the arrangement. This area was one of missed opportunity in the 2008 reforms to the legislation in the UK and in many state jurisdictions in Australia which have recently introduced new surrogacy legislation, such as New South Wales.

A more logical approach is to explicitly recognise that a surrogate mother can, does and should profit from her surrogacy. Surrogate mothers have profited in many of the cases decided by the courts in the UK and Australia. Legal recognition of this reality involves respecting a woman's reproductive autonomy which 'demands that surrogacy laws be reconsidered and radically altered' (Nelson, 2013). Framing the payment to the surrogate mother positively will eradicate the necessity for the judiciary to resort to artificial constructs and tortured reasoning. The role of the courts thus far is also rendered morally difficult as international concepts of 'reasonable expenses' and of 'profit' fluctuate widely. In Australia the average cost of altruistic surrogacy has been estimated at $45,000. The average cost of surrogacy in India (including travel) is $77,000, while an arrangement in the US costs on average about $176,000 (Walsh Halligan Douglas, 2012). In the UK, while section 2(1) of the Surrogacy Arrangements Act 1985 prohibits the negotiation of a surrogacy agreement 'on a commercial basis' and makes the facilitation of a surrogacy arrangement through advertising a criminal offence, ambiguity remains as to what actually constitutes commercial surrogacy. The highest payment (so far) to a surrogate mother retroactively approved by the UK court is $56,750 (American dollars), plus expenses.[27] Recognition of profit as one possible goal of commercial surrogacy will also rid the courts in both the UK and Australia of the legal conundrum of defining acceptable expenses. For example, in

25 *AB and DE* [2013] EWHC 2413 per Mrs Justice Theis at [24].
26 [2013] EWHC 2328 (Fam) at [16–19].
27 See *J v G* [2013] EWHC 1432 (Fam).

Australia the distinction between commercial and altruistic surrogacy is confusing as three states expressly recognise the intended parents' obligation to reimburse the birth mother for reasonable expenses associated with pregnancy and birth.[28]

Explicit public policy approval of commercial surrogacy will also remove existing tensions created around inequities in global reproduction. Such public policy approval would involve an organised state-run system – whether through legislation or state-based agencies. Such a regulated version of commercial surrogacy may reduce the dangers of international surrogacy and result in less pursuit of commercial surrogacy in countries which are less well developed than the UK or Australia. This will also assist the judiciary. Courts have been required to take new steps in relation to international commercial surrogacy with which the judiciary has expressed discomfort. Explicit public approval of their role would assist clearer judicial reasoning. For example, the rise of international commercial surrogacy in jurisdictions such as India and Thailand raises complex cross-jurisdictional issues of motivation and exploitation (Panitch, 2013). International surrogacy cases are uncontested with an imbalance in wealth and country of residence advantage. As stated by Cronin J:

> All of the evidence points to the fact that this child is going to be brought up in a very happy and secure environment with many of the benefits that I suspect he would not have had had he been born and raised in India. The unusual feature of this particular application is that it has been served on the respondent who I suspect, from looking at the signature, has very little knowledge of what this is really all about. But having regard to the fact that my concern is that she has at least been made aware of the application justifies proceeding in her absence. The expression 'gestational parent' or 'gestational mother' seems to me to really belie the fact that she is the mother of this child in some biological senses, but she has not appeared and nothing has been filed on her behalf.[29]

Courts in both jurisdictions acknowledge that in placing the child in the legal care of the commissioning parents the consent of the surrogate mother must sometimes be assumed. In Australia, Ryan J stated that:

> The contract provided that the total compensation Rs 2,25,000 (Rupees two Lakhs twenty five thousand) for a vaginal birth or Rs 2,60,000 (Rupees two Lakhs sixty thousand) if the mother had a caesarean delivery. It is not necessary to summarise the entire agreement but it should not pass without comment that the provisions which limit the birth mother's ability to manage her health during the pregnancy and make decisions about delivery of her babies, are troubling. It is also troubling that this 29 page document is written in English. It is signed by the applicant and, because she is illiterate in English

28 *Surrogacy Act 2010* (NSW) s 6(2); *Surrogacy Act 2010* (Qld) s 15(2); *Surrogacy Act 2008* (WA) s 7(3).
29 *Edmore v Bala* [2011] FamCA 731 per Cronin J at [2].

> and Hindi, the mother's attestation is her thumb print. There is nothing in the document which suggests that before the birth mother signed it that it was read and translated to her.[30]

In the UK, placement of children with commissioning parents has taken place in the absence of consent of the surrogate mother. Consent was dispensed with in *Re D and L (Minors Surrogacy) (Surrogacy Parental Order)*[31] when the Indian surrogate mother gave a false address and could not be located.

While change in public policy to allow the practice of international surrogacy may not redress such global inequities, it is clear thus far that prohibition is unsuccessful. It is also clear that people will continue to seek international surrogates while their domestic laws are in disarray. As discussed above, despite the application of criminal law in Australia and a public policy disapproving of commercial surrogacy in the UK, the courts in both jurisdictions complete these arrangements through placing the child in the legal care of the commissioning parents. The Australian experience shows that:

> ... prohibition of surrogacy does not work... Such regulation is difficult in a globalised world where travel from continent to continent is no longer difficult. Added to this, in some parts of the western world, there is wealth to the extent that funding of surrogacy (whether commercial or altruistic) is easily achieved.[32]

Similarly in the UK, Hedley J observed that 'if it is desired to control commercial surrogacy arrangements, those controls need to operate before the court process is initiated i.e. at the border or even before'.[33]

Conclusion

International commercial surrogacy is a problem garnering international attention (Hague Conference, 2012). It is a practice which both intensifies 'old' surrogacy debates and raises new questions. The interaction between public policy and family law in this area has resulted in the judiciary either attempting to constrain the new elements of the practice within traditional doctrine such as the welfare of the child test or else incorporating the public policy requirements to develop 'new' legal concepts such as altruistic commerce. It may be that either or both these approaches are acceptable to society. However, despite the existence of prohibitive public policy there have been few attempts to gauge public opinion within either the UK, including as recently as the review of the law leading to the 2008 Act (Horsey, 2013), or Australia (Poote and van den Akker, 2008), yet the practice

30 *Mason & Mason and Anor* [2013] Fam at [3].

31 [2012] EWHC 2631.

32 *Lowe & Barry and Anor* [2011] FamCA 625 per Justice Benjamin at [5].

33 *Re L (A Minor)* [2010] EWHC 3146 (Fam) at [10].

is judicially acknowledged to be an issue which merits ' the widest public debate'.[34] While international commercial surrogacy may yet have a long road to trek before it is legislatively sanctioned, what is clear is that the current approach of disapproval and prohibition does not work. Individuals continue to turn to commercial surrogacy in the UK and Australia despite the lack of support from their own state and medical structures – leaving the courts to reconcile legal, moral and ethical tensions and in doing so, creating new families.

References

Blyth, E., Crawshaw, M. and van den Akker, O, (2014) 'What are the Best Interests of the Child in International Surrogacy?' *BioNews* 742 (17 February 2014, Progress Educational Trust).

Crawshaw, M., Blyth E. and van den Akker O., (2013) 'The changing profile of surrogacy in the UK – Implications for national and international policy and practice' 34(3) *Journal of Social Welfare and Family Law* 267.

Department of Immigration & Citizenship, (2013) International Surrogacy Arrangements' Submission to Family Law Council Surrogacy Inquiry.

Emmerson, G., (1996) 'Surrogacy: Born for Another' (Research Bulletin 8/96 No Queensland Parliamentary Library).

Family Law Council, (1985) *Creating Children: A Uniform Approach to the Law and Practice of Reproductive Technology in Australia* (AGPS, Canberra).

Gamble, N., (2013) 'The HFEA Gets into Gear on Surrogacy' *BioNews* 703 (7 May 2013, Progress Educational Trust).

Hague Conference on Private International Law, (2012) *Preliminary Report on Issues Arising from International Surrogacy Arrangements.*

Hibino, Y. and Shimazono, Y., (2013) 'Becoming a Surrogate Online: "Message Board" Surrogacy in Thailand' 5(1) *Asian Bioethics Review* 56.

Horsey, K. and Sheldon, S., (2012) 'Still Hazy After All These Years: The Law Regulating Surrogacy' 20(1) *Medical Law Review* 67–89.

Horsey, K., (2013) 'Swept under the Carpet: Why Surrogacy Law Needs Urgent Review' in Priaulx, N. and Wrigley, A. (eds), *Ethics, Law and Society*, Vol. V 235–255 (Farnham, Ashgate).

Jackson, B., (2014) 'Surrogacy: A guide to the Current Law (Part 1)' *Family Law Week*, http://www.familylawweek.co.uk/site.aspx?i=ed127038.

Keyes, M., (2011) 'Cross Border Surrogacy Agreements' 26 *Australian Journal of Family Law* 28.

Millbank, J., (2011) 'The New Surrogacy Parentage Laws in Australia: Cautious Regulation or "25 Brick Walls"?' 35 *Melbourne University Law Review* 165.

Millbank, J., (2013) 'Resolving the Dilemma of Legal Parentage for Australians Engaged in International Surrogacy' 27(2) *Australian Journal of Family Law* 135.

Millbank, J., (2014) 'Rethinking "Commercial" Surrogacy' 11(2) *Journal of Bioethical Inquiry*, advance access DOI 10.1007/s11673-014-9557-9.

Nelson, E., (2013) *Law, Policy and Reproductive Autonomy* (Oxford: Hart Publishing).

Pande, A., (2009) 'Commercial Surrogate Parenting in India: Nine Months of Labour?' (PhD thesis, Amherst: University of Massachusetts).

34 *Re X and Y* [2008] EWHC 3030 (Fam) per Mr Justice Hedley at [29].

Panitch, V., (2013) 'Global surrogacy: Exploitation to Empowerment' 9(3) *Journal of Global Ethics* 329.

Poote, A.E. and van den Akker, O., (2008) 'British Women's Attitude to Surrogacy' 24(1) *Human Reproduction* 139.

Smith, M., Willmott, L., Trowse, P. and White, B., (2013) 'Back to the Future: Prohibiting Surrogacy for Singles, Same-sex and Shorter-term Heterosexual Couples in Queensland' 20 *Journal of Law and Medicine* 638.

Storrow, R., (2010) 'Travel into the Future of Reproductive Technology' *79 UMKC Law Review* 295.

Storrow, R., (2012) 'The Phantom Children of the New Republic: International Surrogacy and the New Illegitimacy' 20 *American University Journal of Gender, Social Policy & The Law* 561.

Storrow, R., (2013) 'Global Trade and Assisted Reproductive Technologies: Regulatory Challenges and International Surrogacy' 41 *Journal of Law, Medicine & Ethics* 240.

Stuhmcke, A., (1996) 'For Love or Money: The Legal Regulation of Surrogate Motherhood' 3(1) *Murdoch University Electronic Law Journal.*

Stuhmcke, A., (2004) 'Looking Backwards, Looking Forwards: Judicial and Legislative Trends in the Regulation of Surrogate Motherhood in the UK and Australia' 18 *Australian Journal of Family Law* 13.

Stuhmcke, A., (2011) 'The Criminal Act of Commercial Surrogacy in Australia' 18 *Journal of Law and Medicine* 601.

Unnithan, M., (2013) 'Thinking through Surrogacy Legislation in India: Reflections on Relational Consent and the Rights of the Infertile Women' 1(3) *Journal of Legal Anthropology* 287.

Van Zyl, L., and Walker, R., (2013) 'Beyond Altruistic and Commercial Contract Motherhood: the Professional Model' 27(7) *Bioethics* 373.

Victorian Committee to Consider the Social, Ethical and Legal Issues Arising From In Vitro Fertilization, *Report on the Disposition of Embryos Produced by In Vitro Fertilisation*, 1984.

Walsh Halligan Douglas, (30/10/12) Family Matters Blog http://www.whd.com.au/familymattersblog/tag/altruistic-surrogacy/.

Warnock, M., (2002) *Making Babies: Is There a Right to Have Children?* (Oxford: Oxford University Press).

Warnock Report, (1984) *Report of the Committee of Inquiry into Human Fertilisation and Embryology* Cmnd 9314 (London: HMSO).

Whittaker, A., (2011) 'Cross-border Assisted Reproduction Care in Asia: Implications for Access, Equity and Regulations' 19(37) *Reproductive Health Matters* 107.

Index